W9-BGS-372

P.A. STOLYPIN AND THE THIRD DUMA

An Appraisal of the Three Major Issues

George Tokmakoff

UNIVERSITY
PRESS OF
AMERICA

LANHAM • NEW YORK • LONDON

University Press of America,™ Inc.

4720 Boston Way
Lanham, MD 20706

3 Henrietta Street
London WC2E 8LU England

Printed in the United States of America

Library of Congress Cataloging in Publication Data

Tokmakoff, George.
P.A. Stolypin and the third Duma.

Bibliography: p.
Includes index.
1. Soviet Union–Politics and government–1904–1914. 2. Stolypin, Petr Arkad'evich, 1862–1911. 3. Land reform–Soviet Union. 4. Agriculture and state–Soviet Union. 5. Finland–Politics and government–1809–1917. I. Title.
DK262.T59 947.08'3 81–19677
ISBN 0–8191–2058–8 AACR2
ISBN 0–8191–2059–6 (pbk.)

All University Press of America books are produced on acid-free paper which exceeds the minimum standards set by the National Historical Publications and Records Commission.

To The Memory

of

Baron Alexander F. Meyendorff

TABLE OF CONTENTS

PREFACE

Stolypin was the only statesman in Tsarist Russia who held simultaneously the two most important posts of the empire, the Premiership and the Ministry of the Interior. During those five years he seemed invulnerable to all weapons of revolutionary terrorism. While there can be no doubt that he deserves a unique place in Russian history because he was one of the outstanding statesmen Imperial Russia produced and because of the critical role he played before the fall of the monarchy, he has remained an enigmatic figure, noticed by historians, but unassessed in his full value and significance.

To understand the tumultuous course of Russian history in the decade before the First World War is a singularly difficult task. Misconceptions abound and popular ignorance has been abetted by professional neglect of what I would call the "Ten Forgotten Years of Russian History." The need to write a comprehensive and dispassionate history of this epoch, one that seeks to be a thorough synthesis based on the present mass of disparate knowledge, has long been recognized. Historians only very recently have begun showing an interest in this epoch coincident with the opening of archival materials by the Soviet Government. A biography of Stolypin is long overdue; however, it cannot be done since access to many of the vital materials in the Soviet archives is still restricted, and those that are open are encumbered with numerous difficulties. There is now, however, enough material scattered throughout the Western world to allow a historian to come to broad if not definitive conclusions on this all-important epoch.

To the student of Russian history who scrutinizes the diversified career of P. A. Stolypin, and the pronouncements made on that career, it is clear that he was a crucially important and controversial person in his age. The following are some of the diverse opinions the reader may encounter. The leading Soviet specialist on the Third Duma, for instance, refers to Stolypin as a "rabid reactionary."[1] A former Socialist-Revolutionary said, "to call him a reactionary would be obviously unjust."[2] Count S. Witte, a contemporary and a rival of Stolypin, maintained that the latter was selfishly concerned for securing his "position, esteem, and all material benefits which were reaped from this post."[3] L. Tikhomirov, a former revolutionary, wrote in his diary after Stolypin was assassinated: "He was one of the best, the most honest, noblest of all his rivals."[4] V. Gurko, a high state official of those times and an admirer of Witte, stated that "Stolypin was the only outstanding man of all the collaborators of Nicholas II."[5] Such pronouncements show glaringly the controversial nature of Stolypin's reputation.

The pages which follow are not an attempt at biography. Stolypin was involved in numerous issues in his day, such as agriculture, health, local self-government, industry, Siberian colonization, the nationalities issue, and many others covering virtually the whole spectrum of Russia's economic, social, and political life. I am limiting myself here to a study of the only major legislative issues that Stolypin initiated in the Third Duma, carried through the debates within the walls of the Duma and the State Council, and promulgated into law--the agrarian, the Finnish, and the western zemstvo issues. These, which involved Stolypin so intimately, brought out his political philosophy, his plan of action, and his vision of Russia's future. I am here mainly concerned with his actions within the Duma and his political maneuvers within the constitutional limits established by the Fundamental Laws.

In addition to the materials drawn from the bibliography referred to elsewhere, paramount attention has been paid to the stenographic reports of the State Duma and the State Council, the Special Journal of the Council of Ministers (*Osobye*

Zhurnaly Soveta Ministrov), the unpublished documents of the British Foreign Office, and the Finnish National Archive (Valtionarkisto). These materials are in a sense the backbone of the mass of material covered for this study. I have taken years after the completion of the Ph.D. to sift through, and peruse, numerous published and unpublished materials which I had not seen before. I felt strongly that there was a need for time to reflect upon the issues studied.

This volume is an abridged version of my Ph.D. thesis submitted at the University of London under the supervision of Professor G.H.N. Seton-Watson, to whom I am indebted for advice and guidance. I am particularly indebted to the first cousin of P. A. Stolypin, the late Baron A. F. Meyendorff, to whom this work is dedicated. He gave his time generously during the course of the three years that this work was researched in London, and he shared freely his reminiscences of Stolypin and the epoch which this work covers. I am also grateful to Sir Isaiah Berlin and Dr. John Keep who, during the same period, gave me their time and encouragement. Dr. Martin Kilcoyne read the manuscript at various stages, and Dr. Osmo Jussila of Helsinki University read the chapter on the Finnish question. Both contributed helpful suggestions. Many thanks go to Stolypin's eldest daughter and son, Mrs. Maria Bok and A. P. Stolypin, both of whom made themselves available for interviews. I am also indebted for the photographs which the latter supplied me. Thanks go to the following deceased individuals who discussed with me various topics of this work either by correspondence or interview: A. Bilimovich, N. Kastel, Professor V. Leontovitsch, Boris Nikolaevskii, Prince A. Obolensky, I. Tsereteli, Prince F. Usupoff, and A. Zenkovsky. I also owe thanks to my colleague Dr. Manfred Hagen of the University of Goettingen, who throughout the last ten years freely exchanged thoughts and ideas on the topics here discussed. The responsibility for any errors in fact or interpretation rests entirely upon the author.

I would like to express my appreciation to the staffs of the following libraries and archives, who were more than cooperative in making materials available: The British Museum Library, The Finnish National Archive, Helsinki University Library, The Hoover Institution, The Public Record Office, The London School of Economics Library, The School of Slavonic and East European Studies Library, and the Bodeleian. Special thanks go to Mr. L. Magerovsky of the Russian Archive at Columbia University and to Mr. J. Phillips of the London Times Archive. Every academic author owes thanks to the librarians of his institution. I owe a debt to Mr. Gordon Martin, the former head Librarian, and Mr. John McClure, of its Social Science Division, both of whom have always been most helpful in acquiring materials and aiding my research efforts in every way possible.

As for technical matters, I adhere to a modified Library of Congress transliteration system, having omitted all of the hard and soft signs. All translations from the Russian are mine. I use the Julian, or the Old Style, calendar for all dates connected with Russian sources; for events derived from Western materials, I use the Gregorian. To convert the Julian to the Gregorian, the reader should add to it thirteen days.

California State University Sacramento

George Tokmakoff

Summer, 1981

NOTES

1. Avrekh, A., Tsarism i Tretieiiunskaia Sistema (Moscow, 1966), p.27.

2. Karpovich, M., Imperial Russia, 1801-1917 (New York, 1932), p.77.

3. Witte, S., Vospominaniia Tsarstvovanie Nikolaia II (Berlin, 1922), Vol. II, p.393.

4. Krasnyi Arkhiv, Vol. 74 (1936), p.190.

5. Gurko, V., Features and Figures of the Past: Government and Opinion in the Reign of Nicholas II (Stanford University Press), p.515.

CHAPTER I

THE PRELUDE TO THE THIRD DUMA

The convening of the Third Duma in November 1907 may well be considered the end of the 1905 revolution. The dissolution of the Second Duma was followed by the arrest of those of its former Social-Democratic deputies who were charged with treasonable revolutionary activity, as well as by the detention of revolutionaries of various conviction. Most important of all, peasant disturbances abated so drastically that, by the end of 1907, the revolutionary movement was at its lowest ebb and the country was returning rapidly to a more settled condition.

The Duma epoch showed that the Russian monarchy was seeking to adjust to the change in circumstances brought about by the emancipation and the ensuing plight of the peasantry, the decline of landlordism, and increasing industrialization. By the end of the nineteenth century Russia was confronted with two major simultaneous revolutions--the agrarian and the industrial. The social and the political upheaval which followed was to a great extent possible because the Russian monarchy did not have a single class upon which it could lean, other than a largely self-regarding aristocracy that lacked a deep and consistent interest in the well-being of the land and its peoples.

In February 1904 Japan had attacked Russia. The war that followed was highly unpopular in Russia, and as defeat became evident it was easy for those opposed to the monarchy to foment dissatisfaction, which, as the months went by and the Tsar's armies failed, turned into active and violent resistance to the government. On 15 July 1904 the reactionary Minister of the Interior V. Plehve was assassinated and Nicholas II, seeking to quiet public opinion, appointed Prince P. Sviatopolk-Mirsky to the post. The latter sought to win support for the government by indicating that his ministry would uphold the principle of "confidence in the public." Between 6 and 9 November 1904, a congress of the zemstvos, under the chairmanship of D. Shipov, gathered in Moscow and issued an eleven-point resolution calling for a national assembly.[1] Henceforth city Dumas, local zemstvo councils, municipalities, organizations and political groups of all types began to meet freely and to publish resolutions clamoring for constitutional reform. This movement spread so rapidly that the government was taken by surprise and did little to counter the wave of public criticism.

The fall of Port Arthur in January 1905 added more fuel to the fires of unrest, and a feeling of anarchy gripped not only the masses and the politically conscious, but official ranks as well.[2] Further support rallied to the opposition after Bloody Sunday on 9 January 1905, when a procession to the Winter Palace, led by a priest named Father Gapon to present a petition to the Tsar stating grievances and asking for redress, was fired on by troops, causing a panic and hundreds of casualties. The immediate reaction was a wave of strikes throughout the empire.[3] Sviatopolk-Mirsky and higher police officials resigned, and the former was replaced by A. Bulygin. The assassination of senior officials and public figures increased, culminating in the assassination of the Emperor's uncle the Grand Duke Sergei, on 4 February 1905, an event which made a deep impression on the Tsar, and prompted him on 18 February to issue the Bulygin rescript, which announced his intention of summoning a consultative assembly.

The next blow to the government was the sinking of the Russian fleet in the Straits of Tsushima in May 1905. Public reaction to this took the form of meetings of local organizations at which further protests, resolutions, and petitions were issued. Then came a series of mutinies in the armed forces, the best known of which was that of the cruiser *Potemkin*. Russia was inflamed with revolutionary fervor as never before, and the administration, more than ever, lacked popular support. On 26 May,

President Theodore Roosevelt took the initiative and invited both belligerents to a peace conference. Negotiations began on 28 July, at Portsmouth, New Hampshire, with Count S. Witte leading the Russian delegation. Within less than a month the conference ended in the signing of the Peace Treaty.

Meanwhile, the revolution at home gathered momentum. Even though the Manifesto of 6 August, instituting the Bulygin Duma, sought to pacify the liberal elements, it was greeted with utter derision. By September the situation had become yet more tense; strikes and student demonstrations increased, and the crowds in the streets grew ever more prone to engage in sparring with the troops and the police. On 24 September, Moscow's fifty printing concerns went on strike. The next day the bakers went on strike, and the first serious clash with the troops occurred. Then St. Petersburg followed suit.

In the last days of September the Congress of Railway Workers, representing 750,000 workers, met in St. Petersburg. Suddenly on 6 October, rumors spread in Moscow that the Congress delegates had been arrested. This rumor was enough, despite the denial by the delegates themselves,[4] to provoke a strike which brought European Russia to a standstill by 12 October. The Tsar was forced to reconsider whatever plans he might have had and turn to Witte. The latter seemed quite sure of himself and made all possible efforts to let it be known that he considered himself the only man who could lead Russia out of the chaos.[5]

On 13 October Nicholas sent Witte a letter empowering him to form a Cabinet. In his discussion with the Tsar Witte stressed that there were only two options open: either rule by force or by means of national representation. He advised the second course, because he felt that the monarchy would find a strong supporter in a representative body. To this the Emperor replied that he was perfectly aware that he was not creating a collaborator but an enemy, and that he did so with the hope of creating a government which would guarantee Russia a peaceful development.[6]

On the afternoon of the 17th, Nicholas signed the October Manifesto, and late that evening Witte returned from Petershof to St. Petersburg. Witte showed a considerable naivete, or even recklessness, in not informing the branches of government most vitally concerned before making the document public, though even Nicholas had warned him that repercussions would be inevitable if he did not make preparations beforehand.[7] It was not until the next morning that Minister of the Interior Bulygin learned of the manifesto for the first time through the newspapers. Thus Witte did not take account of the repercussions that the manifesto would have among the masses--especially in the cities of the south, where serious riots followed.[8]

The October Manifesto promised the following: the granting of basic rights, the summoning of the Duma (National Assembly) without delay, and the prior approval of the Duma before new laws were put into effect. When the manifesto was printed on the 18th it provoked a new surge of revolutionary energy. In the cities millions of people roamed the streets restlessly, and the revolutionaries insisted that the battle should continue until full freedom was finally secured by written law.[10] As the news reached all parts of the empire this scene repeated itself over again. The streets of the capital were teeming with thousands of people carrying revolutionary placards and red flags and singing the Marseillaise. However, demonstrators also paraded with portraits of the Tsar and with icons, and sang the national anthem.

The intelligentsia greeted the manifesto with mixed emotions. While the conservatives, fearing the effects of the manifesto, were dismayed, the liberals and the radicals rejoiced, kissing each other, holding meetings, making liberal speeches, and drinking champagne. But for the most radical elements, working towards their final aim of an armed uprising, the manifesto was only a step towards their ultimate goal. P. Miliukov, the leader of the Kadet Party, exclaimed that, as far as the Duma was concerned, there was a great difference between the August and the October Manifestoes.[11] Such was the mixed reception that prevailed among the opposition and other elements on this historic occasion. The revolutionary movement had now created effective methods of organization, which it did not intend to abandon. In an untidy way, the manifesto split the ranks of the opposition, and the first disturbances were but the spontaneous and confused reactions of the masses who had been waiting frenziedly for the news of freedom.

The St. Petersburg Soviet organized itself less than a week before the promulgation of the October Manifesto. It at once began to play a leading role in political affairs because of its bold and forceful posture during the time of growing anarchy. It won wide acclaim when it called for the removal of troops from the city and for the handing over of arms to the proletariat.[12] Dissatisfied elements tended accordingly to look to it for leadership, to rally to it, and to support causes and actions it sponsored. Because of its great influence among the workers, it was able to control the streets of the city and to make or end strikes. By the end of October it had become so successful that there seemed no limits to what it might accomplish. The central authority was by this time so disorganized that the Soviet began to perform like a separate government, acting of its own accord and with little regard for the wishes of the existing authorities. On 22 October the Soviet ordered the railway workers to return to work and Witte became conscious of its pacifying influence.

Witte now applied himself to the task of drawing liberals and moderates into his cabinet. His negotiations with D. Shipov, A. Guchkov, M. Stakhovich, and Prince E. Trubetskoi came to nothing because of Witte's insistence on the appointment of P. Durnovo, a noted reactionary, as Minister of the Interior.[13] In the end, Witte had his way, and even though Durnovo was appointed only as acting Minister of the Interior, this action on the part of Witte alienated the liberals, and all hope was lost for any further negotiations. As Miliukov was later to remark, public men no longer went to Witte because they no longer believed him.[14]

The month of November was an uneasy one for Witte and a decisive one for Durnovo. Because of the Premier's vacillation people began asking one another whether G. Khrustalev-Nosar, the Chairman of the St. Petersburg Soviet, would arrest Witte, or Witte Khrustalev. Durnovo, realizing that the St. Petersburg Soviet was the main obstacle to restoring order, arrested Khrustalev on 27 November. The Soviet promptly issued an appeal that same day to the armed forces, and another on 2 December, urging the non-payment of taxes and the withdrawal of gold from the banks. Having obtained the approval of the Emperor, Durnovo surrounded the St. Petersburg Soviet during its plenary session on 3 December and arrested 267 of its deputies.

After the arrest of the Soviet, a strike was declared in Moscow on 6 December, and on the morning of 9 December, armed workers' groups, hastily summoned by the executive committee, appeared in the streets of Moscow. An exchange of fire took place between them and the garrison, and an armed uprising followed. The first stage of the fighting lasted until 14 December, when Admiral F. Dubasov, the head of the Moscow Garrison, visited Tsarskoe Selo, and, after explaining the gravity of the situation, was given the Semenovsky Regiment as reinforcement.[15] By 20 December, after the arrival of this regiment in Moscow under the command of General Min, the rebels had been crushed.

By this time Witte had become a mere figurehead. Durnovo was made full Minister of the

Interior on 1 January 1906 and, under the direct orders of the Monarch, continued to act independently of Witte.[16] The Tsar, aware of Witte's position with regard to the opposition and his inability to act effectively, was disposed to replace him. On 12 January he wrote to his mother: "Now he [Witte] wants to hang everyone. . . No one believes in him any more. He is absolutely discredited with everyone."[17]

On 14 April, Witte sent the Emperor a letter of resignation. Even though he mentioned his health and other reasons for stepping down, the main one was the increasingly powerful position which Durnovo assumed.[18] Witte probably felt that by submitting his resignation he would force the Emperor to retain him and to discharge Durnovo. The opening of the Duma was only two weeks away and as the main figure behind the October Manifesto he may well have felt that his presence would be essential. The Monarch nevertheless accepted the resignation and by the 16th Witte had the acceptance in his hand. An official rescript was issued on 22 April, announcing Witte's resignation and the simultaneous dismissal of Durnovo.

I. Goremykin was then called upon to form a new Cabinet, and the attention of the country was focused on the post of Minister of the Interior. Two names were immediately rumored in the topmost circles--B. Sturmer and P. Stolypin.[19] It was presumably Goremykin who brought Stolypin's name to the Tsar's attention.[20] On 22 April 1906, Stolypin was summoned to St. Petersburg by Goremykin, who just a day before had accepted the post of Prime Minister. It is unlikely that Stolypin was overjoyed, for the post of Minister of the Interior appeared more like a crown of thorns than a wreath of triumph.[21] On the day of his arrival in the capital Stolypin was called to Tsarskoe Selo, where Nicholas offered him the post of Minister of the Interior. Stolypin himself suggested that, because of lack of experience, he should perhaps assume the post of Deputy Minister; however, the Tsar insisted, saying, "I order you to take the post."[22] Stolypin had no alternative but to accept.

In conformity with the October Manifesto the government reorganization took the form of the Electoral Law of 11 December 1905, under which voting rights were extended to the majority of the population.[23] This was followed by the issuance of the Manifesto of 20 February 1906, converting the State Council into a state chamber which was now to serve as the upper house, half its members to be appointed by the Tsar and the other half elected. On 23 April the Fundamental Laws were issued to serve as a constitution of the new political system and to set out the form of the new legislative body. All laws passed by the Duma had to go to the State Council; if accepted by the latter they would be handed for signature to the Monarch, who in turn possessed the power of veto. The two most important provisions concerning the Duma were Articles 87 and 105.[24] Though the Fundamental Laws diluted the powers of the Duma, they were, nonetheless, an attempt to transform the former autocracy into the "more complicated politics of constitutionalism."[25] The monarchy hurried to issue the Fundamental Laws before the Duma met, out of a fear that without them the latter would turn into a constituent assembly.[26]

The First Duma met on 27 April, just a day after Stolypin was officially proclaimed Minister of the Interior, and a national holiday celebrated with great expectations. The Tsar received the newly elected deputies in the Winter Palace, where he delivered his speech of greeting from the throne. The deputies then proceeded to the Taurida Palace, the new home of the Duma, which was formally proclaimed open that afternoon.

Goremykin was certainly not the man for the post of Premier at such a critical time. He appeared before the Duma on 13 May and elaborated on his Cabinet's future legislative intentions, which proved totally inadequate. He spoke in specific terms only on an income tax proposal and some changes in hereditary and poll taxes.[27] This performance was received by the opposition as a declaration of war, since it offered no liberal measure. Every faction attacked the government in the strongest language, discrediting it in every way.

Stolypin's appearance before the Duma was far superior to Goremykin's. He showed himself capable of behaving firmly under the fire of intimidation within the Duma walls. Amply possessed of personal courage, a necessary prerequisite for ministers of the period, he was also an excellent orator. He spoke clearly, powerfully, and with a feeling and intonation rarely heard in the Duma.[28] He was the only minister capable of replying to the shouts and stings of the opposition. On this first appearance before the Duma a member of the Kadet Party remarked, "This time the government has put up a strong man. He cannot be ignored."[29] In his most important speeches he captivated the House and audience, compelling applause even from his enemies.

As Minister of the Interior he was primarily preoccupied with bringing back law and order to an empire seething with unrest. Goremykin was utterly crushed after his first encounter with the Duma, and from this moment, as far as the Duma was concerned, Stolypin carried the Premier's burden. The opposition hurled abuse at the government in interpellations during which ministers were constantly harassed with shouts of "Dismiss! Resign!" Such behavior remained a typical feature of debates as every occasion was exploited for immediate party and revolutionary gain. The introduction on 19 May of the agrarian question, which occupied the Duma until its dissolution, brought about a clearer definition in the policies of the opposition parties. This only further revealed, however, the tempestuous nature of the Duma, and the government became even more convinced that common ground between it and the majority of the Duma could not be found.

It was at about this time that Stolypin was instructed to meet with Miliukov and Shipov in an attempt to feel out the possibility of forming a coalition ministry. These negotiations failed because the government was not in a position to accept the Kadet demand for a Kadet ministry. There was no clear evidence to show that the Kadets would in any case have been in a position to lead the Duma if they had been given the reigns of power. Nicholas and his ministers came to the conclusion that the government would be in a better position to deal with the revolutionary turmoil if it did not give cabinet posts to the Kadets.

The Duma was going from bad to worse in its denunciations of established institutions and in its calls to revolution. It tried to invest itself with some of the executive functions of the government, and many of its deputies were carrying out revolutionary propaganda in the provinces. Nicholas referred to it as a "hotbed of revolt" and was ready to dissolve it long before the middle of the year. On 7 July Stolypin was called to the Aleksandrovskii Palace and informed of the Tsar's decision to dissolve the Duma. The Emperor appointed Stolypin Prime Minister and urged him to retain the Ministry of the Interior, since it was a better position from which to handle the difficult task ahead. Stolypin was then asked when would be an appropriate time to dissolve the Duma. He replied that it should be done as soon as possible for fear that word might get out and thus precipitate disturbances. On the morning of 9 July, after precautions had been taken to prevent public disturbances, the ukase dissolving the Duma and announcing the opening of the new assembly on 20 February 1907 was published, together with the news of Stolypin's appointment to the premiership.

It is quite clear from the evidence available that Stolypin was not party to the decision to dissolve the First Duma; it was done entirely on the initiative of the Monarch and Goremykin. Before taking leave of the Tsar, Stolypin revealed his faith in the idea of having a representative body by seeking to create a Cabinet capable of working with the Duma. In order to be able to carry out his policy he stated that he would have to ask for the resignation of the two ultra-reactionary members, A. Stishinskii and Prince P. Shirinskii-Shikhmatov, for, "they are outrightly hostile to the idea of national representation."[30]

On hearing the news that the Duma was dissolved, the Kadets gathered at the home of I. Petrunkevich, the leader of the Kadet faction in the Duma, where Miliukov drew up an appeal. A debate ensued as to how the delegates should react to this coup de main. They resolved to go to Vyborg and to appeal to the nation from there. By that same evening some 178 deputies of the dissolved Duma had gathered at the Hotel Belvedere in Vyborg,[31] and on the following day the Appeal was signed, exhorting the people to resort to passive resistance, non-payment of taxes, and a refusal to supply recruits for the army. This move failed, however, to awaken any response in the general populace. The Vyborg Appeal rebounded against the Kadet Party and dealt it a serious blow.[32]

The deputies, after signing the Appeal, returned to the capital fearing that some action might be taken against them. Stolypin ignored them for the moment, aware that eventually he would have to censure, or at least reprimand, them. The government, of course, felt that in dissolving the Duma it had acted within the framework of the Fundamental Laws, and that the Duma deputies had acted outside the law.[34] With the Vyborg Appeal the drama of the First Duma came to an end, and the gathering of the new Duma was awaited with considerable apprehension.

In the two hundred days between the first two Dumas the government negotiated with the liberal elements, attempted to quiet the country, passed new laws, and prepared the program which Stolypin was to submit to the new Duma. Having dissolved the first legislature without serious repercussions, apart from a number of unsuccessful mutinies incited by the revolutionaries, Stolypin was partially satisfied that the opposition was still too weak to oppose the government by force. Though the country as a whole was still in a state of considerable chaos, some semblance of order was being steadily restored in both Moscow and St. Petersburg. With the ebbing of the influence of the Kadet Party following the Vyborg fiasco, Stolypin felt that his chances for drawing the liberals into the Cabinet had been increased, and he made immediate plans to invite more influential persons to accept office in his Cabinet.

Shipov, with his impressions of only a few weeks ago, and his conviction that Stolypin had been the one who dissolved the Duma, could not control his hurt pride. On 15 July, he and N. Lvov, a Progressist, came to see Stolypin, who asked both of them to join his Cabinet. The group of which Shipov was a leader was still very much in a minority in the Duma, but it constituted a useful body of opinion which Stolypin would have liked to incorporate in his Ministry. Shipov insisted that half of the ministerial posts should be given to his colleagues, a demand that neither Nicholas nor Stolypin could possibly accept at this time. Stolypin, conscious of his superior bargaining position, did not expect to hear any requests on this scale. Shipov, on the other hand, continued to feel that the Tsar and Stolypin would yet accede to his demands and that all problems would then be solved. As for the Kadets, Stolypin complained to the British Ambassador that they were vacillating and very uncertain, lacking the courage to take a decisive course.[35] As might be expected under such circumstances, nothing substantive resulted from these talks.

Less than a month after negotiations with the liberals, revolutionary terrorism climaxed in a bomb attempt on Stolypin's life at his summer home. Stolypin was unharmed, but over thirty people were killed or injured, including Stolypin's daughter, who almost lost her legs. Stolypin maintained his composure and, when V. Kokovtsov, the Minister of

Finance, arrived on the scene shortly after the explosion, declared: "This shall not alter our program. We shall continue to carry out our reforms. They are Russia's salvation."[36] Stolypin won widespread sympathy even from his political opponents as a result of the attack. This shift in public opinion considerably weakened the position of the revolutionaries and strengthened that of Stolypin.

A few days after this incident, while he was in session with his ministers, Stolypin received from the Monarch a letter which he took the liberty of reading aloud. The letter expressed the desire of the Tsar to institute immediately a law to combat the acts of terrorism which were so numerous throughout the country.[37] It is reasonable to assume that Stolypin read this letter before the ministers to show that it was a direct order from Nicholas, and that he was not seeking revenge for the happenings of the few days before. Hence the law relating to the specially constituted military court was passed on 19 August as an emergency measure under Article 87 of the Fundamental Laws.[38] This decree gave provincial governors power to deal with terrorists who were caught redhanded. The accused were to be tried before military courts, they were not permitted any defense, and executed--in most cases the penalty--within twenty-four hours of the pronouncement of sentence.[39]

Throughout the interim period Stolypin and his Cabinet concentrated their efforts on preparing new legislation to be placed before the next Duma. An impressive list of measures was drawn up, the most important expanding civil rights and those relating to national minorities; increasing the responsibilities and rights of local zemstvos and administration; improving local judicial systems; reforming education; granting freedom of worship; bettering the conditions of the workers, and expanding the rights of labor unions. All these measures were to be dwarfed by the issuance of a series of agrarian laws in October and November of that year.

Possible change in the Electoral Law of 11 December 1905 was another problem which Stolypin had to face during this crucial period. He did not revise its provisions for the new elections, even though he was as well aware as the rest of the Cabinet that the new Duma was likely to be as radical as the previous one, if not more so.[40] The most reasonable explanation of this behavior seems to be that Stolypin, remembering that Goremykin had come before the First Duma empty handed, felt that there had been a possibility that the last Duma would have been cooperative if a concrete program had been presented to it.[41] He seems to have considered that he might gain rather than lose if he were to leave the electoral law as it was and to present the Duma with a constructive program. With this tactic he could see if the representatives would work in harmony with him. If not, then they never would, and the electoral law would have to be changed in order to diminish the size of the extreme left wing opposition. In this way he would then obtain a workable legislative body.

At this stage it seems plausible that Stolypin did not feel that his effort in the direction of liberal reform would be hindered by the majority of the opposition, once it could see that he was earnestly striving towards reformist goals. In particular, he was determined on his agrarian proposals, for he was convinced that they were an essential foundation for the rest of his program. When he had been interviewed by the correspondent of the Associated Press in December 1907, Stolypin said that he was ready to meet the Duma half way with a battery of bills, that the work ahead was colossal and complicated. He emphasized that if the Duma would cooperate he and they could work together, but if not, he would not hesitate to dissolve it.[42] With these convictions and on this basis Stolypin prepared to face the newly elected assembly.

The composition of the Second Duma, which gathered on 20 February 1907, was somewhat different from that of the first. The left wing had increased its representation at the expense of the Kadets. Since the former now had over two hundred votes in the assembly, they felt that with the help of the national minorities and some Kadet votes they would be in a position to muster a majority, and thus drew a sharper line between themselves and the Kadet Party. Stolypin, on the other hand, strove throughout the session to draw the Kadets to his side. If he could win their favor, they, with the right wing and the Octobrists, plus sympathetic national minorities, might in turn be in a position to gather a majority which would make the Duma a workable institution.

The first two weeks of the Duma were quite uneventful, with everyone awaiting the appearance of the new Premier with his program. Stolypin's opening speech on 6 March 1907, which outlined his program, was in marked contrast in content and delivery to that given by Goremykin less than a year earlier. He elaborated on the bills which his government intended to introduce during the current session, dealing with the agrarian question, basic civil rights, workers' welfare, education--both higher and lower--local government reforms, judicial reforms, and bills concerned with the reorganization of the police, not to speak of bills of secondary importance.

Stolypin's speech was met with silence by the left wing as well as by the Kadets.[43] According to I. Tsereteli, the spokesman of the Social-Democratic Party in the Duma, this reaction was an expression of "indignation." Stolypin's program, which was aimed at improving the lot of the masses, nevertheless satisfied the demands which had been made by the opposition in the First Duma. As V. Maklakov, a leading Kadet, rightly observed, the Duma had no reasons to be offended, for Stolypin "spoke not of the past, but of the impending work of the Duma."[44] What is, of course, clear is that the radical left would have nullified its political role if it had supported Stolypin's program. It was also evident from the start that the opposition had no intention of cooperating with the government, an intention which was made emphatic when Tsereteli returned to the tribune and called upon the masses to "awaken to the struggle" against the existing order.[45]

Stolypin came back to the rostrum to respond to the thunder from the left, which he more or less anticipated but hoped would not materialize. He declared that, under his leadership, the government would "keep strictly to legality" and would seek to find a basis upon which mutual cooperation could be established. Stolypin ended his speech by saying that,

> Any section of the State Duma which wishes to work, which wishes to lead people to enlightenment, which wishes to solve the agrarian needs of the peasants, will be able here to get their views accepted, even if they are contrary to those of the government.[46]

At this point Stolypin thus stood as the "defender of constitutional government, not of autocracy."[47]

On 5 May 1907, the apartment of I. Ozol, a leading Social-Democrat in the Second Duma, was raided by the police and some thirty-five Social-Democratic deputies present at the meeting there were detained. Stolypin appeared before the Duma on 1 June and informed the assembly that an investigation of the Ozol case had revealed the existence of a revolutionary organization in which certain deputies were involved.[48] Stolypin then requested the Duma to waive the immunity of the Social-Democratic faction in the Duma and to agree to the removal of the entire group from the assembly and to the immediate arrest of the sixteen Social-Democratic members.

Such a request took the Duma by surprise. By midnight, after an emotional debate, the Kadets, with the aid of the Trudoviks and the Socialist-Revolutionaries, succeeded in transfering the question to a Duma committee. In the end, Stolypin decided to dissolve the Duma before the verdict of the committee was heard, probably because of a misunderstanding which occurred between Stolypin and Maklakov on the night of 2 June.[49]

In conjunction with the dissolution of the Second Duma one final point should be brought out regarding Stolypin's parliamentary strategy. He might well have supposed that, if he removed the Social-Democrats and came to some kind of workable agreement with the Kadets, he would have a workable majority for his policy of reform, and in consequence would not have to dissolve the Duma. Stolypin's aspiration to gain a majority and save the Second Duma was revealed in his discussion with Maklakov towards the end of March. At that time Stolypin asked Maklakov whether the government had a chance of gaining a majority. The latter replied that it was worth the effort to try to get one, and if a majority were obtained from so revolutionary an assembly it would certainly be a great victory.[50]

The Second Duma was dissolved by Stolypin on the morning of 3 June. The decision was entirely his, and should not suggest that his advocacy of the Duma was insincere.[51] Though the reactionary elements greeted the dissolution as a victory, it was not what Stolypin had hoped for. There is no doubt that he had hoped the Duma would collaborate with him in the implementation of his program; however, that was not to be. Here, as later, Stolypin had to fight against both streams which threatened the development of a parliamentary tradition in Russia--the revolutionary and the reactionary. As he told Sir Arthur Nicolson, the British Ambassador, shortly after the dissolution: "Reaction must not be allowed to gain the upper hand, and moderate liberal measures must be carried through."[52] It is important to note that it was Stolypin who succeeded in calling the Third Duma, which Nicholas and the Court camarilla would have preferred not to have summoned.

Even though the new electoral law, which was published on 3 June, limited the franchise, the peasantry still remained the majority of the electorate.[53] Under the new conditions and the new circumstances, the Third Duma, which convened on 1 November, began discussing the most important and decisive issue confronting the nation--the agrarian question.

NOTES

1. Leontovitsch, V., Geschichte Des Liberalismus in Russland (Frankfurt, 1959), p.289.

2. Tverskoi, P., "K Istoricheskim Materialam o Pokoinom P.A. Stolypine," Vestnik Evropy (April, 1912), p.188.

3. Martov, L., Maslov, P., and Potresov, A., Obshchestvennoe Dvizhenie v Rossii v Nachale XX veka (SPB, 1909-14), Vol. I, Part I, p.51. (Hereafter O.D.).

4. Ibid., p.78.

5. Sir Donald Mackenzie Wallace, Correspondence, Printing House Square, London. Letter dated 9 December 1906. (Hereafter Wallace Correspondence). Trotsky, L., 1905 (Moscow, n.d.), p.114.

6. Kryzhanovskii, S., Vospominaniia. Iz Bumag S.E. Kryzhanovskago, Posledniago Gosudarstvennago Sekretaria Rossiiskoi Imperii (Berlin, 1930), p.66.

7. Kurlov, P., Konets Russkogo Tsarizma (Petrograd, 1923), p.33. See also Wallace Correspondence, Letter dated 6 December 1906.

8. Shulgin, V., Dni (Belgrade, 1925), p.72. The Times (London), 31 October 1905, p.5.

9. *Polnoe Sobranie Zakonov Rossiiskoi Imperii. Sobranie Tretie*, Vol. XXV, No. 26805. (hereafter P.S.Z.).

10. *O.D.*, Vol. II, Part I, p.92.

11. Miliukov, P., *God Borby. Publitsisticheskaia Khronika 1905-1906* (SPB, 1907), p.72.

12. Miliukov, P., *Vospominaniia (1859-1917)* (New York, 1955), Vol. I, p.318.

13. Shipov, D., *Vospominaniia i Dumy o Perezhitom* (Moscow, 1918), pp.344-347.

14. Miliukov, P., *op. cit.*, p.325.

15. Oldenburg, S., *Tsarstvovanie Imperatora Nikolaia II* (Belgrade, 1939), Vol. I, p.334.

16. Witte, S., *Vospominaniia Tsarstvovanie Nikolaia II* (Berlin, 1922), Vol. II, p.97.

17. Bing, E., ed. *The Letters of Tsar Nicholas and Empress Marie* (London, 1937), p.212.

18. Witte, S., *op. cit.*, pp.294-297.

19. Bogdanovich, A., *Tri Poslednikh Samoderzhtsa. Dnevnik A.V. Bogdanovicha* (Moscow, 1924), p.379. Petr Arkadevich Stolypin was born on 21 April 1862 in Dresden, the son of General Arkadii Dmitrievich Stolypin, a hero of Sevastopol and a man of liberal views; his mother was born Princess Natalie Mikhailovna Gorchakova. Stolypin spent most of his childhood on the Srednikovo estate near Moscow, until his father returned to Vilna where the boy finished his secondary education at the Gymnasium. He then went to the University of St. Petersburg to continue his studies in the Faculty of Natural Sciences, from which he graduated in 1884. In November of that year he married Olga Borisovna, one of the daughters of General Neydhardt, the Lord Steward of the Imperial Household.

After leaving St. Petersburg University he gained a post at the Ministry of the Interior. Approximately two years later he transferred to the Ministry of State Domains, where he occupied various positions chiefly concerned with agriculture. Shortly afterwards, tired of the bureaucratic routine, he decided to settle down as a young squire on the family estate in the Province of Kovno (Bok, M., Vospominaniia o Moem Ottse P.A. Stolypine (New York, 1953), p.43), being seemingly content with life on his estate, improving agricultural methods and participating in the social life of the district. In 1889 Stolypin was elected Marshal of the Nobility for the district of Kovno, and ten years later, in 1899, was promoted to the same post for the whole province. This gave him a closer acquaintance with local needs, further developed the ability as a speaker, a gift he already had, and gave him considerable administrative experience. In May of 1902 he was appointed governor of the province of Grodno (Bok, M., op. cit., p.112). His superiors observed his activities closely, for here seemed a young man of promise, possessed of the qualities required of an administrator of a difficult province. A year later, in February 1903, Stolypin was appointed governor of Saratov, a traditional hotbed of revolutionary activity, an area of dissatisfaction going back to the days of Pugachev. For a lesser man the new appointment would scarcely have been a promotion. When the 1905 Revolution set in, Saratov outdid all the other provinces in violent agrarian disturbances, many estates being burned and pillaged and landlords killed. Sir Bernard Pares, who visited the province on more than one occasion during Stolypin's term of office, noted that what struck him most was that both Stolypin's friends and enemies respected him (In the private notes and letters of Sir Bernard Pares, School of Slavonic and East European Studies Library, London).

A man who was able to maintain order in Saratov in such a manner was clearly a man destined for a yet more important post and all this was without doubt reported to the Emperor. By the time Stolypin was finally assigned to St. Petersburg he had developed his character and personality in the face of the magnitude and diversity of his experiences during the turbulent years of Saratov. In appearance he was tall, with a large head, impressive and penetrating eyes, a high forehead and a striking beard and mustache. Stolypin was a witty and genial host; in his personal relations he preserved a natural simplicity, mingling easily with all classes. He was a good talker and listener, eager to learn, vividly interested in everything and everybody (Conversation with Baron A.F. Meyendorff, first cousin of P.A. Stolypin. Hereafter Baron Meyendorff). A lifelong asset of great importance in the various positions he held was his remarkable memory, and his swift ability to grasp the difficulties of a fresh problem (Zavarzin, P., Rabota Tainoi Politsii (Paris, 1924), p.143). Prior to achieving prominance in Russian politics Stolypin found time to travel extensively in Europe and was much more Western in outlook than is suspected. He had a good command of English, French, German and a fair knowledge of Polish (Conversation with Mrs. M. Bok, Stolypin's oldest daughter).

20. Bok, M., *op. cit.*, p.220.

21. Stolypin told Baron Meyendorff, as regards this appointment, "They have put a horse's collar on my neck." Baron Meyendorff also noted that Stolypin was lost in the St. Petersburg bureaucratic world. The Baron's exact words were, "on byl v lesu," that is, "he was all at sea."

22. Bok, M., *op. cit.*, p.159.

23. The franchise was granted to those who owned property, or paid house or business taxes. These property qualifications limited the urban franchise, so that few workers were represented in the Duma. Some twenty large cities enjoyed separate representation, which gave the workers some degree of representation. The electoral law had been designed to give the peasantry a representative majority.

24. Article 87 provided that the Monarch might enact emergency laws on urgent matters when the legislature was not in session. However, this legislation ceased to function unless the enactment was brought before the Duma within the first two months after the opening of the next session. Article 105 stated that the Duma could be dissolved by the Tsar before the completion of its five year term, but that the decree of dissolution had to contain the dates for a new election for the convening of the next Duma.

25. Hosking, G., _The Russian Constitutional Experiment: Government and Duma 1907-1914_ (Cambridge, 1973), p.12.

26. Sidelnikov, S., _Obrazovanie i Deiatelnost Pervoi Dumy_ (Moscow, 1962), p.98.

27. _Gosudarstvennaia Duma, Pervogo Sozyva, Stenograficheskie Otchety_, 13 May 1906, pp.321-325. See also _Public Record Office_ F.O. 371, Vol. 127, No. 27544, 6 August 1906 (Hereafter P.R.O.).

28. Maklakov, V., _Vtoraia Gosudarstvennaia Duma_ (Paris, 1944), p.14.

29. Tyrkova-Williams, A., _Na Putiakh k Svobode_ (New York, 1952), p.347.

30. Kokovtsov, V., _Iz Moego Proshlago. Vospominaniia 1903-1919 g.g._ (Paris, 1933) Vol. I, p.214. Stishinskii occupied the post of Minister of Agriculture and Shirinskii-

Shikhmatov was Attorney General of the Holy Synod.

31. Oldenburg, S., *op*. *cit*., p.363.

32. Kizevetter, A., *Na Rubezhakh Dvukh Stoletii: Vospominaniia 1881-1914* (Prague, 1929), p.435.

33. It was not until December 1907 that they were tried and sentenced to three months imprisonment and barred from taking any active part in the assembly.

34. *P.R.O.*, F.O. 371, Vol. 126, No. 26843, 25 July 1906.

35. *P.R.O.*, F.O. 371, Vol. 324, No. 18906, 29 May 1907.

36. Gurko, V., *op*. *cit*., p.498.

37. *Krasnyi Arkhiv*, Vol. 5 (1924), p.103.

38. *P.S.Z.*, Vol. XXVI, No. 28,252.

39. During the two years 1906-1907, over four thousand persons were killed by Maximalists through acts of terrorism, while those executed under this law during the eight months it was in full force numbered 638 persons. See *O.D.*, p. 65; Maklakov, V., *op*. *cit*., p.18; *Krasnyi Arkhiv*, Vol. 8 (1925), pp.224-243; *P.R.O.*, F.O. 371, Vol. 728, No. 13,600, 7 April 1909.

40. *P.R.O.*, F.O. 371, Vol. 126, No. 26,843.

41. *P.R.O.*, F.O. 371, Vol. 127, No. 27,544, 6 August 1906 and Vol. 321, No. 5229, 7 February 1906.

42. *Vestnik Evropy*, *op*. *cit*., p.193.

43. It had presumably been arranged in advance to receive the address in absolute silence. See P.R.O., F.O. 371, Vol. 514, No. 3642, 29 January 1907.

44. Maklakov, V., *op. cit.*, p.86.

45. *Gosudarstvennaia Duma, Vtorogo Sozyva, Stenograficheskie Otchety*, 6 March 1907, Col. 126.

46. *Ibid.*, Col. 169.

47. Maklakov, V., *op. cit.*, p.95.

48. Tsitron, A., *103 Dnia Vtoroi Dumy* (SPB, 1907), p.178. The government had at its disposal numerous incriminating documents which were confiscated at the home of Ozol and Alexinsky. See P.R.O., F.O. 371, Vol. 324, No. 21,209, 27 June 1907.

49. For details see my article "P.A. Stolypin and the Second Duma," *The Slavonic and East European Review*, Vol. 50, No. 118, January 1972, pp.60-61.

50. Maklakov, V., *op. cit.*, p.228. Maklakov felt that, after the October Manifesto, people like himself, were able to work against autocracy, in the form it was then found, within the framework of the law. He also felt that the Fundamental Laws of 1906 were far more dependable than Miliukov's irreconcilable tactics, which leaned towards revolution. If, as he says, Miliukov was in favor of constitutional monarchy, it was imperative for the Kadet Party to look for and to find the limits of cooperation. But he decided that the government was not sincere and found an ally in Acheron. By so doing Miliukov, according to Maklakov, deprived liberalism any reform of any foundation. See letters dated 21 February 1956 (Items No. 85-88), 16 March 1956 (Items 113-115) in the unpublished Maklakov-Elkin Correspondence, The Bodeleian.

51. P.R.O., F.O. 371, Vol. 512, No. 30,901, 4 September 1908.

52. P.R.O., F.O. 371, Vol. 326, No. 29,515, 16 August 1907.

53. For more on the electoral law and the elections, see Levin, A., The Third Duma: Election and Profile (Connecticut, 1973).

CHAPTER II

THE AGRARIAN QUESTION

The issue which occupied Stolypin throughout the whole course of his political career in St. Petersburg was the agrarian question. It was also the most debated question in the Third Duma and one which took the Duma and the State Council four years to enact into law. For that matter, in few other countries has the agrarian question played as important a role as it did in Russia in the two decades preceding the First World War. The agrarian unrest which reached its climax against the background of revolution in 1905 was daringly challenged by Stolypin with the series of reforms which bear his name.

With the shameful and chaotic results of the Russo-Japanese War and subsequent domestic events, it became clear to most knowledgeable Russians that an extreme had been reached requiring the introduction of drastic and unmistakable reforms. The driving force of the change lay within the increasing pressure from the oppressed peasantry, who had started to ravage the countryside with gathering fury. The government had spent its time in endless discussions of agrarian reform and had now studied the question with complete thoroughness. Nevertheless, though the government realized the problem, no government representative was bold enough to initiate the colossal task of attempting a radical reform of agriculture. It had become more than obvious that any further postponement of reform would mean a complete catastrophe for the monarchy and the entire established regime. With no definite program, the government merely intensified its measures of repression, thus increasing discontent and encouraging the revolutionaries to further action. Many in the government may perhaps have felt that the agrarian reforms, and how they were to be executed, were far from clear.[1]

To relieve the peasant condition as best it could, the government issued a series of enactments which can be considered as forerunners of Stolypin's subsequent agrarian legislation. On 12 March 1903,[2] it issued an ukase abolishing the *krugovaia poruka* (mutual guarantee). This was followed by the Ukase of 11 August 1904,[3] abolishing corporal punishment by the volost courts; and the Ukase of 3 November 1905,[4] by which the balance of outstanding redemption payments was cancelled as of 1 January 1907, thus making each peasant the legal owner of his plot.

Even though these three enactments altered considerably the legal status of the peasantry and were intended to meet their demands, their effect seemed to be only to stimulate the peasantry to further violence. In the middle of February 1905, serious peasant disturbances broke out in the provinces of Kursk, Orel, and Chernigov, and by the summer of the same year embraced almost thirty provinces, including outlying areas like the Baltic, Bessarabia and the Caucasus.[5] The leaders of this mass movement included not only active revolutionaries, but also sympathizers from the learned professions, usually called the "third element," who helped organize the movement.[6]

An imaginative and effective reform remained a prerequisite of the highest order if peace and tranquility were to be restored. It could no longer be denied that the prime motive of any such reform should be to satisfy the peasants' hunger for land. The main point of contention was the most feasible path of reaching this aim, so as to avoid and not engender a revolutionary upheaval. This question in turn depended on the attitude adopted towards the commune--that crux of the agricultural situation. Broadly, on the eve of the 1905 Revolution two distinct views were held within the government hierarchy. One group sought the preservation of the commune at all costs and wished to restrict reforms simply to improving and assisting methods of cultivation; the other advocated the breaking of the commune into individual farms.

It is of interest to relate Stolypin's own opinions on these questions against this background. Immediately after being appointed governor of Grodno in 1902, Stolypin had stressed, in his first speech before the provincial committee, that the practical means to improve agriculture lay in settling peasants on individual _khutors_ (enclosed farmsteads) and in abolishing the strip system, with the grant of financial aid from the government for land improvement.[7] These views had in fact already been clearly expounded by his uncle Dmitrii Stolypin and this circumstantial factor suggests that Stolypin himself had been influenced by his uncle's experiences. D. Stolypin had attacked the communal system as early as the 1870's, insisting that only individual ownership could raise the standards of Russian agriculture, by encouraging initiative and the full use of the land. He had also experimented with _khutors_ which he had separated from his own estate and rented to peasants for twelve year periods. These projects, which had been carefully recorded and had reached a successful conclusion,[8] must have reached the ears of the young Stolypin and convinced him that they contained a practical alternative to the Russian agrarian problem, a view which he later advocated with such persistence.

In a report to the Tsar in 1904, while still governor of Saratov, Stolypin first officially formulated his ideas on the agrarian question:

> The only counterbalance to the _obshchina_ land organization is the individual peasant homestead. Private peasant ownership is a guarantee of order, because each small owner represents the nucleus on which rests the stability of public order . . . Such a type of peasant is already in existence in the western provinces and he is particularly desired now.[9]

Later in that year, in reply to a telegram from Durnovo--then Minister of the Interior--asking for an explanation of the agrarian disturbances in

Saratov, Stolypin attributed the peasant disturbances largely to revolutionary incitement. He added, however, that in his view land hunger could not be adequately satisfied merely by adding new strips to the existing allotment holdings with the aid of the Peasant Land Bank. Stolypin noted that in most cases the rebellious ones were those with sufficient land, whereas the land-hungry peasants did not in general break the law. In his reply he emphasized that the basic solution to the problem lay in the establishment of a class of small land owners, who, as he expressed it, "are by nature organic enemies of all destructive theories."[10]

The unanimous replies of the provincial governors to Durnovo's telegram, which made clear that revolutionary propaganda was the immediate cause of the disturbances,[11] formed the basis of a report to the Tsar. This, together with a memorandum of the Council of Ministers containing the minutes of their discussion of the problem, was handed to the Emperor on 4 March 1906.[12] On the same day an ukase was issued establishing provincial and district agrarian commissions for the purpose of dealing with land settlement problems.[13] Even at this late stage the Council of Ministers only established these local commissions in order to study the problem; no plans were made to tackle the agrarian issue radically.

Immediately after the dissolution of the First Duma and his appointment as Premier in July 1906, Stolypin set about preparing for the agrarian reform which was intended to change the structure of Russian agriculture. Although Count Witte and others had suggested replacing the commune by individual homesteads, it remained for Stolypin to take the decision and to obtain the Emperor's consent to implement such a step. What distinguished Stolypin from his predecessors was the fact that he brought with him to the ministry the idea of turning the Russian peasant into a truly free, individual small landowner; it was not a conviction that he picked up casually, or had had imposed upon him, but one which he had long held and deliberated upon. Within the first weeks after the dissolution, the Monarch discussed the land issue with the members of his immediate family and with the ministers most vitally concerned.[14] In these discussions, though himself well informed, Stolypin was aided by an impressive retinue of agricultural experts, such as A. Kofod, A. Krivoshein, S. Shidlovsky, V. Gurko, A. Rittich, A. Lykoshin, and N. Demchinsky, not to speak of an important staff of specialists and officials.[15]

In Stolypin's view, the keynote to all future political development lay in the solution to the agrarian problem. He therefore sought to make the land-hungry peasant a law-abiding citizen, and, hand-in-hand with this, an independent farmer whose interest in his plot, together with his competitive instinct, would improve methods of cultivation.[16] Through these basic means he felt that the Russian agrarian question could be solved without revolutionary upheaval. A really contented peasantry would, in the end, safeguard the rights of individual property and respect the laws of the state. The fate of Russia therefore depended on shaping or influencing the attitude of the peasantry, and Stolypin was only too well aware that the revolutionary parties would stop at nothing to rouse the peasant masses against the existing order.

Stolypin expressed the views of his Ministry to an Associated Press correspondent in a vivid and concise form. The government, he said, had no other alternative but to hurry through its reforms in order to distract the appetites which had been incited and to guide the masses towards the only practical path:

> Time flies quickly, and the nation is stirred with a colossal agitation--whereas the agrarian reform, simply by its nature, can move forward at a very slow pace. This is the reason for the haste of the Act and form given it. In essentials the commune is a greater hindrance to our political and economic development than all the

> other factors taken together. It hinders the welfare of the peasants and their opportunities for individualism, as well as the formation of a middle class, a class of small land owners which constitutes the power and well being of most advanced Western countries. What, if not the individualism of the small farm ownership, so quickly pushed America out to the fore? Our land commune is a rotten anachronism. . . Give the strong personality of the peasantry an outlet, free it from the influence of ignorance, indolence and drunkenness, and you will have a firm and stable foundation for the development of the country without any utopian, artificial and harmful leaps. The commune in its present state does not help the weak, but crushes and destroys the strong and ruins the nation's energy and might.[17]

Stolypin's agrarian reform came into effect in the period between the first two Dumas with the enactment in quick succession of his three most important ukases under Article 87 of the Fundamental Laws. The Ukase of 5 October 1906[18] abolished the restrictions placed upon the personal rights of the peasantry; the Ukase of 15 November[19] revised and extended the functions of the Peasant Land Bank, so that its credit operations extended to reach the more impoverished peasants and helped them to buy and improve private land; and, lastly, the most important of the three, the Ukase of 9 November[20] provided that every head of a household within the commune could claim his share of the land as private property in a single and entire plot, and at the same time the right to leave the commune.

It would be undiscerning to argue that Stolypin had no respect for the legislative powers of the Duma, since the Duma debated a bill which was already being promulgated. What has to be borne in mind is that the status of the peasantry was to change drastically as of 1 January 1907, and it was imperative for the government, or Stolypin, to define their position and their newly acquired rights. This reason, more than any other, dictated the introduction of Stolypin's agrarian enactments under Article 87, prior to the convening of the Third Duma.

Elected under the restrictions of the new electoral law, the Third Duma met on 1 November 1907, with a conservative majority.[21] Although the conservative element was more prominent than in the preceeding two Dumas, the third, if a workable Duma was the only hope for the development of parliamentary government, may be regarded as a continuing step in that direction, comparing not too unfavorably with corresponding developments in Germany and Austria-Hungary. It would be wrong, however, to lump together the Octobrists, the largest single party, with the right wing reactionaries.[22] The Monarch in fact personally despised Guchkov, their leader; more unequivocally, the right wing opposed his nomination as chairman in 1910, although the Progressivists, Moslems, and Poles supported it.[23] The opposition, strictly speaking, was nevertheless composed of some fifty Kadets and a mere handful of Socialist-Revolutionaries and Trudoviks.

Stolypin's first appearance before the Third Duma was on 16 November 1907, when he reaffirmed the Ukase of 9 November 1906, with some added clarification. He repeated what he had said before the Second Duma and then summarized his attitude as follows:

> By setting on its feet the large rural population and giving it an opportunity to achieve economic self-sufficiency, the legislative institutions have established the foundation upon which a sure transformation of the structure will be attained.[24]

The representatives of the right and center, occupied by the Octobrists, gave a favorable reception to Stolypin's reform program.[25] The left wing deputies declared that the Duma, like the government, represented only a privileged minority which had no interest in the progress of the country and reiterated that the government had misused its powers under Article 87, having illegally dissolved the first two Dumas. Representatives of the national minorities spoke in comparatively mild terms and seemed generally to sympathize with the government's stand for reform. As for the Ukase of 9 November, they showed indifference perhaps because their nationals would not benefit by it.[26] Nevertheless, the national minorities failed in the main to oppose the agrarian reform with any passion and only joined the opposition ranks when their interests seemed directly affected.

Briefly, but energetically, Maklakov, though criticizing some aspects of Stolypin's speech, then stated that if the government would comply with what had been promised in the October Manifesto, there would be only minor differences between his party and the official line: "We stand on the same grounds and in details we will be able to come to terms."[27] Throughout the Third Duma the Kadets never denied that communal land tenure was obsolete and implied strongly that it would be necessary to replace it with private ownership. Their main point, however, was that the process of agrarian reform should be evolutionary and not enforced, even by the intervention of law.

Stolypin returned to the tribune for a second time, stating that, though he had noted the accusations and criticism which had been made, he did not intend to enter into further apologia for the government. However, he said that he could not ignore the accusations of a deliberate policy of rule by force,

> . . . that the government is aiming to establish in Russia some kind of a police state, that it aims to clench the whole nation in the clutches of some arbitrary rule and coercion. That is not so.[28]

In the interest of the country, at an exceptional time, the government had been forced to use measures outside the category of normal procedures. Nevertheless,

> The government, simultaneously with the suppression of revolution, is carrying out the task of making it possible for the population actually and truly to use the rights recently granted them--as long as the peasant remains impoverished, as long as he finds himself forcibly in the grip of the commune, he will remain a slave and no written law will give him the benefit of civil liberty. . . The small landowner will no doubt become the nucleus of the future zemstvo's smallest unit; for he is hard working, possessing a feeling of dignity, and will contribute culture, enlightenment, and sufficiency to the village. Only then will the written freedom turn and be realized in real freedom.[29]

The fact that Stolypin was able to meet the opposition's case on the issue of "arbitration and coercion" with an unprecedented degree of success, deserves special mention and should have sufficed to convince the opposition at least of his logic and personal integrity. Their reaction, however, was a mixture of ill-founded attacks and apathy. The latter may perhaps be attributed to the fact that the opposition felt that their numbers were too few to be effective in debate and that the passing of the agrarian law was a matter of time--a virtual fait accompli. Miliukov attacked the Premier's speech as based on intimidation rather than on trust and confidence, and cast stray darts at the Octobrists.[30] He concluded his speech on a historico-sociological note: "The ideal of small individual ownership is not a Russian ideal, and still more, not a Russian reality."[31]

On 22 November 1907, the Third Duma elected an agrarian committee which proceeded to debate the provisions of the Ukase of 9 November 1906. It was not until October 1908 that the ukase was finally brought back to the plenary sessions.[32] The report of the agrarian committee was presented by Shidlovsky, an Octobrist who had been its chairman. He began by covering the main articles of the Land Statute of 1861, showing the parallels with the new ukase; he then explained the pros and cons of the system of communal land tenure and emphasized the significance of the Manifesto of 3 November 1905, which had abrogated redemption payments as of the beginning of January of 1907, showing the urgent need for a law which would serve to outline the peasants' new legal rights to their plots. Turning to the Ukase of 9 November 1906, he said that the agrarian committee looked favorably upon it since it promoted the individual ownership which was indispensable to the raising of agricultural productivity. Shidlovsky then stressed with emphasis that anyone who sought sincerely to bring the existing system of government into a permanent framework of law could not argue against the private ownership of land--for land in itself, he said,

> . . . is only a field for the application of individual labor and capital, and labor can only be productive when the person performing it is placed in a favorable position. The most important conditions, are, I feel, personal initiative, the liberty of creative energy, security from non-interference, and, finally, individual self interest.[33]

In the opinion of the committee, Shidlovsky continued, the solution of the agrarian problem depended largely on the creation of small individual farmers placed on a footing which would insure the development of the inherently creative forces of the cultivator.[34] Though he agreed with the slogan malozemele (land shortage), the main obstacle lay in the ever increasing population. From either viewpoint, however, it was necessary to tackle the problem not only from the standpoint of quantity of land obtainable, but also from that of quality of cultivation. The commune was a deterrent to the improvement of the soil on both grounds, he announced, a formerly progressive unit which had outlived its day. To the opposition's proposals of socialism, municipalization, or nationalization he added that these proposals, "have not come out of their theoretical stage as yet and cannot represent an accomplished means of solving the agrarian question simply by transferring a definite amount of land to a definite number of people." In conclusion he pointed out the importance of climatic factors in Russia, which rendered over half of the year unproductive. The villages spent in the winter months all that had been earned during the summer, and only the expansion of industry could overcome this economic drawback.[35]

Thus commenced the general debates on the agrarian question which continued until the end of November. The left wing, greatly reduced both in numbers and quality, continued to attack the government in the same vein as during the previous two Dumas. A.Kropotov, a Trudovik, attacked the bill on the usual grounds that it supported the pomeshchiks, that it was attempting to convert certain peasants into <u>kulaks</u> and that the rest of the peasantry would be pauperized.[36] The speech of I. Tomilov, another Trudovik, typified the replies of the left. He first maintained that the ukase would bring only chaos to the village and benefit only the privileged class. He drew a grim picture of a future in which most of the land would go, at the expense of the commune, to the capitalists or to the new class of "pomeshchik peasants," thus transforming the landless peasants into a class of agrarian proletariat (<u>batraki</u>) who would move to the cities and cause further unemployment and price hikes. He then announced that the main aim of the legislation was to stamp out revolution by sowing antagonism among the peasants, thus distracting their attention from expropriating land from the landed gentry, and concluded by calling upon the Duma to reject the proposal.[37]

E. Gegechkori, speaking for the Social-Democrats, once more attacked the government for passing the ukase under Article 87, on the grounds that it benefited only the gentry. Having covered events from 1861 in exhaustive review, he pronounced that, "the peasant does not rebel because of hunger, but because he is a member of the commune--a communist."[38]

In the face of these extreme attacks, the Kadets took an appreciably more lenient stand than had been the case in the earlier Dumas; they were the opposition party which made the most constructive criticism and took an active part when detailed amendments were considered. A. Shingarev, the agrarian spokesman for the Kadet Party, said that land owned by peasants privately was a "just" concept, and went on to criticize the reform for its rapid application.[39] F. Rodichev, another Kadet, spoke in favor of the disintegration of the commune and the institution of private ownership of land. If the more pertinent constructive statements are considered, it appears that Rodichev had no real basis of disagreement with the government's policy; if anything, there is a certain congruency. For example, he insisted that the government should try to eliminate the various hindrances in the way of agricultural development, although this was precisely what the government was trying to do. However, like the rest of the opposition, Rodichev insisted that it was his duty to reject the law and to help prepare a new one.[40]

P. Dvorianinov, a non-party peasant from the province of Tver, no doubt expressed the view of a fair section of the peasant population when he said that he regretted to see the new bill being opposed as it stood, for, as he said, "this law is indispensable to us." He could not, likewise, accept the contention of some deputies who argued that land could be consolidated without any laws or agrarian committees, or without the aid of the government. When he had attempted to consolidate his own strips, the village assembly had prevented him. In his view, the law was being rejected not because of its defects, but simply because it was being promulgated by the existing government.[41]

The government was rather thorough in answering the attacks and accusations of the opposition speakers. Lykoshin, the assistant to the Minister of the Interior, began by reiterating Shidlovsky's explanation of the urgency in issuing the ukase, namely, the desire to abrogate redemption payments effective 1 January 1907. This factor had placed the ukase within the category of Article 87 of the Fundamental Laws, as a measure which could not be postponed. The pessimistic views which had been expressed were refuted by the fact that some 300,000 peasants had already enclosed their plots by 1 August 1908, and over 700,000 applications for such enclosures had been received by the government before 1 September. Lykoshin also emphasized that the main object of the ukase was to eliminate the strip system. He then developed his two most important points: first, that the principles and aspirations expressed in the government's agrarian policy had found a response among the peasant masses; and second, that these measures had brought about a considerable amount of tranquillity in the country, a fact which could be explained only by the general realization that order and tranquillity alone could guarantee any type of ownership.[42]

Lykoshin returned on another occasion to answer some new points which had arisen in the course of the debates. Here he repeated Stolypin's assurance that wherever the commune was strong the ukase would have little effect; in reply to a statement that the decaying communes should be left to die of their own accord, he replied that those who expressed such views could have no idea what a "decaying commune" was like. He continued,

> It is strange, gentlemen, to hear when such a commune is brought to us as an ideal in fairness, and as an institution which could further some kind of an equalizing distribution of land when precisely the very fact of the existence of such a commune strengthens the landlessness of the peasantry.[43]

This reply was aimed at the Kadets' insistence that the commune should be left to perish by inertia, without the aid of legislation. It was undeniable that the agrarian problem had to be dealt with immediately, for even under usual conditions and normal rates of industrial growth, the question could only grow more complex over the coming years--a view which even the most left wing writers could scarcely deny.[44]

Concerning the opposition's view that the Ukase of 9 November would cause dissension amongst the different classes of the peasantry, Lykoshin said that,

> These accusations spring from an erroneous notion of what is presently happening within the commune. It cannot be unknown to anyone who knows a village, what redistribution in a decaying commune represents. . . what quarrels and clashes come into being, sometimes leading to bloodshed; what crying injustices are done in redistributing, what malice accumulates in those who have to give up the land which was tilled and brought up to the high level of fertility by them.[45]

Listing the government's efforts towards reform, he admitted that each item could be criticized, but it was undeniable that there had never been a time in the entire history of Russia when such an effort of official energy and means had been directed to raising the welfare of the masses.[46]

On 10 November, Krivoshein, the Minister of Agriculture, himself made a long and informative speech, expanding upon some of the issues which had been left outstanding. He emphasized the need to increase per capita output, since Russia was lagging behind most European countries, and stressed that economic development would be the government's main concern.[47] If productivity could be increased by 8 to 9 puds per desiatin (one pud equals 36 pounds) this would enrich the nation by some 400 million rubles; only by improving methods of cultivation and eliminating all the obstacles between the cultivator and his land, however, could such a solution be found.

Krivoshein denied emphatically that the government supported the interests of the large landowning class to the exclusion of all others, and stressed that the ukase was meant to help the ever growing class of small landowners.[48] He acknowledged that the law of 1861 had stopped short of turning the peasants into full private proprietors, but argued that the Ukase of 9 November would make the peasants the real owners on their plots. Thus, in his view, the ukase complied with the basic notion of the Land Statute of 1861 and constituted a further emancipation of the peasants from the soil. "We are told that the land should belong to the one who tills it," said Krivoshein on 10 November 1908, "but that in the interest of the state every patch of land should be in the hands of those best able to gain the utmost from it." This remark was even greeted with cries of "Correct!" from the left, and "With this we can agree!" However, he continued, the present growth of population made it impossible to give every peasant an adequate plot of land, and that the ukase had permitted those who wished to leave the soil to do so freely. For one reason or another, individual peasants might feel that it was possible for them to do better elsewhere, but at least those who had the desire to remain on the land would not be constrained in the application of their creative labors. Lastly, referring to the argument that the government was more sympathetic to the more wealthy peasants, Krivoshein said that this accusation was misleading; those persons who had succeeded, at least in a little way, in emerging from the slumbering inert mass of the peasantry, deserved a measure of admiration and encouragement rather than reproach, for they had also benefited the community. He concluded,

I see no reason to fear the development of individuality in the peasantry and am convinced that this development will not in the least threaten us with the ruin of social and collective beginnings.[49]

Shidlovsky returned to the rostrum and implored the opposition to raise questions during the detailed reading of the ukase, stressing that it would be wrong to make the ukase a phase or object of class warfare. The Duma should respond with fairness and with the interest of the state primarily in mind.[50] To the opposition's call for expropriation and equalization, Shidlovsky asked, "Do you think that it will stop at that?"[51] In his opinion expropriation could not possibly satisfy the demands of the peasantry, for there was more need than there was land to be had. Moreover, the principle of "absolute equality" among the peasants themselves was absurd; some would always have more land than others, who would in turn resent that fact. If matters were ever carried so far, he continued, the peasants would then realize for themselves "No, this is impossible, we have to settle it in some other way."[52] The commune, moreover, was defective and unable to meet changing conditions. It would be wrong he held, to assume that each peasant found the commune a refuge in his hour of need, for in many cases, for instance where the head of a family died, the commune would interfere and often leave the family destitute by taking the plot away: "That is why one cannot treat the commune as a mother, for very often she becomes a step-mother."[53]

With this speech the major debates on the agrarian question in the Third Duma drew to an end. As early as mid-November the atmosphere in the Duma was one of impatience among the right wing and Octobrist deputies who felt that the question had already been adequately discussed. The opposition, however, countered all motions to proceed to the reading of the ukase.[54] Even S. Wankowicz, speaking for the Polish group, produced a short and energetic speech in which, to the surprise of all, he announced that the Polish deputies supported the motion to proceed to the reading of the ukase.[55] This brought applause from the right and the center, and commotion on the left. The Moslems, to the surprise of the Poles, announced their group was against the reading of the ukase.[56]

Taken against the general background of these debates, it becomes clear that the emphasis of the extreme left opposition was mainly upon intimidating the peasantry and convincing them that economic doom, impoverishment, and exploitation were upon them, and that the few were to be enriched at the expense of the many. By this time, the opposition on the left appeared to lack stamina, or, more correctly, an ability or willingness to focus on the practical point at issue and to score points at that level--here the government, lead by Stolypin, had the best of it.

The Kadets, in the final analysis, were never closer to the government views than they were at the close of the debates in the Third Duma. It is no wonder that the left accused the Kadets of joining hands with the right wing. The Kadets' main point of disagreement was over the question of the tempo in which the reform was being carried out. However, this question could be reduced to what Maklakov had earlier referred to as a matter of detail on which both sides could come to terms.

On 22 November, the Duma finally decided by a majority vote in favor of an article-by-article reading of the ukase, which was then read and debated.[57] Proposed amendments were voted upon at once. While the Duma was still at the initial stages, Stolypin appeared in order to give a further resume of the government's attitude towards the measure. The meaning of the ukase, he declared, was no doubt clear to all, but he wished to stress the importance of the individuality of the peasant,

> In those areas of Russia where the individualism of the peasant has already received a definite development,

> where the commune, as a compulsive union, hinders his individuality, there it is essential to give the peasant the freedom to apply his labor to the soil, there it is essential to give him freedom to work, to get rich and to manage his own property; he has to be given authority over the soil, he has to be freed from the bondage of the moribund communal system.[58]

Stolypin, it must be repeated, was not opposed to the commune as an institution of the agrarian economy as such. He was only against the commune in those cases where, and to the extent that, it had degenerated into a system which hindered the development of agriculture and of the economy as a whole. A private proprietor in the light of the new law was a peasant who had his plot at his sole disposal, so that he could do whatever he pleased with it. On this occasion Stolypin made an important and significant statement which was misinterpreted not only by the members of the opposition but also by subsequent Soviet historians of the period.

> The government took this great responsibility of passing the Ukase of November 9, 1906, under Article 87; for it put the wager not on the wretched and the drunk, but on the strong. Close to half a million such householders were found in a short time, who have consolidated over 3,200,000 desiatins of land. Do not paralyse, gentlemen, the future development of these people, and remember, while you are legislating, that such strong people are in a majority in Russia.[59]

From the context, it is apparent that Stolypin, when referring to the strong, did not limit himself to any class or breed, nor even to the "already" strong. He referred to all amongst the peasantry who had the will and the desire to improve their lot. But the usual implication of left wing writers that Stolypin was referring to the kulaks when he spoke of the "strong" is inaccurate. His remark was more general and his aims more far reaching than this criticism implied.

Stolypin also took this opportunity to read the Social-Democratic resolution which had been issued in London, emphasizing that if his reforms were successful they would spell doom to the chance of revolution.[60] He concluded,

> It is necessary to lift our impoverished, our weak, our exhausted soil, for soil is the guarantee of our strength and future; soil--that is Russia.[61]

It was not until 24 April 1909 that the article-by-article reading of the ukase came to a close and it was finally passed by a majority after almost five months of deliberation. It was thereupon handed to a commission, to be drawn up anew with appropriate corrections, and then returned to the Duma for a second reading.[62]

The first session of the Duma after the summer recess of 1909 was the last important session during which general debates on the agrarian question took place, after which the Duma plunged into the second reading of the ukase. Krivoshein opened the debate by congratulating the deputies on having passed the legislation. Yet it was not enough, he noted, to create millions of new landowners; their possessions must now be turned into a productive whole. He then elaborated the main points of the law and outlined the government's activity in the distribution of land and financial aid. Krivoshein also produced fresh figures of applicants for that year. To the opposition's argument that only the rich peasants were in a position to take advantage of this law, he responded,

> Do not think that most of these applicants are individual cases who are running off from communal ownership

> because they might be wealthier or perhaps more adroit. No, over 75% of those who have applied up to January of this year were from whole communes who wished to enclose, and have expressed their decision by a two-thirds majority vote.[63]

At this point the opposition, although conscious that this was probably their last stand on the topic, appear to have lost heart, feeling it would be futile to argue further. The Kadets were the only ones who still had anything significant to say. The Kadet A. Berezovskii, for instance, stated that increasing the productivity of the land had nothing to do with the elimination of the strip system; in any case, the main issue at hand was the enlightenment of the peasant masses. His main criticism of the law was its forced application, although he agreed, in contradictory fashion, that compulsion was essential.[64] After this formulation it is hard to discern just how much disagreement there was among Kadets with Stolypin's proposals.

Kropotov, a Trudovik who also expressed the views of the Socialist-Revolutionaries, once more accused the government of going hand-in-hand with the pomeshchiks and bureaucrats--the majority in the Duma--who had no wish to listen to the voice of the people. He repeated Rodichev's demand to "First of all bring about order, give the people a just legal system which will be efficient and just; give the people equality, I mean in rights, and then people will themselves settle the land issue."[65] These words speak for themselves, for eloquent as they are, the country certainly could not wait for a free parliamentary evolution before solving its economic ills and raising the bulk of its population from a subsistence level.

T. Belousov, for the Social-Democrats, repeated the usual attacks upon the latifundia as an obstacle to progress, upon the Peasant Land Bank, and upon the time which it would take to carry through the reform. He could not let pass the remark made by the Kadet N. Kutler against the followers of Marx, however, saying that in the last elections the Marxists had frightened the Kadet Party to such an extent that "The Kadet Party had lost all its intellectual baggage." Even the "Kutlerite" scheme for the forced expropriation of land, he warned, could not be attained without the aid of the proletariat, meaning, in this context, the parties of the extreme left.[66] The right wing and Octobrist deputies answered some of the attacks made upon them, although the majority refused to speak as a sign of protest.

After the last speaker the proposal of the chairman that the Duma proceed to the second reading of the bill was quickly carried. The Duma was preoccupied henceforth with the second reading, debating the bill article-by-article and introducing further amendments. The main participants were, of course, the Octobrists and right wing groups, although the Kadets, while against the bill in principle, offered constructive criticisms. From here on events moved at a fast pace, and by 2 November 1909 all of the articles of the bill with the additional corrections had been accepted by a majority vote. Count I. Kapnist, a member of the agrarian committee, then requested the Duma to grant four days in which the committee might consider the bill and make the appropriate corrections. This was granted.[67]

On 25 November 1909, at 2:15 p.m. commenced the third and final reading of the agrarian bill. It continued until 27 November.[68] Upon completion, the opposition parties were given an opportunity to make their last comments. Miliukov declared,

> The state in which the bill is being accepted by the Duma in its final form will not serve the economic needs of peasant agriculture, nor the political aims of implanting individualist ideas for landownership, for the means of accomplishing these aims are derived

from the law of arbitration and coercion. Under such conditions the Party of People's Freedom with all of its sympathy for the agrarian law when properly enacted, is forced to vote against this bill.[69]

Kropotov said that the present bill infringed wholly upon the interests of the commune and of the laboring people. The Trudovik Party therefore voted against the bill.[70]

The Chairman of the Duma then put the bill to the vote in its final form. It was passed by a majority. The most controversial and important issue which had troubled the Duma for nearly four years was thus finally resolved by a law. The chairman's announcement that the bill would now be transferred to an editing commission was met with continuous applause from the center and right, with hissing from the left.[71] The agrarian debates in the Duma then closed and the legislation was directed to the State Council.

It was not until mid-March 1910 that the debates on the agrarian question commenced within the State Council.[72] Although there were approximately twenty sessions devoted to it, the views of both the government and the opposition were only fully expounded in three of them, the others being largely occupied by a detailed article-by-article reading of the bill. The session of 15 March 1910, the opening day of the agrarian debates within the State Council, was perhaps the most important of all. Stishinskii first read the report of the agrarian committee and traced the history of agrarian developments since 1861. He then turned to the Ukase of 9 November, elaborated the corrections which had been introduced by the Duma, and enumerated what had taken place since the institution of the ukase. Nearly a million households had enclosed their property before September 1909, and over 350,000 new applications had been received from individuals who wished to settle on individual farms. Comparing these figures with the mere twenty thousand who had enclosed their plots between 1861 and 1906, Stishinskii noted that there was no doubt that the measure had given a strong impetus towards private enclosures and could not be reconciled with the employment of official coercion.[73]

Stolypin was next to mount the rostrum to answer some of the more important questions which had been raised by the Third Duma. He, too, rejected the opposition's accusation that the government had used a policy of force to ensure the success of the ukase; the reaction had been too great and too spontaneous for that. He then recalled the circumstances under which the ukase had come into being:

> Those were troubled times, when country estates were still burning or nearly burnt, when freedom was regarded as the freedom of violence. . . During this period the government had to push through a whole series of laws concerning the peasantry. These measures were taken by many as an act of political confusion by a weak government which had instantly squandered to no purpose all of its ballast; private lands, state lands, the communal system--all in sacrifice to the hydra of revolution.[74]

In diagnosing this period, Stolypin acknowledged that political sedition and revolutionary propaganda, as well as anarchical social unrest, had begun to spread among the masses. Hence arose the natural conclusion: the necessity to eliminate the primary cause by giving the peasants the opportunity to emerge from poverty and ignorance.[75] From this it is clear that Stolypin's cardinal insistence was upon satisfying the needs of the nation, a point of view comparable to that of Witte, who noted that all revolutions arise when the government does not satisfy the imminent demands of a nation.[76] In reply to the familiar attack that there had been no need to pass the ukase under the provisions of the

Fundamental Laws, Stolypin commented:

> Only coupled with social agrarian reform could the political reforms receive life, strength and meaning. That is why, gentlemen, one has to look upon the Ukase of November 9, from the social point of view, and not from the political; then it will become clear, that it did not come as the fruit of a confused decision, but that precisely with this law was laid a foundation based on a new socio-economic peasant system. But as troubled times are a time of decision and not of meditation, it becomes quite clear why this question was carried out in accordance with the Article 87. . . By January 1, 1907, the question of turning the peasant plots into private property had to be decided upon, as by this date redemption payments were to end, and Article 12 of the general statutes was to come into force.[77]

In ending his speech, Stolypin stressed that he had too much regard for the nation's intelligence and common sense to accept the notion that the Russian peasantry was changing its way of life through government pressure and not by personal convictions.[78]

The supporters of the bill were the center, representing just over half the members of the State Council. The opposition, on the other hand, was composed of the two extreme groups, the left and right, which comprised 45% of the membership of the Council. It should be noted that the extreme right in fact carried the brunt of the opposition debates.[79] Here Maklakov's statement that "Revolution and reaction are closely interlocked, and feed each other," fits the occasion appropriately.[80] In essence, much of what was said in the State Council was a reiteration of what had already been expressed in the Duma, but a new factor emerged when arguments previously expounded by the revolutionaries within the Duma were now vociferously advanced almost verbatim by deputies of the extreme right.

Although Durnovo was regarded as the leader of the extreme right wing group, Witte, while carefully preserving his independence from allegiance to any faction, played a major part in leading the opposition on the agrarian issue. He was the first to reply to Stolypin's speech. As his speeches are the most important and contain all the elements of the opposition's position, they must be examined carefully. He began by stating that, although a supporter of private property, he could not welcome any bill which would bring about the forced disintegration of the commune. While he was willing to applaud a law which extended to the peasants the same right to private property presently enjoyed by other citizens, there was also another side to the matter--the legal protection of this right.[81]

Turning to the issue of the commune, he did not deny that there were areas where the transition from communal to individual ownership was due. However, "Nothing was done to find out where this fruit is ripe and where it is still green, or where it might still be in its embryonic stage." As for the scope of the law itself, Witte said,

> The present bill is strictly the result of bureaucratic work. . . it pretends to solve one of the most important questions in the life of the empire by means of 60 articles, and attempts to do it throughout the whole expanse of this huge empire with one stroke of the pen.[82]

Lastly, Witte announced that the government had the power, as well as the desire, under this law, to drive the peasants out from the commune, and that it had not even taken the trouble to inquire whether the peasants themselves wished to leave. He therefore felt that the proposed bill had every chance of bringing little benefit, but only considerable confusion and harm.[83] The major argument in Witte's speech was that the government was forcing the peasantry from the commune against their will, although the available figures hardly support such a view. It may also be noted that it was not a complete innovation to allow the peasants to leave the commune, for this principle had already been recognized in the Statute of 1861; the new legislation was largely an attempt to facilitate the procedure for leaving the commune, by opening the doors as widely as possible. Even S. Dubrovskii, a Soviet authority, came to admit that official policy was not to destroy the commune completely, but only to place--or release--as many peasants as feasible onto individual farms.[84]

Witte was followed by a retinue of opposition speakers. Professor A. Manuilov, the Rector of Moscow University who represented the left wing, emphasized that the bill's defect in his view was its resort to force; leaving the commune should be an entirely voluntary act.[85] He was followed by A. Donetskii, who, like all extreme right wing deputies, doubted the urgency of issuing the Ukase of 9 November under Article 87.[86] S. Bekhteev, from the same group but with milder reactionary leanings, conceded that the commune was an outdated institution but doubted whether the ukase would meet the needs placed upon it.[87] Count D. Olsufiev concurred in Witte's contention that there had been no urgency in issuing the ukase and that it was strictly a bureaucratic product. He expressed confusion as to why the government had stood for a policy of communal ownership in 1903, but was now against this communal institution. Though not impressed with Stishinskii's figures, he conceded that there had been no coercion on the part of the government in implementing the reform, and indeed brushed the accusation aside as a "fairy tale."[88]

These utterances reflect the general scope of the opposition's stand. The following sessions were largely taken up with a palemic between, on the one hand, Witte and the extreme right wing, and, on the other, the spokesmen of the agrarian committee and the supporters of the law. As in the Duma, the speeches were usually long and monotonous; on occasion the Chairman of the State Council would be forced to remark, "We cannot possibly waste our time in this manner."[89] Though the deputies drawn from the academies and the professions, as well as from industry, largely sided with the reactionaries in their attacks against the ukase, and their speeches were in many respects comparable, their motives were clearly distinct, less extreme and essentially moderate. Even if theoretical their speeches were never revolutionary in character.

Stishinskii, though previously a staunch supporter of Witte, was the first to answer some of the latter's criticisms. The accusation that the government had failed to consider the ultimate implications of the Act for the life of the citizen was an argument which could be used against any measure. He also found unfair Witte's reproach that the law had a "bureaucratic character"; was that perhaps because of its origin in St. Petersburg? As for the remark that the government had not asked the local peasant populace, not only had the local provincial agrarian committees been consulted and their suggestions incorporated, but the results of the special committee which had studied agrarian needs under the chairmanship of Witte had also been most carefully considered.[90]

Lykoshin, who also spoke in favor, characterized the term "bureaucratic" as relative; in his view bureaucratic laws were those which were inert and failed to leave a mark, whereas this one had already created a profound impact upon the consciousness of the people.[91] In reply to Count Olsufiev's surprise as to why such a drastic change had occurred so abruptly in government agrarian policy, Stishinskii declared that this change of policy had come about long before the ukase was promulgated, the implication being that the change had first taken place when Witte held office.[92]

Witte then returned to answer the remarks which had been cast in his direction. Tension increased as the session seemed to turn towards a duel of temperaments. Witte once more insisted that the ukase could not have been provoked by the abrogation of redemption payments alone, so as to justify promulgation under Article 87. The cause lay mainly in the current political circumstances. To the suggestion that the government had consulted the findings of the special committee of which he had been the chairman, Witte said that to his knowledge only university professors had taken advantage of that piece of work, although the efforts of the committee "were really colossal." His government had not attempted to establish private property in land with one stroke of the pen, and he doubted whether the transition from communal to individual ownership would solve the agrarian problem. He also warned that the ukase was an extremely risky wager which it would have been in the country's interests to postpone for two or three years--although what interim measure would have sufficed he did not specify.[93]

The main points of contention advanced by Witte on this occasion do not appear to have the full weight of conviction behind them. They suggest a struggle which was in large measure concerned, at least on Witte's part, with personalities rather than with issues. The last statement in particular elicits a doubt as to Witte's exact convictions, for what could waiting for another two years accomplish? If anything the situation would only worsen. If Witte's views as expressed in his reports to the Tsar in 1905 are compared with those which Stolypin expressed in the Duma and the State Council, or for that matter with the contents of the Ukase of 9 November, one finds them to be almost identical--a point which was brought up in the State Council debates.[94] It was thus hardly accurate for Witte to insist that his views were as different from Stolypin's as "fire is from water."[95]

Two major points which Witte persistently stressed were directly disputed by Lykoshin and P. Krasovskii. In reply to Witte's steadfast insistence that the Ukase of 3 November 1905, abrogating the redemption payments, had not in fact provoked the Ukase of 9 November, Lykoshin brought to the State Council's attention an imperial edict directed to the State Senate immediately after the issue of the first ukase which explicitly stated that, with the promulgation of the Ukase of 3 November 1905, the peasants were acquiring a right to leave the commune freely and enclose their holdings into private property. The edict further stated that appropriate legislation would be needed to meet the demands of this new legal status.[96]

The other major point of contention, inextricably tied with the first, was disproved by Krasovskii when he replied to Witte's criticism that the Ukase of 9 November was being introduced with the speed of an "express train." Krasovskii said that he had come across a document in the archives of the State Council which indicated that those who had spoken of haste and thoughtlessness in connection with the Ukase of 9 November had themselves previously submitted a proposal for legislative approval almost identical to the Ukase of 9 November. On 10 March 1906 a memorandum of the Council of Ministers signed by Witte had been submitted for the State Council's consideration, largely reiterating the main tenets of the new legislation. The memorandum stated specifically that the measure was "urgent and had to be accepted quickly, for it is a natural and indispensable consequence of the cancellation of redemption payments, announced by the Manifesto of 3 November 1905." Krasovskii concluded from this that what had seemed urgent and indispensable during the critical period of 1905-6 appeared at present, in the state of comparative tranquility, to be both too rapid and too risky.[97]

Both of these replies cast a shadow of mendacity, or at least of doubt, on Witte, for he was probably aware of those documents before making his statements public. In some respects, therefore, unless the government is to be accused of deliberately forging evidence, the exposure of these documents cannot but undermine some of Witte's prestige on the agrarian question.[98] Witte's remark to the effect that the new legislation was provoked by political considerations was not a point at issue, for Stolypin had himself already freely acknowledged that that was so on several occasions.

Seemingly as a reaction to this turn in the proceedings, V. Shebeko, from the Polish faction, then spoke in unmistakable defense of the ukase, claiming that "the commune did in the past, and still does, inflict an irreparable economic harm upon the State."[99] He concluded that he had the honor to announce, in the name of the Polish faction of the State Council, that they would vote in favor of the new legislation in the draft form prepared by the agrarian committee.[100]

The State Council then passed to the article-by-article reading of the bill, followed by appropriate criticisms and amendments. In an effort to proceed faster, the chairman proposed that no speaker should continue beyond half an hour, but this was rejected by a majority.[101]

Witte did come forward to reply to Krasovskii's remarks on 22 March, but largely repeated what he had already said. He reiterated the accusations of coercion, while conceding that the Ukase of 9 November had at least been contemplated during his premiership. He admitted that the memorandum read out by Krasovskii had in fact been submitted by him, but explained that the bill had been deferred at that stage owing to the objections encountered before the State Council. In conclusion, Witte stated that, owing to the compulsory nature of the first eight articles of the bill, he would vote against it.[102]

Though Witte did not expressly admit it, this last speech did not contain his previously emphatic statement that the abrogation of the redemption payments was largely independent from the publication of the Ukase of 9 November 1906. Krasovskii could not therefore refrain from returning to this point. He repeated the nature of the memorandum of 10 March, with such emphasis as to make it too obvious that it was identical with the main tenets of the Ukase of 9 November, and again stressed that the issue of the ukase was inextricably tied to the abrogation of the redemption payments. Then, in answer to Witte's last categorical statement, he repeated that the first eight articles of the ukase did not retreat from the beginnings which were projected under Witte's Premiership. He ended,

> I am completely bewildered as to why under Count Witte's project the proposal can be considered ownership, but under the project of P. A. Stolypin it is considered only a half ownership. Further, Count Witte insists that when the provincial committees gathered under him, for the purpose of discussing the work of the special conference, then the voice of the people was heard. By the coincidence of fate, at that time I was a member and speaker of the uezd and provincial committees. Lately, I find myself in the position of expressing myself during the legislative scrutiny of that same question. I find it hard to explain to myself, as to why my views could be considered as the voice of the people, when I used to express my views in the person of a member of an uezd and provincial committee, and why they suddenly became bureaucratic fabrication when they are being expressed from this rostrum.[103]

Witte did not have a reply and this particular discussion ended here. Prince Trubetskoi, however, the chairman of the agrarian committee, could not bypass Witte's labelling of this legislation as "bureaucratic." This all-important question had been discussed from all sides and by every segment of society. What else could have been done? Should it have been handed down to the peasant communes for discussion and examination, so as to relieve it from its bureaucratic character? He concluded:

> We are offering a law according to which only those who will wish to pass to individual ownership, will be able to do so; and those who do not, may remain within the commune.[104]

From here on the article-by-article reading and the voting on the different corrections continued at a more rapid rate until 27 March 1910. After the Easter interval, the State Council was reconvened to continue the same procedure from 28 April until 30 April, when the chairman announced the ballotting for the bill as a whole. This was passed by a majority at 5:30 p.m. and then handed to an elected coordinating commission, consisting of delegates from both the Duma and the State Council.[105]

After further deliberation by the coordinating commission, the bill was returned to the Duma at the beginning of June 1910 for a scrutiny of the articles which had met with the State Council's disapproval. After appropriate debate, the whole legislation was voted on once more.[106] The legislation was then resubmitted to the State Council for second reading. Here again, only those articles were discussed which had been the subject of conflicting views in both Houses and a majority vote in favor of the bill was quickly obtained. In a concluding speech the chairman declared that the bill would probably be formally enacted within a few days; he also paid tribute to the efforts of the agrarian committee, of its chairman Prince Trubetskoi, and of the two official speakers, Stishinskii and Krasovskii. The Chairman and other members of the State Council then rose and bowed to the committee.[107] On 14 June 1910, the Monarch affixed his signature to the document, which was then officially proclaimed law.

At the end of March 1911 this enactment was returned to the State Council in order that it might consider certain amendments which had already received the consent of the Duma. The law of 14 June 1910, having been approved by a majority of the Council in its corrected form,[108] received the Tsar's signature on 29 May 1911. In this way the statute known to us as the Stolypin agrarian reform received its final legal cast.

NOTES

1. Kofod, A., Russkoe Zemleustroistvo (SPB, 1914), pp. 23-24.

2. P.S.Z., Vol. XXIII, Nos. 22,627 and 22,629.

3. Ibid., Vol. XXIV, No. 25,014.

4. Ibid., Vol. XXV, No. 26,872.

5. See Khrulev, S., "Iz Istorii Agrarnogo Dvizheniia," Krasnyi Arkhiv, Vol. 39 (1930), p. 79.

6. "K Istorii Agrarnoi Reformy Stolypina," Krasnyi Arkhiv, Vol. 17 (1926), pp. 85-86.

7. Izgoev, A., P. A. Stolypin: Ocherk Zhizni i Deiatelnosti (Moscow, 1912), p. 65.

8. Stolypin, D., Ob Organizatsii Nashego Selskogo Byta (Moscow, 1892), pp. 60-71; 78-87.

9. Krasnyi Arkhiv, op. cit., p. 89.

10. Karpov, N., Krestianskoe Dvizhenie v Revoliutsii 1905 goda v Dokumentakh (Leningrad, 1926), pp. 161-2. (This reply was dated 11 January 1906). Krivoshein, then Deputy to the Minister of Agriculture, in a report submitted to the Council of Ministers on 3 February 1906, first reiterates Stolypin's views that agrarian dis-

turbances were largely caused by revolutionary propaganda; he continues, however, by pointing out that the reason why propaganda, and not lack of land, was producing agrarian disturbances was that many of the peasants participating in rebellions were prosperous, owning ample land, and in some cases had even more than their quota. He stressed that as the peasants comprised 80% of the population, it would be impossible to raise their general standards of living in a short time whatever means were used; this could only be accomplished by a long process. He suggested, therefore, that since a central body would be incapable of studying local needs, a number of regional agrarian commissions should be established. In addition Krivoshein, like Stolypin, emphasized the importance of freeing the peasants from the commune and resettling them as individual owners. Then, as he expressed it, the peasants would, "realize the whole monstrosity of expropriation of private property, and would realize the criminality of forced encroachment on another's property." See Karpov, N., Agrarnaia Politika Stolypina (Leningrad, 1925), pp.162-165.

11. Karpov, N., Krestianskoe Dvizhenie v Revoliutsii 1905 goda v Dokumentakh, p.94.

12. Karpov, N., Agrarnaia Politika Stolypina, pp.167-172. This memorandum was signed by Count S. Witte, P. Durnovo, I. Shipov, Count I. Tolstoy, K. Nesselrode, Prince V. Kochubei, A. Krivoshein, and M. Fedorov.

13. P.S.Z., Vol. XXVI, No. 27,478.

14. Dnevnik Imperatora Nikolaia II (Berlin, 1923), pp.249, 251.

15. In correspondence with Prof. A. Bilimovich. See also Oldenburg, S., op. cit., Vol. I, p.375.

16. Oganovskii, N., Individualizatsiia Zemlevladeniia v Rossii i eia Posledstviia (Moscow, 1917), p.83. Baron A. Meyendorff expressed the following view: "Stolypin's agrarian legislation attempted to put upon the land the best possible agent, which theoretically is the owner. It presupposes the existence of the ownership mentality in the peasant."

17. Tverskoi, P., "K Istoricheskim Materialam o Pokoinom P. A. Stolypine," Vestnik Evropy (April 1912), pp.190-1.

18. P.S.Z., Vol. XXVI, No. 28,392.

19. Ibid., No. 28,547.

20. Ibid., No. 28,528.

21. For figures of elected deputies see, Ukazatel k Stenograficheskim Otchetam Tretei Dumy, 1909-10, pp.12-18. Right wing members came up to 51; 91 Nationalists; 131 Octobrists; 39 Progressists; National minorities came to 26; 53 Kadets; 14 Trudoviks; 15 Social-Democrats; and 17 Non-Party deputies.

2. Pinchuk, B., The Octobrists in the Third Duma, 1907-1912 (Seattle, 1974), pp.6-7. Commenting on the membership of the Octobrist Party, Edelman notes that they were "motivated by a concern for legality and social justice." Edelman, R., Gentry Politics on the Eve of the Russian Revolution (Rutgers University Press, 1980), p.38. Sir Arthur Nicolson felt that Guchkov was a "man of broad views and of firm constitutional principles." P.R.O., F.O. 371, Vol. 977, No. 10424, 22 March 1910.

23. Urskii, G., Pravye v Tretei Gosudarstvennoi Dume (Kharkov, 1912), p.32.

24. Gosudarstvennaia Duma, Treteogo Sozyva, Stenograficheskie Otchety (Hereafter G.D.),

16 November 1907, Cols. 307-12. For a more detailed account of what Stolypin said before the Second Duma, see my article "Stolypin and the Second Duma," The Slavonic and East European Review, Vol. L, No. 118 (January 1972), pp.51-56.

25. G.D. 16 November 1907, Cols. 312-318.

26. Ibid., Cols. 327-343.

27. Ibid., Cols. 343-348.

28. Ibid., Cols. 348-354.

29. Ibid.

30. G.D. 17 November 1907, Col. 369.

31. Ibid., Cols. 358-361.

32. G.D. 20 October 1908, Cols. 118, 125.

33. G.D. 23 October 1908, Col. 171.

34. Brutskus, B., Obobshchestvlenie Zemli i Agrarnaia Reforma (Moscow, 1917), pp.29-30. Kliucharev, S., Krestianskaia Nishcheta i Finansovo-Ekonomicheskaia Sistema S. Iu. Witte (Kiev, 1906), p.67.

35. G.D. 23 October 1908, Cols. 145-198. N. Markov (also known as Markov II) noted that in the province of Kursk the peasant worked an average of 85 days a year, and for the rest of the time he did nothing. See G.D. 7 November 1908, Col. 929 and Col. 919.

36. G.D. 23 October 1908, Col. 205.

37. G.D. 27 October 1908, Cols. 409-415. The revolutionary press both within and outside of Russia was stressing the same points. See, for instance, Za Narod (Paris) No. 13, January 1909; No. 17, May 1909. Russkoe Slovo

(Moscow) and Rus'.

38. G.D. 24 October 1908, Cols. 313-324.

39. G.D. 23 October 1908, Col. 239 and 24 October 1908, Col. 262.

40. G.D. 29 October 1908, Cols. 463-489.

41. G.D. 24 October 1908, Cols. 293-295. Brutskus, G., Agrarnyi Vopros i Agrarnaia Politika (SPB, 1922), p.23. Even Brutskus, a dire opponent of Stolypin's reform during its implementation, agreed much later that in the case of the Law of 9 November 1906, the government was much more farsighted.

42. G.D. 24 October 1908, Col. 276-291. Lykoshin refused to accept the accusation that the government was resorting to coercive methods in the face of so many applicants expressing a clear desire to leave the commune, and made it a point to emphasize that the revolutionaries did a considerable amount of agitating within the villages against the Ukase of 9 November. G.D. 24 October 1908, Col. 290. See also Dubrovskii, S., Stolypinskaia Reforma (Leningrad, 1925), p.51.

43. G.D. 7 November 1908, Cols. 902-913.

44. Oganovskii, N., "Ocherki po Agrarnomu Voprosu," Vestnik Evropy (September 1913), p.280.

45. G.D. 7 November 1908, Col. 913.

46. Ibid., Col. 915.

47. G.D. 10 November 1908, Col. 1028.

48. Krivoshein brought out the then current world trend towards smaller farm units. In this connection see the stimulating volume by Prof. F. Hertz, Die Agrarishchen Fragen im Verhaltnis zum Sozialismus (Wien, 1899). On the basis of

figures Prof. Hertz demonstrates a world-wide trend towards smaller farm units, thus refuting Kautsky's contention that the tendency was the opposite, in the direction of large farming units.

49. G.D. 10 November 1908, Cols. 1026-1044.

50. G.D. 22 November 1908, Cols. 1548-1549.

51. Concerning this point see: Peshekhonov, A., op. cit., pp.71-80.

52. G.D. 22 November 1908, Col. 1555.

53. Ibid., Cols. 1558-1560.

54. G.D. 15 November 1908, Cols. 1194-1222.

55. Ibid., Col. 1225.

56. G.D. 17 November 1908, Col. 1308.

57. G.D. 22 November 1908, Col. 1567-1573.

58. G.D. 5 December 1908, Col. 2280.

59. Ibid., Col. 2282.

60. Ibid., Col. 2283.

61. Ibid., Col. 2284.

62. G.D. 24 April 1909, Cols. 2927-2928.

63. G.D. 12 October 1909, Cols. 48-54, 61.

64. Ibid., Cols. 64-65, 80.

65. Ibid., Cols. 94, 100.

66. Ibid., Col. 134.

67. G.D. 2 November 1909, Col. 1136.

68. G.D. 25 November 1909, Col. 2443.

69. G.D. 27 November 1909, Col. 2648. Miliukov was later to explain this stance by saying that the Kadet Party was opposed to the forced dissolution of the commune and against the rapacious sale of land to the "strong elements of the village." Miliukov, P., Vospominaniia, 1859-1917, Vol. II, p.61.

70. G.D. 27 November 1909, Col. 2648.

71. Ibid., Col. 2649.

72. In the meantime two agrarian committees were elected, one, in October 1909, to prepare the bill for presentation to the State Council, and the other, elected on 3 March 1910, to discuss and analyze the problem with the aid of expert witnesses.

73. Stenograficheskii Otchet. Gosudarstvennyi Sovet (Hereafter G.S.), 15 March 1910, Cols. 1117-1125.

74. Ibid., Cols. 1136-1137.

75. Ibid., Col. 1138.

76. Witte, S., Vospominaniia Tsarstvovanie Nikolaia II (Berlin, 1922), Vol. I, p.483.

77. G.S. 15 March 1910, Col. 1138.

78. Ibid., Col. 1144.

79. For comments concerning the intrigues of the reactionaries see: Diakin, V., "Stolypin i Dvoriantsvo (Proval Mestnoi Reformy)," in Nosov, N., ed., Problemy Krestianskogo Zemlevladeniia i Vnutrennei Politiki Rossii (Leningrad, 1972), pp.233-241; Izgoev, A., op. cit., pp.83-84.

80. Maklakov, V., "The Agrarian Problem in Russia Before the Revolution," Russian Review (January 1950), p.4.

81. *G.S.* 15 March 1910, Cols. 1145-1147.

82. *Ibid.*, Col. 1148.

83. *Ibid.*, Col. 1149.

84. Dubrovskii, S., *op. cit.*, p.41. Von Dietze, C., *Stolypinsche Agrarreform Und Feldgemeinschaft* (Berlin, 1920), p.57. Pavlovsky, G., *Agricultural Russia on the Eve of Revolution* (London, 1930), pp.117-118.

85. *G.S.* 15 March 1910, Cols. 1149-1154.

86. *Ibid.*, Col. 1163.

87. *Ibid.*, Cols. 1165-1170.

88. *Ibid.*, Cols. 1179-1183.

89. *G.S.* 16 March 1910, Col. 1206.

90. *Ibid.*, Cols. 1219-1221. A special committee of inquiry into the agrarian question was appointed by the Tsar on 22 January 1902, which carried out its work through local agrarian committees in an attempt to get to the root of the causes of agrarian drawbacks and the need to alleviate the agrarian problem. This committee carried out investigations for over two years, at the end of which Count Witte wrote an official report to the Monarch, expressing identical views to those which were later enacted in the Ukase of 9 November 1906. Witte, S., *Zapiska po Krestianskomu Delu* (SPB, 1905).

91. *G.S.* 16 March 1910, Col. 1240.

92. *Ibid.*, Col. 1226.

93. *Ibid.*, Cols. 1228-1230.

94. Witte, *op. cit.* See especially pages 111-124.

95. G.S. 16 March 1910, Col. 1230.

96. Ibid., Col. 1241.

97. G.S. 18 March 1910, Cols. 1284-1285.

98. Here is what Sir Bernard Pares wrote to the Foreign Office in 1908: "Count Witte commands no confidence whether at the Court or with the public; my own conversation with him this year entirely justified the grounds for this all-round distrust." P.R.O., F.O. 371, Vol. 512, No. 30901, 4 September 1908.

99. G.S. 18 March 1910, Col. 1305.

100. Ibid., Col. 1324.

101. Ibid., Col. 1379.

102. G.S. 22 March 1910, Cols. 1449-1454.

103. Ibid., Cols. 1454-1457.

104. Ibid., Cols. 1465-1471.

105. G.S. 30 April 1910, Col. 2601.

106. G.S. 2 June 1910, Cols. 3096-3143.

107. G.S. 10 June 1910, Cols. 3831, 3841.

108. G.S. 31 March 1911, Cols. 1695; 2 April 1911, Col. 1916.

P.A. Stolypin as a student at the gymnasium (1877).

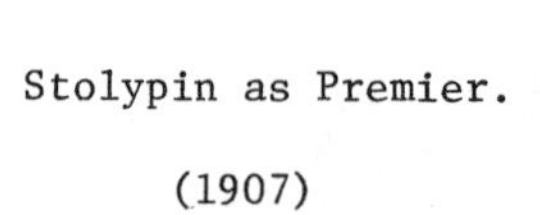

Stolypin as Premier.

(1907)

CHAPTER III

THE FINNISH ISSUE

The two overlapping issues of major importance with which Stolypin had to contend immediately prior to his death were the Finnish and western zemstvo bills. They had certain features in common in that they both invoked the government attitude towards the more advanced of the many racial groups who inhabited the empire. The Finnish bill touched upon the mainsprings of Russian relations with the autonomous region of Finland; the western zemstvo bill, although indirectly, involved official policy regarding Poles living in the western provinces.

Russia's policy towards Finland is the most difficult minority problem to assess. The Finnish question occupies a unique place by reason of the complex constitutional relationship which had evolved over a century, and which had given rise to a dilemma which became acute at the end of the nineteenth century under General N. Bobrikov, the Governor General of Finland, but which was not seriously tackled until 1910. Finland, which had been part of the Swedish dominions for some seven hundred years, had been united with Russia after the war of 1808-1809. The Finnish Diet of Borga, summoned by Alexander I on 27 March 1809, obtained a guarantee that the Finnish Fundamental Laws based on the Swedish Form of Government of 21 August 1772, and the Act of Union and Security of 21 February, and 3 April 1789, respectively, would be maintained.[1] Subsequently, however, Finland acquired a measure of independence, becoming a Grand Duchy with the Tsar as Grand Duke. After the signing of the Treaty of Frederickshamn on 5 September 1809, whereby Sweden gave up her claim to the Finnish territories, Alexander I established a State Council consisting of fourteen members elected by the Diet. In 1816 this council assumed the name of Senate, after which the Tsar selected its members every three years.[2] The Senate acted in an executive and the Diet in a legislative capacity, although neither body had other than advising powers.[3] The head of the Senate was also governor general. In addition there was a Secretary of State for Finland, living in St. Petersburg, whose duty it was to place before the sovereign all matters which required his decision. He also consulted each of the ministries concerned before submitting any bill to the Emperor, whose sanction was needed to validate all Finnish laws; however, this procedure was not always strictly observed. The Tsar also had the right to initiate legislation.[4]

After its meeting at Borga the Diet was not reconvened until 1863, when its sessions were reopened by Alexander II. The Diet thereafter met at regular intervals. The consequence of establishing this Diet was to create feelings of Finnish nationalism and national consciousness which became stronger as the century proceeded and which proved to be the first steps towards national self-determination.[5]

Naturally enough, Alexander III reacted very quickly to this nascent Finnish nationalism and attempted to stifle its ever louder rumblings. However, any attempt on the part of the Russian government to impose restrictions was met by further demands for self-determination. During the first decade of his reign, Nicholas II maintained his father's policy. Nevertheless, a number of legislative questions left over from the 1880's, such as postage, coinage, and customs tariffs, which had aggravated Finnish-Russian relations, now required attention. The difficulties involved were increased by the fact that laws affecting Finland might be enacted on two levels, one general and the other Finnish. To the former belonged laws which were to operate throughout the empire, including Finland, as well as laws concerning Finland alone but which involved imperial interests. The latter, on the other hand, related solely to Finnish internal affairs and were passed by the Diet and confirmed by the Emperor. These categories frequently overlapped and the proper procedure was not always strictly followed. Thus, with time, in the absence of any precise definition as to which laws fell into one or the other category, the legislative process became more obscure and entangled, aided by the growing self-confidence of the Finnish Diet, which attempted to seize jurisdiction whenever it felt it could do so.

The issues involved came to a climax with the promulgation of the Manifesto of 3 February 1899, a first attempt to correct the deficiencies in the legislative procedure. The manifesto's main stipulation was,

> While maintaining in full force the prevailing statutes concerning the promulgation of local laws which relate exclusively to the internal affairs of Finland, We have found it necessary to reserve to Ourselves the final decision as to which laws came within the scope of general imperial legislation.[6]

While those laws which affected the interests of "general imperial legislation," were mentioned specifically, this term itself was not further defined.[7] This omission inevitably caused the deepest concern in the Diet. Finnish political leaders interpreted the manifesto as an encroachment upon their accustomed legislative prerogatives. Henceforth the Finnish Diet had consultative powers only over statutes which affected the interests of the empire, or which were of general application; laws which were solely of local importance, however, remained subject to the Diet, with only imperial ratification being necessary. The Finnish leaders instantly requested a specific designation of whatever fell within the framework of "imperial legislation," for they feared that St. Petersburg would interfere in almost every sphere.[8]

Events followed quickly: a Russification policy was introduced in 1901 with the appointment of the ultra-reactionary V. Plehve, as Secretary of

State for Finnish Affairs; and dictatorial powers were conferred on General Bobrikov, the Governor General of Finland in 1903. His over-enthusiastic endorsement of official policies ended finally in his assassination on 3 June 1904 by Eugene Shauman, the son of a Finnish senator.[9] The period concerned, which overlapped that of internal revolutionary strife in Russia after the Japanese War, forced the Russian government to show signs of leniency which culminated in the issue of the Manifesto of 22 October 1905, suspending the ill-conceived Manifesto of 1899.[10] The Finns regarded the 1905 manifesto as a concession of full liberties; it thus had the same effect on the Finns as the Manifesto of 17 October 1905 had on the politically conscious Russian masses.

Some broad indication must be given at this point of the political situation in Finland and of the aims and motives of imperial policy towards that country. C. Pobedonostsev, the reactionary statesman who had presided over the select committee which drafted the 1899 manifesto,[11] clearly played a dominant role and exercised a strong influence upon the inexperienced Tsar. Strategical considerations also influenced events after the Finnish Senate passed military legislation in 1896 without prior consultation with the Russian government in St. Petersburg. The Army Act which was enacted by the imperial authorities in 1898 ensured that Russian control over Finnish forces remained paramount.[12] This was followed by the Manifesto of 1899, resulting in a policy which reduced the Finnish Diet to a provincial assembly with no sovereign powers. However, the policy of Russification, which was introduced simultaneously, caused the greatest apprehension on the part of the Finns. The imperial authorities, seeing the problem through the eyes of Pobedonostsev, failed to appreciate the transformation of a Finland conscious of its national and cultural heritage. The Finns were ready to oppose any restriction placed on the rights to which they were accustomed, whatever the legal position might be.

The last three decades of the nineteenth century had drastically altered Finland's attitude towards the Russian empire. Political life in Finland had taken a firm root since the early sixties when Alexander II had summoned the Diet for the first time. Nationalism and a desire to leave the Russian empire had gone hand-in-hand.[13] The Finnish upper and middle classes were strongly influenced by European ideas, thus further alienating them from Russia.[14] Moreover, the country had experienced a wide degree of local autonomy for over three decades. Consequently, the new generation of Finnish leaders could not comprehend or accept the principle of drastic Russian intervention. The crisis involved a conflict between two cultures, mutual misunderstanding, economic and military matters, and a dispute over constitutional legality.

By the turn of this century the Finns were politically educated and united under an efficient leadership. When the Russo-Japanese War broke out, certain Finnish leaders, largely activists and constitutionalists, approached the Japanese Government through its representatives in Sweden for financial help to be used for revolutionary activities.[15] This was followed by the General Strike in Finland, which coincided with the turbulent events in October 1905 in Russia and forced Nicholas to change his policy by issuing the manifesto of 22 October. In July 1906, the Emperor sanctioned universal suffrage for all Finns aged over twenty-four, although he in no way restricted his prerogatives in so doing. Finland was the first country in Europe to enfranchise women and was claimed to have the most democratic parliament in the world. The results of the new general elections held in March 1907 were highly significant, since the Social-Democrats, a new element in the political life of the country, gained eighty out of the two hundred seats, thus becoming--to the alarm of the Russian Government--the largest single party in the Diet. The situation at this stage was somewhat paradoxical, for it meant that within the empire a territory in which advanced democratic principles were practiced was existing side by side with an outdated autocracy. But now, at least, the aim of the Russian Government was to introduce a defined legislative process whereby the interests of the empire would be protected and, at the same time, an attempt would be made to satisfy the basic political demands of the Finns as a nation.

The chaos and turmoil which prevailed in Russia during the years immediately following 1905 left Finland almost entirely to herself as regards legislative procedures, until the law of 1910 was published. It is important to note, in order to understand succeeding events, that the 1905 manifesto did not abrogate the Manifesto of 1899, but simply suspended it until such time as the question was finally determined. In the meantime, however, the central government merely established joint commissions in the hope that some sort of compromise could be reached. These committees proved fruitless; the diametrically opposed views which were held prevented any reconciliation. This situation persisted until the beginning of 1908, when, to the surprise of Stolypin and the government and before any agreement had been reached with the Finns, the extreme Right, the Nationalists, and the Octobrists within the Russian Duma demanded that the government explain its attitude towards Finland over a number of issues. This prompted Stolypin to appear before the Duma early in May 1908, and forced the government to quicken its tempo in preparing a law which would establish, once and for all, the Finno-Russian legislative process.

The questions raised were answered by Stolypin on behalf of the government on 5 May 1908, and were followed by heated debates which lasted until 13 May. These debates provided an opportunity for the deputies to expound their views in much greater detail than was the case in 1910, when the actual bill was discussed by the Duma. These sittings also acted as a barometer of the assembly's attitude towards Stolypin's intentions, and enabled him to test the strength of feeling involved over this highly controversial question, prior to committing himself too firmly towards any definite policy.

Stolypin first cautioned the Duma by stressing the need for calm and self-control in considering the question. He stated, however,

> From the very beginning I should like to establish that the imperial government considers, and will consider, herself responsible for Finnish events, as Finland is an organic part of the Russian empire, and the empire is governed by a united government, which is responsible to the Emperor for all that transpires within the state.[17]

He then dwelt on the Red Guard, a Finnish revolutionary organization, on the Voima, a supposedly revolutionary society, on the laxity of the Finnish Government towards the smuggling of arms into Finland, and on the imperial government's appeals regarding activities of Russian revolutionaries on Finnish soil.[18] Stolypin queried whether the Secretary of State for Finland was in fact in a position to decide matters of imperial interest, for, without consulting the War Ministry, the Finnish Senate had in 1896 revised certain sections of the statutes involving military matters. In 1906, the Finnish Diet had passed a law concerning the use of the Russian language in Finnish Government offices, again without any inquiry being made of the Russian authorities. In Stolypin's opinion some of these changes affected the interests of Russia and infringed upon the prerogatives of the Monarch. However, the most important incident, which had alarmed the Russian Government considerably, was that of February 1907, when the Secretary of State for Finland, without consulting the government, had informed the Tsar that the Finnish Senate had begun drafting a bill which would introduce a new form of government for Finland, severing the ties between the two countries. Stolypin felt, therefore, that the uneasy relations between the two governments should be thoroughly analyzed; the problems involved could not be solved mechanically.[19]

Stolypin considered that the matter could be solved only through a legislative intervention on the part of the Duma which would give proper consideration to the Finnish point of view. He did not, however, indicate whether the government was in fact preparing a bill of a general nature, such as he appeared to envisage. Nevertheless, he gave an assurance that Russia did not intend to violate the measure of Finnish independence which had already been granted by the Monarch, for, he said, "in Russia might does not stand above the law." He hastened to note, however, that the fact that the slightest mention of Russia's rights was interpreted as an insult in Finland constituted an intolerable situation. Lastly, Stolypin expressed the hope that the Duma would reject the interpellations,[20] thus reinforcing its confidence in the present administration.

The debates which ensued for the next three sittings were passionate, often interrupted by the shouts of both extremes, and such that the chairman was forced to ring his bell at frequent intervals to bring the assembly to order. The Russian press followed the debates closely and the Finnish question resulted in a literary polemic.[21] All the main parties of the Duma had an opportunity to expound their views on the issue even though no bill in fact lay before them.

Miliukov was one of the few representatives of the Kadet Party who delivered a competent reasoned speech, although he was also critical of the government's attitude. Analyzing Stolypin's speech, he traced historical events since 1809, quoting excerpts from utterances of Alexander I and stressing that Finland was a special kind of state, which had been governed in a special manner. In his opinion relations between the two countries were not a *tabula rasa* on which anything could be written, although he agreed that a solution could not be found mechanically.[22] Nevertheless, no serious or calm discussion was possible if the Finns were to be labelled as traitors by the reactionary elements every time they introduced a bill. Although Miliukov assumed that Stolypin intended to submit a new law for the Duma's approval, he asked for greater clarification of the future path which the government intended to follow. In conclusion, he declared that Stolypin's terminology was that of the Manifesto of 1899 and that he was taking the Duma on the same course as Bobrikov once had, namely complete annihilation of Finnish autonomy.[23]

Gegechkori presented the views of the Social-Democrats in a long and provocative speech, full of revolutionary turns of phrase. The questions posed to the government were of a political character and were designed to rouse Finnish public opinion. He created an uproar in his attack upon the Octobrists by implying that they were synonymous with the Black Hundreds. He insisted that the remarks made about the Voima were extremely exaggerated--for the impression was being given that hundreds of thousands of arms were being shipped into Finland and that such allegations could lead only to grievous consequences.[24] Gegechkori added that since the Finnish democrats could not come to any agreement with the Russian reactionaries, they would in any case have to show their solidarity with Russian democracy.[25] The last part of his speech was mainly devoted to revolutionary slogans, and he concluded with an exhortation:

> Let the Finnish people know that the Russian people, not you and 130,000 pomeshchiks, but the proletariat and the peasants, warmly sympathize with their struggle for sublime aspirations, for a democratic state, for socialism.[26]

The Trudovik A. Bulat had less to say than Gegechkori; his speech lacked any fruitful criticism, and his remarks only served to weaken the position of the extreme left before the Duma. Defending the passive attitude of the Finnish Government towards Russian revolutionaries hiding in Finland, he pointed out that these revolutionaries had committed their crimes in Russia and not in Finland and that the Finnish Government therefore had no grounds for their arrest. He blamed the political crimes on the Bobrikov regime and the extraordinary measures which had been imposed on Finland at that time. As for the shipment of arms on the John Krafton, he laid the blame on the Japanese, and said that the Finns should not be held responsible.[27]

The position of the extreme rightists was expounded by two ultra-reactionaries:N. Markov and V. Purishkevich. The former rebuked Stolypin for not having set out the issues involved in any detail, thus rendering it necessary for his party to do so. When Finland was under Sweden, she had not in fact been an independent country, but a Swedish province; there had not been any Finnish Constitution nor Fundamental Laws at that time, for the Finns used to send their representatives to the Swedish Reichstag. Alexander I had not been in a position to grant any prerogatives to the Finns at Borga, for the peace treaty had not yet been signed and Alexander was not then the titular head of Finland. Markov also accused the Finns of 1809 of being traitors, for they had no right to attend the Diet at Borga, when they were still legally Swedish citizens. Trying to incite the national sentiment of his audience, he pointed out that Finland had received not only a measure of independence, but deliverance from military service as well. For while Russian soldiers fought and died, and did so for Finland, the Finns stayed at home. The Russian Government contributed an estimated 18 million rubles annually to Finland, money which, if used in Markov's own province of Kursk, would benefit the people there greatly. He summed up his position, to the disgust of the left wing, when he said, "I maintain that the Finns, for the past 100 years, have grown fat on Russian money. . . Russian blood, and Russian sweat."[28]

He then called attention to the fact that throughout Russia Finns were treated as Russian subjects without any restrictions being placed upon them and that a number of Ministers were in fact Finnish subjects. In Finland itself, on the other hand, he noted that Russians were denied electoral rights of any kind--whereas the Finns had the right to vote for the State Council and Duma--and employment in Finland. Doctors, for example, who graduated from Russian universities were not allowed to practice in Finland. Listing a series of restrictions, he stated that the Finns had introduced some 171 laws directed to limiting the rights of Russians on Finnish soil, whereas in Russia not a single restriction existed against the Finns.[29] Speeches with such a nationalistic tinge easily produce a stirring response, and these above remarks went a long way toward recruiting enmity against the Finns. Markov then rebuked Stolypin for the inertness that the government had shown and called on him to halt the actions of obvious insurgents "with an iron fist."[30]

The impetuous reactionary Purishkevich, like Markov, produced his usual mixture of bigotry and ultra-chauvinism. He considered all the previous speeches devoid of all true Russian national feeling, and then proceeded to attack the leftists and the Octobrists for demanding more freedom for a country which already enjoyed more than the Russians themselves. In the opinion of his group the crux of the present crisis lay in the lack of a consistent policy on the part of Russia. Insisting that the government inaugurate a nationalistic policy towards all her border regions, he ended by stressing that the rightists had no intention of withdrawing their interpellation.[31]

Within the right wing, however, there was a sprinkle of those deputies who, through devout nationalists, still held comparatively liberal views. One such deputy was G. Zamyslovskii, who wholeheartedly agreed with Stolypin and opposed the views, expressed by the left and the Kadets, that the interpellations were an insult to the Finns and that the government was encroaching on the cultural independence of minorities.[32] G. Shechkov was another; turning to Miliukov, who insisted on the existence of a Finnish constitution, he demanded, "Show us this constitution, where did you see it?" He also contended that there had been no constitution under the Swedes, nor a Diet, for the Finns had sent their representatives to the Swedish parliament. He alleged that what might be termed a constitution had been introduced solely through Russian legislation.[33]

Although more were swayed by greater nationalist sentiment than the Octobrists, the Nationalist Party nevertheless came closer to the Octobrists than the rightists on this issue. Speaking for the Nationalists, V. Vetchinin acknowledged that persons acting as intermediaries (he instanced Count A. Armfelt, a nineteenth century Secretary of State for Finland) might abuse their positions in order to gain privileges in the field of Finnish legislation. The Nationalists, he said, had no interest in taking away from the Finns any rights which they presently enjoyed within the framework of the Russian Fundamental Laws; however, an end had to be put, once and for all, to any attempts by the Finns to broaden their rights to the detriment of Russian interests. However, they were satisfied with Stolypin's reply and would withdraw the interpellation. Finally Vetchinin expressed the hope that the government would, in the near future, submit a bill defining a new legislative process.[34]

Another deputy of the same faction, N. Ladomirskii, with closer sympathies towards the right, complained that the Finns did not accept the legal rights of the imperial authority and thus systematically violated the principle of state unity. He could not refrain from badgering Gegechkori by saying that it was difficult to contradict one who demonstrated so laboriously that a peaceful corner of the empire was one in which bombs were manufactured and where political assassinations were planned. Though his party did not support a policy of forced Russification, it could not permit the separation of outlying regions.[35]

The Octobrists delivered moderate speeches in the main. Count E. Bennigsen in the name of the party announced that they concurred with Stolypin's reply and that they were withdrawing their interpellation. He also emphasized that the Russo-Finnish question could be solved only by the promulgation of a new statute.[36] Thanking Gegechkori on another occasion for the revelation of revolutionary activity in Finland, he considered it interesting that the Social-Democrat speaker should be so well informed; however, he found it rather surprising that Gegechkori had taken it upon himself to speak for the loyalty of the Finns. Bennigsen then corrected Gegechkori's inference that the calling of the Diet in 1863 had been motivated by the Polish uprising, calling attention to the fact that talks on convening the Diet had started as early as 1858, and that the final decision had already been taken in 1862. As for Miliukov's inference that Alexander I had granted a constitution at Borga, Bennigsen maintained that the Diet at Borga had been merely a consultative and not a legislative body. He pointed out that Alexander I had closed the Borga Diet with a speech in which he had stressed that he had called the Diet in order to become acquainted with the needs and wishes of the people.[37]

V. Petrovo-Solovovo, referring to Miliukov's speech, said that the Octobrists were well aware that "right did not always stand above might;" however, he felt that there was no need of such extreme scepticism as was expressed by the leader of the Kadet Party. He emphasized that "Might must not stand above the law in Russia." He felt that Stolypin was laying the foundation of future relations with Finland, and that the latter's suggestion, as expressed in his speech, could be exemplified in the epithet, "Neminen laedere suum cuique tribuere."[38] Like many others, he was convinced that revolutionary activities in Finland had to be suppressed, but gave a warning as to the methods to be used--for force usually ran out of hand. He felt sure that if the Finns were assured that an act, like that of February 1899, would not be repeated, then the opposition would quickly subside. He emphasized that only the beginning of equal rights could establish satisfactory relations between the empire and the Grand Duchy.[39]

Count A. Uvarov, unlike his colleagues, rose to give a short and comprehensive speech. He attacked the demand of the right wing that the guilty members of the Finnish administration should be punished; he felt that that provided no real answer to the problem. The purpose of the Duma's discussion at this stage was the regulation of relations between Russia and Finland. Like others, he agreed that Russians in Finland should enjoy the same rights as the Finns did in Russia and attacked the left wing for trying, as he said, to confuse the assembly with alternative historical commentaries which might undermine the basis of Stolypin's historical analysis.[40]

On 13 May, after days of debates, the Duma voted on the three interpellations: all three were rejected.[41] This was a distinct victory for Stolypin and one which must have given him considerable relief, for he was now able to push this particular issue to the background and to concentrate his efforts on the agrarian problem, which was then the major issue before the Duma. It may be noted that the rightists voted for retaining the interpellations, while the Nationalists and the Octobrists sided with the Kadets and the extreme left wing, though for different reasons, against doing so. In broad terms, both the Nationalists and the Octobrists were in favor of promulgating a law which would define the limits of general and local Finnish legislation, thus laying the foundation for future good relations between the two governments, although, as their name suggests, the Nationalists were somewhat more inclined to the right so far as Russian interests were concerned. The only major point on which the center and the right wing agreed was that Russians in Finland should have the same rights as Finns on Russian soil, and that action should be taken against Russian revolutionaries in Finland. The

Kadet Party's main efforts were to criticize the government for attempting to encroach on those Finnish constitutional rights which had been granted by the Tsars. The extreme left, however, geared their arguments almost exclusively to revolutionary ends.

As a result of these happenings in the Russian capital, the feeling in Finland became one of apprehension. The Finnish press responded violently. The British Consul in Helsinki reported:

> The general feeling is one of depression. . . The opinion in the whole country is to make passive resistance once more against any attempt to renew the Bobrikov system.[42]

On 20 May 1908, just a week after these debates, the government issued an ordinance, signed by the Emperor, stating that all matters concerning Finland would henceforth have to go through the Council of Ministers in order to ensure unity of action within the administration.[43] This decree was decried in Finland, for it was felt that the Council of Ministers would act as a veto upon the Finnish Senate and thus constitute a further strain upon relations between the two governments. It was intended, however, that the Council of Ministers should act more narrowly as a body with jurisdictional powers, specifying which legislative acts or bills would affect the interests of the empire.[44] The powers of the Secretary of State for Finland to approach the Monarch directly on legislative matters were thus removed.

Following these disturbed events the Finnish question did not reappear on the national scene until almost two years later, when the government had begun to prepare a bill defining the correct legislative procedure regarding legislation affecting the interests of both Finland and Russia. In the spring of 1909 a joint committee of Finns and Russians was set up to draft proposals for delimiting general legislation.[45] This committee considered the reports of an earlier series of committees which had been called to discuss the Finnish question between 1891-1905, but it unfortunately proved unable to reach unanimity and had to be dissolved after only four meetings.[46]

It was not until 17 March 1910 that the Chairman of the Duma announced the submission of a bill concerning Finland and that the rostrum was vacated for those deputies who wished to speak on the proposal. Miliukov was the first to attack the introduction of the bill on the grounds that it uprooted completely the legal constitution of Finland.[47] The chairman retorted that the contents of the bill were not yet known to members of the Duma, as it was to be distributed later in the day. Miliukov insisted, however, that he and his comrades could not but consider the bill unlawful since any statute on the subject concerned had to go through the legislative institutions of Finland first.[48] After Miliukov had stated that the Kadets would not vote against placing the bill before a commission, the chairman referred him to article 61 of the Duma statute, which affirmed that no bill could in fact be rejected by the Duma until it had been examined and reported on by a commission.[49] Miliukov's attitude seems to indicate that the Kadets were either already familiar with the details of the bill or were determined to oppose any legislation pertaining to Finland which the government might submit.

The Social-Democrats attacked the right and the center and insisted that the bill should be rejected, as did the Kadets, without handing it to a special commission.[50] The Trudoviks, on the other hand, accused the government of deft double dealing, designed to put the blame on the Duma for any decision taken regarding Finland. They also called upon the peasant and clerical deputies to vote against the bill and the commission.[51]

The Octobrists and the rightists insisted on the need for studying and debating the bill. The right wing made a special point of attacking

Miliukov sharply for his participation in the Vyborg incident, accusing him of treason and asserting that the only reason he showed such anxiety over an autonomous Vyborg was because he wished to use it a second time.[52] Finally, the Octobrists advocated that the bill should be sent to a Duma commission for scrutiny. The chairman thereupon presented a motion for the election of a special commission, which was carried by a majority and followed by the election of twenty-one members.[53]

This special commission had a full two months at its disposal for discussion of the bill and for preparing the customary report to the Duma. On 19 May 1910, the Duma agreed to set aside 21 May for initial discussion of the Finnish bill and simultaneously declared the commission's report to be urgent.[54] The latter action reflected the anxiety of the supporters of the bill that it should be passed before the summer session.[55] The opposition parties made their last attempt during this sitting to reject discussion of the problem, or, at best, to postpone the debate until the fall session.

On 21 May the Duma met as planned to discuss the Finnish question. Although the speeches quickly gathered force and momentum, the real debates lasted for only three sittings. The atmosphere was tense, with a constant ringing of the chairman's bell and frequent shouts which made it impossible to hear the speakers.[56] Much of what the opposition and the supporters of the bill had to say had already been said during the debates of May 1908; however, on this occasion the government presented additional clarification regarding its intended policy towards Finland. The commission's report, which was read by Count Bennigsen, began by saying that for some eighty years after Finland's annexation by Russia no definite rule had existed concerning legislation of general significance (<u>obshchegosudarstvennom znachenii</u>). Such laws were passed according to local imperial procedures, although no definite rule existed. When the Finns had attempted in 1891 to pass legislation of a general nature, Alexander III had summoned a commission consisting of Russian and Finnish representatives, each of which had independently worked out a solution. Nevertheless, although all concerned had agreed on the need to regulate the procedure for passing laws of general significance, no agreement had been reached on what that procedure should be.[57]

In 1893 Alexander III had therefore contemplated settling the question through the Council, but the matter had been set aside at his death in 1894. Thereafter the matter had been discussed by a commission, under the chairmanship of Grand Duke Michael Nikolaevich, which had produced the manifesto of 3 February 1899. As will be recalled, this stressed that the initiative in raising legislation of general significance lay in the hands of the sovereign. Legislation of local significance, however, was to be placed in the hands of the Finns. Like Bennigsen before him, Stolypin felt it necessary in his bill to enumerate those items which would fall under the heading of general significance. Imperial authorities took up this suggestion and summoned a Finnish Senate commission, followed by a Russian commission under the chairmanship of Senator N. Tagantsev, and set both to the task of drawing up the enumeration concerned. However, after the publication of the 22 October manifesto, Tagantsev's commission was disbanded at the request of the Finnish Senate.[58] As could be expected, the particular problem involved continued to exist, until it had arisen again in 1908, affirming the need for a law which would define once and for all the correct legislative process. The bill which was submitted to the Duma in 1910 had in fact been prepared by a Russo-Finnish commission under the chairmanship of deputy P. Kharitonov.[59]

The Finns, Bennigsen continued, contended that a special Finnish constitution existed and thus ignored the application of any alternative procedure. However, no legislative act existed to support this point of view and for the past hundred years all laws of general significance had been enacted on the basis of Article I and II of the Russian Fundamental Laws. Bennigsen then listed the legislation so passed. He asserted that,

> From the above it is enough to maintain that the Russian legislative sphere always overlaps that of Finland, and that the Finnish legislation does not exclude our legislation; consequently the present bill is based on lawful origins and its realization without infringement of the Finnish constitution seems perfectly feasible.[60]

Pointing out that education in Finland was encouraging animosity towards Russia, he suggested that such efforts should be checked. He concluded by calling upon the Finns to put themselves in the place of Russians, for even with the introduction of the law proposed, the Finnish people would have their national and cultural interests assured.[61]

Miliukov briefly ascended the tribune to announce that the Kadet Party washed its hands of what was proposed, insisting that it was nothing but an act of coercion.[62] Gegechkori, on the other hand, recapitulated his earlier speech with added vituperation. However, he was the first of the deputies to acknowledge frankly that the minorities were Russia's internal enemies, and accused the government of inciting the Great Russians against them in order to divert attention from social problems. He ended his speech with the usual revolutionary call,

> I leave this tribune with an appeal to all the creative forces of society to unite and to reject decisively the misanthropic propaganda and agitation which you are spreading throughout the entire nation, so as to end it for ever.[63]

Zamyslovskii, presenting the main arguments of the rightists, emphasized as he did in 1908 that Russia could not permit the separation of a territory which was within easy reach of the capital, was openly aggressive, and had organized armed uprisings and given refuge to revolutionaries during the 1905 crisis. Turning to the legal aspects of the problem, he defended Russia's prerogatives over Finland by citing Article II of the Fundamental Laws, which stated that Finland was an inseparable part of the empire; this, in his opinion, categorically destroyed the theory that a Finnish State existed. He once more called upon the opposition to produce the Finnish constitution and argued that the word "constitution," which Alexander I had used at Borga, now carried a different meaning from that which it had in 1910, when it had meant simply "Code," or "Statute." He pointed out that throughout the nineteenth century Finnish writers had referred to Finland as a province of Russia. The Form of Government of 1772 and the Act of Union and Security of 1789 (to which reference was being made as the Finnish Fundamental Laws) were really part of the Swedish constitution, for during that period Finland had been part of the Swedish empire.[64]

V. Fon Anrep, speaking for the Octobrists, insisted that the problem could be approached only by objective analysis of a series of historically created relationships. In his judgment, the whole issue lay in answer to this question: was it conceivable that one part of the empire could have a disproportionate role in questions which concerned the interests of the whole? He concluded an intelligent speech by touching on a salient point:

> I am ready to admit that this law was introduced into the Duma inopportunely, not from the standpoint of prematurity, but from the standpoint of its belatedness. . . it should have been introduced exactly fifty years ago, i.e. at the moment the Seim statutes were established.[65]

These were the initial outbursts of party views prior to Stolypin's appearance; after his speech the debates began in earnest. Stolypin presented the government's point of view in a long address which mingled statesman-like impartiality and national feeling. The written norms which had defined Finland's position within the empire and the legislative acts which had concerned Finland over the past hundred years reflected the most diverse political and historical streams, often contradicting one another and usually depending on temporary events and conditions. There was ample material available concerning Finno-Russian relations to substantiate any attitude which might be adopted.[66] Stolypin noted that many were still uncertain why the government had raised the Finnish issue at this juncture. He explained that in 1905 the law on general military service in Finland had been temporarily suspended and then abolished. In 1908 this particular question had cropped up again, and required re-examination. The imperial government considered that military service and its supportive taxation were of general interest, because involving the number of recruits to be enlisted from the Russian provinces and the amount of taxation to be paid by the Russian population. The Finns, on the other hand, considered that these questions lay at the unilateral discretion of the Diet.

The wisest course, declared Stolypin, might be to make Finland a completely free, independent state, tied to Russia only by common external bonds and to create, as he said, "At the threshold of St. Petersburg, a noble and happy nation."[67] The question was, he proceeded, "What are the interests of the state without yielding, under such circumstances, to feelings of false pride or to those of national chauvinism?" In answer he scrutinized, in an almost pedantic manner, the legislative events of the previous decades, with the hope of substantiating the validity and legality of the action of the Russian Government. The Finns had relied on the words of Alexander I, pronounced a century before, in order to reach the conclusion that Russia only had powers as regards foreign relations; all internal affairs were to be dealt with by the Finnish legislature, even if general interests of the empire were involved. On this view Russia had only the passive right to veto any acts which might be harmful to her, through the role played by the Tsar. Stolypin then emphasized:

> I would not wish to conceal a single word of the arguments which speak in favor of the Finnish point of view. I will not take it upon myself to seek out words, expressions which might discredit such acts; one cannot present an historical argument by constantly presenting words pronounced by historic figures long gone to the grave, especially words and arguments which are dependent on the rhetorical dexterity of an advocate.[68]

Finland enjoyed a wide measure of local autonomy under its provincial constitution. However, Stolypin wished to assure the Duma of the government's conviction that those issues which embraced the whole empire, or those Finnish laws which affected Russia's interests, were beyond the Diet's competence. Any other understanding of this point would, he said, "bring us to an historic impasse." He pointed out that under the British Colonial Legislative Act the decisions of colonial parliaments were recognized provided they did not conflict with the legislative acts of the British Parliament.[69] During the nineteenth century,

> . . . Because of the uncertainty of the Finnish laws, they clouded understanding of the Finnish Fundamental Laws, and because of the obscurity of the boundaries between local and general legislation, our monarchs implemented their authority nonchalantly, by means of imperial commands, in accordance

> with subordinate legislation as well as with that of the Diet. Such legislation, as you have seen, even encroached upon the field of purely Russian legislation at times; but what is clear and undeniable is that our emperors themselves were conscious, that they, and they alone, had the power and the prerogative to implement general legislation within the limits of the Grand Duchy of Finland.[70]

Stolypin mentioned that in all his manifestos, even the most liberal ones, Alexander I had always considered Finland subordinate to the Russian state. Thus, Stolypin concluded, it was impossible to interpret a prolonged practice as an aberration. He then stressed to the deputies that "the Tsar confided this matter to you, and not to the administration, and no imperial law will bypass you."[71]

The main opposition speakers were the Kadets and the Social-Democrats. There was also a handful of deputies who expressed liberal opinions, but their influence upon these debates was insignificant. Since the majority of the opposition chose to boycott the rostrum as a sign of protest, most of those who spoke did so in favor of the bill. Few deputies had anything new to say and, though there was considerable tension in the assembly, the actual speeches were largely undistinguished.

The Kadets were the first to oppose the government's point of view as presented by Stolypin. Miliukov accused him of deviation from his principle that "right should be above might!"[72] Brushing aside the suggestion of the reactionaries that Finland was a military threat to Russia, he declared that Finland was too small and weak to nourish any bellicose feelings towards Russia.[73] Branding the bill as illegal, unjustified by present needs, and presenting a serious danger to the state, he implied that Stolypin's policy was even more reactionary than that of Bobrikov and Plehve.[74]

Although Miliukov spoke at greater length than any other opposition speaker, his words do not appear to have contained the seeds of conviction. Maklakov did more than any of the other Duma deputies to present a constructive argument from the legal point of view. Unlike others, he gave precise reasons why it would be unjust to pass the bill and did not confine himself to violent attacks as a substitute for balanced arguments, as his colleague Miliukov had done. He began by noting that the bill itself had nothing to do with general legislation. That it in effect took the Duma back to 1809 since it gave an exact definition of Finland's political position for the first time. The prolonged duration of the present situation made it especially acute and any mistake now would be tragically irreparable. From a legal standpoint Article Two of the Finnish bill meant that the Duma would be in a position to change any Finnish legislation; in the final analysis, therefore, Finland might even lose her provincial self-government. Maklakov firmly believed that the whole evil of the bill lay in a wide disparity between its aims and the means to which it resorted. The essence of the Finnish question, he stressed--and he was the only opposition speaker to admit this--lay in the necessity of establishing a new procedure for general legislation.[75]

Appealing to the Octobrists, he declared that their methods would destroy Finland and the Russian constitution at the same time. While he conceded that Finland would no doubt be at the mercy of the Russian legislative body with the passage of the bill, he suggested surprisingly that the bill should first be submitted to the Diet; if the Finns, upon consideration, rejected the measure, "then," said Maklakov, "I would say with you, no matter how much I value legality, there are moments when _suprema lex salus populi_." In those circumstances he considered that the government would be entitled to use force. The government would then be consciously in the right, for, having exhausted all means, it would be compelled to act. Thus the government would not have to lower itself to what he termed, "a lie, a deceit, and the denial of a constitution which was guaranteed to the Finns."[76]

Maklakov's speech, full of eloquence, well and precisely presented, could not but win him admiration. But his final words appear to contradict the sense of his preceding exposition. In either case the government would be resorting to force, but if a public rejection by the Finnish Diet could first be obtained, then Maklakov's sense of moral values would be satisfied. However, the final result would still be equally unconstitutional according to his own earlier analysis. To an impartial listener it would appear that the perennial conflict between Realpolitik and morality had led Maklakov into an inconsistent position.

The Trudovik Bulat, openly declaring that he intended to speak over the heads of deputies in the interests of the welfare of the workers and the peasants, observed that if Finland were really preparing an attempt to overthrow Russia, then all the Duma parties would undoubtedly support the government in bringing Finland to submission. However, he quickly explained that if such attempts were being organized in Finland, they were not directed against Russia as such but against its government. If the bill were passed it would be disastrous for Finland and dangerous and disgraceful for Russia. He then ended with the usual call for revolution,

> We know that only when we have overthrown the autocratic regime will the minorities which comprise the Russian state, and Finland in this case, have full freedom, and only then will we be able to strive together towards a better future.[77]

The Social-Democrats, in the person of N. Chkheidze, spared no words in attacking the rightists and the Octobrists as one and the same. He even castigated the liberal Maklakov, saying sarcastically that the latter "always raises alarm at the tragedy of the situation whenever the question of a constitution arises, and on each occasion dramatically acts out the role of a tragic hero of Russian constitutionalism."[78]

He insisted that the minorities loved Russia and the Russian people which had produced such great creative forces as Tolstoy, Turgenev, Griboedov, and others. Noting that the minorities knew whom to respect, for they had allies within Russia, he ended with an appeal to the Finns:

> We are sending our comradely and friendly greetings to the Finns and will say: Hail Finnish freedom! Hail the free Finnish people! Away with barbarians and barbarian government.[79]

Another member of the same party, A. Kuznetsov, exclaimed that it would be a crime to be silent, not only before the working class of Russia and Finland, but before the world proletariat. He stressed that both the Russian and Finnish proletariat should unite under the slogan "Fraternity, Equality, and Liberty," and added that the Social-Democrats were determined to restore independence to the Finns and to gain further rights for the Russian people.[80]

W. Zukowski, speaking for the Polish factions, felt that the legal and historic aspects had been amply set out and therefore abstained from any detailed elaboration. Surprisingly enough, he declared that his group sided with the views expressed by the Octobrists. Though the bill was an infringement upon the national rights of Finland, nevertheless he felt that it was essential to establish rules to solve the existing legal predicament. His only emphasis, or appeal, was for the government to adhere to a policy of statehood.[81]

Those Octobrists who disagreed with the bill were too few to have any great effect upon party unity. In any case, most opposed only this or that feature of the bill and not the entire proposal. Most of them supported two main arguments in its favor: the establishment of a definite legislative procedure and the safeguarding of Russian national interests. Those who spoke in favor of the bill presented the same arguments as had been put forward in 1908, with only a few variations.

By 24 May the Duma was becoming restless with the reiteration of old arguments. There was growing indifference and apathy on the left and a mood of confidence among the supporters of the bill. Though there was still a long list of speakers, a motion was introduced to limit them to fifteen minutes; despite objections, the motion was passed by a majority.[82] It was simply a matter of time and procedural etiquette before the debates could be closed and the Duma proceed to the reading of the bill.

Baron A. Meyendorff, the Octobrist with a liberal reputation which had won him the respect of even the ultra-revolutionaries, spoke objectively and critically.[83] He declared that most of the speeches had revealed a passionate nationalism. "Love for Russia," he said, "does not ensure us against erroneous proposals or erroneous projects." He called attention to the fact that,

> The basic element of a constitution does not consist of an oath alone. . . the fundamental and decisive moment of every constitution is a simple and clear rule: that no law can be passed, changed or revoked without the consent of the representative body.[84]

The Baron further noted that Stolypin was attempting to minimize the significance of the Finnish bill by alleging that what was involved was not an agreement but simply a promise. In his view, the

Monarch's promise should be more strictly observed than any agreement. He did not deny, however, that Stolypin's bill was a question of political necessity and his only insistence was on the need to show consideration and fairness, lest separatist feelings only become intensified. Concluding his speech, he said that he had no intention of sharing responsibility for this nationalist exploit (he was the only Octobrist to make this declaration), thus earning the applause of the left, hisses from the right, and silence from the Octobrists themselves.[85]

The right wing reiterated the same arguments they had delivered in the 1908 debates. Their main points of emphasis were again that Finland was an inseparable part of the Russian empire, that it had never been granted a constitution by Alexander I, that the Borga Diet was simply a consultative and not a legislative body, that Russians in Finland should have the same rights as the Finns in Russia, that the Finnish Diet should not be allowed to pass laws in opposition to imperial interests, that the Finns were a potential military danger within a stone's throw of the Russian capital, and, finally, that a new bill which would enumerate the subjects falling into the category of general laws was essential.[86] This last was their major argument, and was also pressed by the Octobrists.

The debates continued until 25 May, when the Chairman of the Duma submitted a motion which was immediately carried, to pass to the reading of the bill.[87] On 26 May the Duma proceeded to an article-by-article reading of the bill. On 28 May, after the completion of the second reading, the chairman presented the whole bill for a vote.[88] After a majority had been obtained, the chairman announced that the bill would then be sent to the editing commission,[89] which reported on 31 May on the corrections made. This third reading of the bill was then voted on again and passed by a majority.[90] With the Finnish bill thus ratified by the Duma, the chairman declared that the bill would now be handed to the State Council.

Within the State Council the debates on the Finnish question were greatly simplified, for the majority was sympathetic towards the bill, and its passage was inevitable from the start. In their criticism of the nineteen points enumerated in Article Two, the small opposition minority attempted to convince the Council nevertheless of the need for a complete revision of this section. Though they had very little hope to turn the tide, they made all possible efforts to win their way. There was also a sprinkling of right wing and center deputies holding liberal views, but their speeches were comparatively weak and ineffective. As in the Duma, the far right was dominated by feelings of extreme nationalism. The center, although supporting the bill for varied reasons, did not agree in particulars with the right wing on this occasion.

The State Council commission began its scrutiny of the bill on 18 May and, on 8 June 1910, after the report of the commission had been read, the Council itself started its discussion of the Finnish question.[91] V. Dietrikh, to whom the report had been entrusted, stressed that Finland was an integral part of Russia, with a broad degree of self-government over internal affairs. The main aim of the bill, he emphasized, was to define the legislative boundaries of Finnish institutions and to establish finally the legislative process regarding statutes which concerned Finland, and those which fell into the category of general legislation (obshchegosudarstvennago znachenie).[92] The commission decided that such a step--the defining of Finnish legislative or constitutional rights--should really have been undertaken (in 1809 with the granting of special state and legislative rights by Alexander I) when Finland was occupied. Unfortunately, the granting of special rights, without defining their extent, brought about an inevitable collision of interests. Dietrikh pointed out that the idea of Finland as a distinct independent State had been developed in the nineteenth century by professors of the University of Helsingfors. He recalled that laws concerning Finland were always passed by imperial command or manifestoes, simply promulgated by the issue of an imperial decree based on the opinion of the State Council, or contained in regulations issued by the Committee of Ministers. These had never been considered illegal or a breach of Finnish privileges.[93]

As for the origins of the present issue, Dietrikh said that in 1878 a statute concerning military service in Finland, which had violated the most vital interests of the empire, had been passed in the Diet in spite of protests from the Minister of War, Count D. Miliutin. This statute established a Finnish army, separate from that of the Russian, with large reserves, special military outposts, and headquarters under the exclusive command of Finnish officers. It also introduced the taking of a special oath, special military courts, and even a special military criminal code. The government, realizing the danger, had attempted to introduce legislation to curb the newly established order, but in each case had been met with the Finnish "*non possumus*."[94] Besides the military statutes, another question had also arisen which touched on the interests of the empire, namely the passing of a new Finnish Criminal Code, which infringed on the unity and rights of Russia. The need to confine legislative boundaires was thus further accentuated. The unacceptability of the criminal code forced Alexander III to demand changes to be made in it. The Diet, however, had considered the imperial command illegal. Although amendments had again been suggested in 1891, the Diet had once more deemed them unacceptable. Finally, in 1894, the Diet had been obliged to accept the alterations desired by the imperial government. The Finnish question had then been set aside until 1899.[95]

Turning to the 1899 manifesto, Dietrikh noted that this had been the first statute to establish the procedure for general legislation, leaving to the Tsar to decide which laws were of general, and which of local significance. During the troubled period of 1905-1907, the Finns had attempted to pass laws pertaining solely to Finnish affairs, without imperial participation, although state interests were very much involved. Such action, more than anything else, forced the government to hasten a suitable bill.[96] If laws of general significance were in fact to be turned over to the jurisdiction of the Diet, this body would be transformed from a local into an all-state institution and the State Council and the Duma would no longer be in a position of authority over Finland. The Finns demanded that any law which concerned the Duchy of Finland should be passed first by the Diet and then by the State Council and the Duma. This meant that any bill would become law prior to submission to the full legislative bodies of the empire. Dietrikh considered this ridiculous. According to the existing statutes, any bill which concerned Finland could only become law when it was ratified by the Emperor. He concluded that the Diet's demand violated the Fundamental Laws of the empire and was an attempt to deprive the State Council and the Duma of their legislative prerogatives over the total expanse of the empire. These were the main reasons why, he emphasized, "we refuse categorically to agree to the Diet's point of view."[97]

Stolypin spoke next, without going into details, for he considered that the commission's report had been detailed enough. He concentrated on reiterating certain points of principle involved in government policy. Both Russian and foreign opponents of the bill considered it an infringement of the present law. However, he declared that the government had to look first and foremost to the interests of Russia and that he was fully convinced that to give way fully to the demands of the Diet would constitute a flagrant infringement of the Russian Fundamental Laws. There were now in fact two alternatives open: one was to give Finland a completely free hand in the sphere of matters affecting her even if they involved imperial interests (he instanced the promulgation of the criminal code in 1899 and the preparation of new draft rules for the Finnish State in 1906, which had come to his attention by accident, through the newspapers), the other was to rely on a resolute safeguarding of imperial well-being, with a due respect to Finnish autonomy and privileges.[98] Throughout his speech, however, Stolypin emphasized the supremacy of Russia's interests. From this standpoint, the government had no alternative but to follow the course which it had in fact already chosen.

Three consecutive sittings of the State Council then followed, devoted to general debates on the bill. The first to come to its defense was Tagantsev, a Professor of Jurisprudence, a man of moderate nationalist views. He had sat as chairman of the Russo-Finnish commission in 1905 and was perhaps the only member in the State Council who had closely studied the subject. He stressed that, from the point of view of Russian interests, the bill was imperative. As late as 1800 the Swedes had played a prominent role in the cultural, political, and economic life of the country, and it was not until Finland had come under Russian rule that her whole physiognomy had changed. Finland had been a constant arena of wars between Russia and Sweden, and as contacts with the Western world increased, the position of Finland had gained in significance.[99] Tagantsev then read Article 4 of the Fredrickshamn Treaty, which stated that the King of Sweden renounced for himself, and his successors, all rights over the Finnish provinces and, in Article 6, any rights over the citizens living there. He pointed out that this was not an international agreement and that Russia herself had not assumed any international obligations. At Borga, he said, the Finns had been brought together to take an oath of citizenship at the solemn opening of the Diet. However, "no oath was taken by the Emperor to give a constitution." His main assertion was that, historically, no constitution had been granted at Borga and that "constitutional rights were only granted, little by little, by our emperors."[100]

P. Kobylinskii, a moderate right wing member, presented a speech the contents of which were only too familiar to the audience. He reproduced the usual argument showing that Alexander I had not granted a constitution at Borga, and traced the history of Finno-Russian relations.[101] N. Sukhotin, another rightist member, lived up to the traditions of reactionary chauvinism. He, too, traced the history of Finland from earliest time, stressing the Swedish influence, and cited numerous comments made by Alexander I and M. Speransky to prove conclusively that a constitution had not been granted at Borga.[102]

A somewhat different speech was presented by the Ukrainian Archpriest Butnevich, who asserted that the arguments against the bill did not convince him, for he could well argue that the Ukraine was an independent state, and yet it had not been conquered like Finland. Attacking the remark made in the Duma and the State Council that, "Russian barbarians were destroying the rare Finnish culture, this jewel of the imperial crown," he noted that in Helsingfors, where he had lived for many years, Russian priests had been spat upon simply because they were Orthodox clergy. He also elaborated several incidents in which Orthodox clergy and parishioners had been abused by Finnish citizens, who had not been punished by the authorities.[103]

Speeches such as these, and others, filled with nationalistic metaphors, were plentiful and perhaps the easiest to deliver, for they promptly produced the desired excitement and indignation. By the second day of the debates, both the speakers and the audience were highly tense; an attempt to limit speeches to twenty minutes was quickly brushed aside.[104]

The opposition presented speeches of a consistently higher quality, criticism being concentrated largely on Article Two of the bill. D. Grimm, a liberal member of the center, criticized the nineteen points on the grounds that they did not define very clearly where local Finnish legislation ended and where general legislation began. His main point, however, was that the bill lacked any formal guarantees of the imperial government's position as regards general legislation. He considered the bill so inadequate in this respect that he declared he would vote against it, and requested the Council to reject it without passing a reading.[105]

Professor M. Kovalevskii, a left wing opponent of the bill, cited a number of examples from European and United States history which had some similarity to the problem under discussion. The parallels, which he drew, however, like those of the right wing, had little direct relevance to the Finnish bill and largely pointed to the need to set legal limits to the exercise of sovereignty within the state.[106] Among other opposition speakers, P. Kamenskii felt that the government's sudden haste could be justified only by military considerations. He suggested that, even in the previous winter of 1909-1910, rumors had prevailed that relations with one of the European powers were extremely strained and might be broken off.[107]

Baron A. Korf, speaking for the Poles, said that they would vote against the bill. Nevertheless he agreed on the points relating to state defense, military service, the payment of certain general expenses by the Finns, and the equalization of rights for Russian subjects residing in Finland. He repeated Maklakov's argument that it would have been wiser to submit the bill to the Diet first, to have taken the final stroke only if it had been refused.[108]

A. Koni, a liberal lawyer with a reputation for great integrity, delivered some positive and telling arguments against the bill in a short speech of exceptional quality which received the unusual tribute of applause and "bravos" at the end. He conceded that Finland had already received a broad measure of self-government, but argued that the bill as drafted, with its sweeping terms, would constitute a threat to the political liberties already gained. The famous Article Two, for example, interfered in the spheres of education, communications, travel and with the monetary system. The sections dealing with the right of assembly and with the freedom of the press should be clarified, if the old issues of general versus local legislation were not to rise again and once more threaten the unity of the empire.[109] The Duma had not really considered the bill but had only sought to use it in order to castigate the government. However, although the present heads of state were fair minded enough, a great deal of damage could be done through the bill if an extreme reactionary element were to head the cabinet. True "peace-makers," as he evidently considered Stolypin, were few and far between, and "thoughtless optimism" over the future was not enough. He therefore called for a thorough revision of the bill by the commission, and announced that he would vote against it if such a revision were not carried out.[110]

Dietrikh, the spokesman for the commission, then reappeared to make a number of clarifications. To the main criticism, that the points enumerated were not clear, he declared blandly that this defect was no reason for rejecting the bill outright; the State Council had full rights to introduce any necessary amendments. If the assembly turned to the article-by-article reading of the bill it would be possible to introduce such corrections. He denied that there was any special haste over the bill, but suggested that the whole question had perhaps been discussed often enough over the previous twenty years. The present commission had gone over the bill with extreme thoroughness already, but if the State Council decided to introduce changes it could still go to the coordinating commission in the following fall.[111]

By 11 June the debates were over and an air of impatience overtook the assembly. Motions were now being introduced to pass on to the article-by-article reading.[112] Finally the chairman announced the conclusion of the debates and read a motion by four opponents to reject the bill outright, which was immediately voted down.[113] Durnovo, the leader of the reactionary clique, appeared to suggest that the Council should proceed to the detailed reading in order to put a stop to the press agitation.[114]

The press campaign to which Durnovo referred, and the foreign interference mentioned by Stolypin, deserve attention;[115] both the opposition papers in Russia and the foreign press exhibited a great deal of interest in the bill, reflecting considerable sympathy for the Finnish cause. In Finland itself there was intense feeling against the action of the Russian Government, with vehement press attacks, political meetings, and popular demonstrations.[116] Finnish political leaders travelled throughout Europe rallying support for their cause; well known lawyers gathered to deliberate on the issue, before concluding that Russia was guilty of encroachment on her subjects' rights; parliamentary members of France and England sent notes of protest to the Russian legislative bodies.[117] Political circles in Russia thus became well aware of their isolation, and the government's organ _Novoe Vremia_, was forced into repeated attacks on this "foreign interference in domestic affairs."[118]

The chairman's motion to pass to the reading of the bill was therefore passed by a standing vote;[119] the size of the majority could not but have impressed the opposition that the passing of the bill was a virtual _fait accompli_. Nonetheless, when Article Two was reached they made a last stand. Stolypin therefore took the opportunity to clarify further government policy over this part of the bill. He assured his audience that, as long as future laws did not overlap general legislation, the present Finnish legislative process and existing Finnish liberties would both be maintained. Bills would have to be submitted to the Diet prior to going to the Duma and the State Council, which would both receive Finnish representation. He agreed that the Finnish delegationwould be in a minority, but pointed out that they would be listened to with particular attention. All bills which dealt with questions of local Finnish interest would be handed over to the Diet and passed strictly by the Finnish legislative bodies; it was only legislation affecting the general interests of the empire which would be decided upon by the Russian legislature.[120]

The State Council then turned to the reading of Article Two; the sitting closed at 10 p.m. after the first four points had been voted on.[121] The reading of the bill was resumed on 14 June, and the rest of the article was approved without amendment.[122] The remaining eleven articles of the bill were then agreed to within fifteen minutes, after which the State Council went into recess for half an hour. The whole bill was then presented for the final vote and accepted by a majority.[123]

The Tsar signed the bill on 17 June 1910, the day that the summer recess of the Duma and the State Council began. This, the first law of its kind in Finno-Russian relations since 1809, provided that legislation affecting Finland, but which involved imperial interests, would be enacted by the Russian legislature.[124] The nineteen points of Article Two listing what was covered by "general or imperial interests," over which so much of the debating battle had raged, read as follows:

> In addition to the Fundamental Laws of the empire, and to the other laws and ordinances affecting Finland by way of general legislation before the enactment of this present law, as well as to enactments altering and supplementing these laws and ordinances, the following subjects shall be dealt with in accordance with section 1, subsection 1:[125]

1. The participation of Finland in the expenditure of the empire, and the establishment of payments, charges, and duties necessary for this purpose;

2. The discharge of military service of the population of Finland, and the fulfillment of other military duties;

3. The rights of Russian subjects residing in Finland who are not Finnish citizens;

4. The employment of the imperial (official) language in Finland;

5. The fundamental principles for the internal administration of Finland, on the basis of a special procedure of legislation;

6. The rights, obligations, and procedure of action of the public institutions of the empire in Finland;

7. The carrying into effect in Finland of sentences, verdicts, and orders of courts of justices in the empire, of demands made by the authorities there, and of contracts and agreements therein entered into;

8. The making of exception, from the point of view of imperial interests, to the criminal laws and laws of procedure in Finland;

9. The safeguarding of state interests in regard to establishing a program of education and its supervision;

10. Regulations concerning public meetings, associations, and societies;

11. The rights and conditions of Finnish business companies established in parts of the empire, and the conditions for their activities in Finland and abroad;

12. Legislation on the press in Finland, and on the importation of foreign literature;

13. Customs and tariffs in Finland;

14. Protection of commercial and industrial trademarks and privileges in Finland, and likewise the rights of literary and artistic copyright;

15. The monetary system in Finland;

16. The post, telephones, aeronautics, and similar means of communications in Finland;

17. The railways in Finland, in regard to the defenses of the empire and to the traffic between Finland and other parts of the empire, as well as to the international traffic; railway telegraphs;

18. Navigation, piloting, and lighthouse services in Finland;

19. The rights of aliens in Finland.[126]

From this it is clear that, as a number of speakers had pointed out, notably Koni, the Russian Government could restrict Finnish legislative prerogatives. Stolypin's government, in the person of Stolypin himself, had been at great pains to indicate that the classification of subjects under the nineteen points would be conducted fairly and equitably. This principle was also proclaimed in article one of the law.

To any observer with liberal sympathies it is only natural to conclude that Finland, a distinct cultural and geographical entity, should have been given complete independence; the accepted dictates of humanity are that every national group has the right to self-determination.[127] On the other hand, the desire of Stolypin's Cabinet to preserve existing state boundaries is also one with which modern man is perfectly familiar. In both cases moral grounds and considerations of Realpolitik played their part, although much of the argument turned on superficial legal issues.

The Finnish case, in essence, was that a Finnish constitution, promised by the Tsars, was now being encroached upon as part of a general policy of Russification.[128] The opposition in the Duma and State Council broadly accepted this argument and developed it in the course of the debates. The government, on the other hand, was driven by somewhat more complex factors;[129] in addition to the powerful force of Russian nationalism, there was a great deal of social unrest, not to mention the intricate cross currents of reactionary and revolutionary intrigue and the pressure of international opinion. The government therefore adopted a position of formal legality to combat the Finnish claim for justice, and stressed that Finland had never truly been an independent state;[130] prior to Russia's annexation it had been a Swedish province and thereafter an integral though privileged part of the Russian empire.[131] Owing, however, to the lack of detailed statutes, the Finns had been in a good position to undermine the edifice of imperial legislation in an attempt to gain an independent position for themselves, thus equalizing Finnish with Russian national interests. As national feeling had grown, new situations had arisen constantly and complications had increased. The Finns had gone far beyond the fears of the imperial government in the use they had made of their privileges and had begun to infringe upon Russian prerogatives and interests. This inherent incompatibility of interests had been evident to the Russian Government even before the Finnish

Diet of 1863 when it had been referred to by Alexander II in his opening speech.

This raised the question of legislation which dealt with matters of "all-imperial scope." The concept itself was disadvantageous to the Finns because it gave the Russian Government the privilege of determining which laws fell within the imperial scope.[132] The Finns naturally denied that their country had ever formed an integral part of the Russian empire, although they accepted the fact that they were a Grand Duchy of Russia and therefore her protectorate.[133] Again, the immediate difficulty lay in the lack of legal or statutory documentation which defined the prerogatives and limits of both the Finnish Diet and the Russian monarchy. It could be argued, as the Finns did, that every aspect of Finnish life fell within the category of matters of "all-imperial scope" and that the Finnish Diet would be reduced to the level of a minor provincial assembly, thus disfranchising the Finnish electorate. The nineteen points passed by Stolypin, however, were intended only as a framework upon which Finno-Russian relations could be established. With time, improved arrangements could be made through legislative amendments to fit the needs of the future. The present bill did not treat everything as "all-imperial," but simply reserved the constitutional right to interfere in the matters listed in the nineteen points, should the Finns jeopardize the interests of the empire regarding them. Stolypin intended the bill as a safety valve, not as a constitutional infringement. Without acceptance of such a framework the result would be a continuous and intricate judicial duel, finally involving the _ultima ratio_ of the litigants. The Finns, not unnaturally, were distrustful of Stolypin's policy and feared a return to the Russification policy of the Bobrikov period. However, the text of the bill and the points stressed by Stolypin in the Duma and the Council indicate a change of policy and a desire to establish an agreed base upon which both governments could build.

It is noticeable that Stolypin's speeches on the Finnish question lacked enthusiasm by comparison with his other orations. The spark and eloquence which he showed in his speeches on the western zemstvos, which were also linked with the problem of national minorities, were not repeated. But on that occasion he believed firmly in what he had to say; by contrast, his speeches on the Finnish question suggest that he was to some extent an unwilling party to the policy adopted, influenced by the fear of a greater evil and perhaps also by the forces at work within the Court, as has been suggested.[134]

NOTES

1. Finland and Russia (London, 1911), p. 9. For Alexander's manifesto on the Finnish Senate and other documents pertaining to Finno-Russian relations, see Kirby, D., ed. and trans., Finland and Russia 1808-1920 (London, 1975).

2. Renwick, G., Finland To-day (London, 1911), p. 309.

3. For a succinct account see, Raeff, M., Michael Speransky: Statesman of Imperial Russia, 1772-1837 (The Hague, 1957), pp. 70-75.

4. Chertkov, V., Finliandskii Razgrom, (England, 1900), p. 10.

5. Alektorov, A., Inorodtsy v Rossii (SPB, 1906), p. 8. According to him anti-Russian propaganda, agitating for the freedom of Finland from Russian encroachment, began in the early 1870's; See also Stenback, M., Finland: The Country, its People and Institutions (Helsinki, 1926) pp. 121, 123, and 183; Feodoroff, E., The Finnish Revolution in Preparation 1889-1905 (SPB, 1911), p. 71; Finlianskaia Okraina v Sostave Russkago

Gosudarstva (SPB, 1906), pp.26-30; Wuorinen, J., Nationalism in Modern Finland (New York, 1931), pp.201-202. He places the first stirrings of Finnish nationalism as early as the 1840's.

6. For a full text see: P.S.Z., Vol. XIX, No. 16447. See also Lipskii, A., O Poriadka Izdaniia Kasaiushchikhsia Finliandii Zakonov Obshchegosudastvennago Znacheniia (SPB, 1910), p.9.

7. Henceforth "Imperial legislation" (obshchegosudarstvennago znacheniia) will be referred to as "general legislation," and Finnish laws as "local legislation." For an excellent summary (in English) concerning Finno-Russian legislative relations between 1808-1863, see Jusilla, O., Suomen Perustaslait Venalaisten Ja Suomalaisten Tulkintojen Mukaan 1808-1863 (Helsinki, 1969), pp.263-279.

8. Harrison & Sons, The Russo-Finnish Conflict (London, 1910), p.10.

9. Alektorov, A., op. cit., p.12, 15.

10. P.S.Z., Vol. XXV, No. 26846; Pushkarev, S., Rossiia v 19 Veke (New York, 1956), p.384. He notes that laws passed under the Bobrikov regime were also rescinded with this manifesto. Novoe Vremia, 19 March 1910 (12219), p.3. It states that the Finnish nationalist Mechelin presumably drew up the Manifesto of 22 October 1905.

11. MacGowan, D., "The Conflict in Finland," The Century Magazine, February 1905, Vol. 69, p.627.

12. Jackson, J., Finland (New York, 1940), p.67.

13. For a brief account of Swedish influence in Finland and the development of Finnish nationalism, see Myhrman, A., The Swedish

Nationality Movement in Finland (Chicago, 1959).

14. Shearman, H., Finland: The Adventures of a Small Power (London, 1950), p.29.

15. Ibid., p.52.

16. Smith, J., Finland and the Russian Revolution, 1917-1922 (Atlanta, 1958), p.5; Reade, A., Finland and the Finns (New York, 1917), p.210.

17. G.D. 5 May 1908, Col. 2920.

18. Ibid., Cols. 2921-23. Stolypin told Baron Meyendorff that the German Government was more helpful in apprehending and handing over revolutionaries who had committed crimes in Russia than was the Finnish Government. Stolypin noted in this speech that, between February and December 1907, 25 conferences and meetings of a revolutionary character had been held in Finland. He also stressed that most of the assassinations which took place in Russia were organized in Finland, and listed those government officials who had been assassinated. G.D., 5 May 1908, Cols. 2923-24. Smith notes that the Voima consisted of nationalists who were "ex-soldiers of the dissolved Finnish Army." Smith, J., op. cit., p.4. The Voima was very active in smuggling arms into Russia, which seems to have been a major concern of the Russian Government. See P.R.O. F.O. 371, Vol. 512, No. 17775, 25 May 1908.

19. G.D. 5 May 1908, Cols. 2924-26.

20. Ibid., Cols. 2928-41.

21. See Rech and Novoe Vremia for the month of May 1908.

22. G.D. 12 May 1908, Cols. 417-27.

23. Ibid., Cols. 439-442.

24. On the shipment of arms to Finland see: Wuorinen, J., *op. cit.*, p.199; Alektorov, A., *op. cit.*, pp.20-21; A. B., *Za Kulisami Okhrannago Otdeleniia* (Berlin, 1911), pp.169-170; Feodoroff, E., *op. cit.*, pp.22-70. Revolutionary activity in Finland was also an established fact. See Stolypin's telegram to the Governor General Gerard in July 1906. "P. A. Stolypin i Sveaborskoe Vostanie," *Krasnyi Arkhiv*, Vol. 49 (1931), p.147; Polivanov, A., *Iz Dnevnikov i Vospominanii po Dolzhnosti Voenogo Ministra i Ego Pomoshchnika*, 1907-1916 g. (Moscow, 1924), p.84.

25. *G.D.* 12 May 1908, Cols. 399-406.

26. *Ibid.*, Col. 416.

27. *G.D.* 13 May 1908, Cols. 653-660. For more detail on the *John Krafton* and the Japanese see Futrell, M., *Northern Underground* (London, 1963), Chapter IV.

28. *G.D.* 12 May 1908, Cols. 365-373.

29. *Ibid.*, Cols. 374-375. Such statements were influential in that they were sympathetically received by Russians, liberals, and reactionaries alike. As Baron Meyendorff noted, such statements turned many of the *dachniki* (summer residents) and Russians living in Finland into eager chauvinists. See also "Vnutrennii Obzor," *Vestnik Evropy*, September 1911, pp.266-371.

30. *G.D.* 12 May 1908, Col. 382.

31. *G.D.* 13 May 1908, Cols. 688-704.

32. *G.D.* 5 May 1908, Cols. 2942-60.

33. *G.D.* 13 May 1908, Cols. 627-628.

34. *G.D.* 12 May 1908, Cols. 390-395.

35. G.D. 13 May 1908, Cols. 624-625.

36. G.D. 5 May 1908, Cols. 2941-2942.

37. G.D. 13 May 1908, Cols. 669-678.

38. "Do not encroach on the interests of others and give each which each deserves."

39. G.D. 13 May 1908, Cols. 636-641.

40. Ibid., Cols. 665-669.

41. Ibid., Cols. 720-723.

42. P.R.O. F.O. 371, Vol. 515, No. 19618, 9 June 1908.

43. Finland and Russia, op. cit., pp.15-16.

44. The Finnish Question in 1911 (London, 1911), p.11; Renwick, G., op. cit., p.326.

45. Borodkin, M., Finland: Its Place in the Russian State (SPB, 1911), p.88.

46. The Finnish Question in 1911, op. cit., p.13.

47. Just a day before, the Kadet organ Rech had stressed the same point, i.e., that the bill was contrary to existing relations with Finland. Rech, 16 March 1910, (73), p.1.

48. G.D. 17 March 1910, Cols. 935-936.

49. Ibid., Cols. 947-948.

50. Ibid., Cols. 952-954.

51. Ibid., Cols. 967-968.

52. Ibid., Cols. 958-960, 961, 966.

53. Ibid., Cols. 969-970, 975. For the list of

elected deputies see G.D., 22 March 1910, Col. 1386.

54. G.D. 19 May 1910, Col. 1862.

55. In the beginning of April Rech reported that the bill would be examined in extenso before the end of this session. Rech, 10 April 1910 (98), p.3. This was also reported in the London Times: 23 May 1910, p.7. The latter also noted that the Emperor wished the law to be passed during the session.

56. "Duma po Finliandskomu Voprosu," Vestnik Evropy, July 1910, p.424. Baron Meyendorff stated that these debates were perhaps the most disorderly and emotional in the life of the Third Duma.

57. G.D. 21 May 1910, Cols. 1928-1929.

58. Ibid., Cols. 1929-1930.

59. Ibid., Col. 1931.

60. Ibid., Cols. 1938-1947.

61. Ibid., Cols. 1952-1953.

62. Ibid., Cols. 1956-1957.

63. Ibid., Cols. 1959-1960, 1982.

64. Ibid., Cols. 1982-84, 1987-89.

65. Ibid., Cols. 1997-99.

66. Ibid., Col. 2025.

67. Ibid., Cols. 2026-27.

68. Ibid., Col. 2035.

69. Ibid., Col. 2036.

70. _Ibid_.

71. _Ibid_., Cols. 2037-41.

72. _G.D._ 22 May 1910, Col. 2073.

73. While the rightist deputies and some Nationalists exaggerated the potential military threat of Finland, this was a live issue at the time, and many took it seriously. The fear was not of Finland, but of an Austro-German combination striking through the North as well as through the South. Botianov, M., _Stati_ (SPB, 1910), pp.7-10.

74. _G.D._ 22 May 1910, Cols. 2079, 2081, 2083, 2089.

75. _Ibid_., Col. 2126-33.

76. _Ibid_., Col. 2143.

77. _Ibid_., Cols. 2092-2104.

78. _G.D._ 24 May 1910, Col. 2223.

79. _Ibid_., Cols. 2232-33.

80. _G.D._ Evening Sitting, 24 May 1910, Cols. 2308-2312.

81. _G.D._ 22 May 1910, Cols. 2146-49.

82. _Ibid_., Col. 2191.

83. Before the debates on the Finnish question began in the Duma, Baron Meyendorff sent the chairman a request to be relieved of his duties as a vice chairman. According to his friends his action was prompted by disagreement with the government's Finnish policy; it was even alleged that he intended to break with the Octobrist Party. See _Rech_, 19 March 1910, (76), p.3.

84. G.D. Evening Sitting, 24 May 1910, Col. 2313-2315.

85. Ibid., Col. 2318-28.

86. For the above right wing views see: G.D. 17 March 1910, Cols. 958-966; 19 May 1910, Cols. 1870-1872; 21 May 1910, Cols. 1982-97; 24 May 1910, Cols. 2233-52; 25 May 1910, Cols. 2353-73.

87. G.D. 25 May 1910, Col. 2426.

88. Novoe Vremia, 29 May 1910 (12288), p.2.

89. G.D. 28 May 1910, Col. 2582.

90. G.D. 31 May 1910, Cols. 2889-90.

91. Rech, 20 May 1910, (136), p.4.

92. G.S. 8 June 1910, Col. 3626.

93. Ibid., Cols. 3627-28.

94. Ibid., Cols. 3629-30.

95. Ibid., Cols. 3631-32.

96. Ibid., Cols. 3633-34.

97. Ibid., Cols. 3639-40.

98. Ibid., Cols. 3654-60.

99. Ibid., Cols. 3678-80.

100. Ibid., Cols. 3681-85.

101. G.S. 9 June 1910, Col. 3772. He did, however, cite an interesting comment made by Alexander II in 1863 when he opened the Diet, and reflected upon the strains which were felt even then regarding the proper legislative process:

"Many enactments of rooted laws of the Grand Duchy of Finland appear to be incompatible with things as they now are, having arisen after their annexation of this Duchy to the empire. Wishing to correct these deficiencies, I intend to instruct the drawing up of a bill which will consist of clarification and additions to these laws." (For his full speech see Cols. 3768-82.)

102. G.S. 9 June 1910, Cols. 3782-93.

103. G.S. 11 June 1910, Cols. 3916-19.

104. G.D. 9 June 1910, Col. 3768. Novoe Vremia, 11 June 1910 (12300), p.1.

105. G.S. 8 June 1910, Cols. 3663-3678.

106. Ibid., Cols. 3692-3704.

107. G.S. 10 June 1910, Col. 3856.

108. G.S. 8 June 1910, Col. 3739.

109. Ibid., Cols. 3869-3877.

110. G.S. 10 June 1910, Cols. 3879-82.

111. Ibid., Cols. 3885-86.

112. G.S. 11 June 1910, Cols. 3921-23.

113. Ibid., Col. 3924.

114. Ibid., Col. 3926.

115. G.S. 8 June 1910, Col. 3654.

116. Novoe Vremia, 23 March 1910 (12223), p.3; Rech, 31 March 1910, (88), p.2; P.R.O., F.O. 371, Vol. 725, No. 21896, 7 June 1909.

117. Oldenburg, S., Tsarstvovanie Imperatora Nikalaia II (Munich, 1939), Vol. II, p.69;

Schybergson, M., Politische Geschichte Finnlands 1809-1919 (Stuttgart, 1925), pp.373-374.

118. Novoe Vremia, 18 March 1910 (12218), p.3; 22 March 1910 (12222), p.3; 24 March 1910 (12224), pp.3-4; 15 April 1910 (12246), p.3; 16 April 1910 (12247), p.3.

119. G.S. 11 June 1910, Col. 3929.

120. Ibid., Cols. 3941-44.

121. Ibid., Cols. 3949-72.

122. G.S. 14 June 1910, Col. 4016.

123. Ibid., Col. 4018. See also Cols. 3997-4018.

124. The rest of the law established the procedure to be taken in the case of general and local Finnish legislation, as well as that for electing Finnish deputies to the Russian State Council and Duma. Two deputies were to be elected to the former and four to the latter; all had to be fluent in Russian. This was done specifically so that the Finns should not be excluded during the discussion of general legislation which might affect Finnish interests. The Finnish legislative bodies remained as they had been in the past.

125. Section I, subsection 1, states that laws and ordinances, the effect of which was extended to the Grand Duchy, should be issued by way of general legislation insofar as they did not refer solely to the internal affairs of the Duchy.

126. For the full text of the Law see: P.S.Z., Vol. XXX, No. 33795; Ioffe, M., Vazhneishie Zakonodatelnye Akty: 1908-12 (SPB, 1913), pp. 268-273; G.D. 31 May 1910, Cols. 2901-2911. For an impartial observation of the bill by the British Ambassador, see P.R.O. F.O. 371, Vol. 976, No. 15173, 3 May 1910.

127. Shelukhin, S., *Ukraine, Poland, and Russia and the Right of the Free Disposition of the Peoples* (Washington, 1919), p.8.

128. For the Finnish point of view see: The Finnish Question, *op. cit.*; Schybergson, M., *op. cit.*; Wourinen, J., *op. cit.*; Jackson, J., *op. cit.*; Korewo, N., *The Finnish Question* (SPB, 1911), Mekhelin, L., *Raznoglasiia po Russko-Finliadnskim Voprosam* (SPB, 1908).

129. Although the debates in the Duma and the State Council reflect the shades of Russian opinion adequately enough, a number of books published in the period are of interest: *The Russo-Finnish Conflict* (London, 1911); Borodkin, M., *op. cit.*; *Finliandskaia Okraina v Sostave Russkago Gosudarstva* (SPB, 1906); Soovoroff, P., *The Finnish Question* (SPB, 1910).

130. Though this point was sufficiently proved in the course of the debates, it is interesting to note the opinion expressed by a Finnish politician, a member of the Old-Finnish Party. W. Churberg, in an interview with a foreign correspondent in December 1910, replied, when asked whether the Russian Government had destroyed the constitution granted by Alexander I, that the Russian Government had not in fact given any promises, and went on to say, "If Finland is a state, as the Finns are always asserting, then it has the right to act as it thinks best for itself. But it is in no position to do so." See Churberg, W., *The Situation of Finland* (SPB, 1911), pp.13, 15, 19.

131. Sliozberg, G., *op. cit.*, p.22.

132. Jussila, O., *op. cit.*, p.274.

133. Jackson, J., *op. cit.*, p.65.

134. Kryzhanovskii, S., *op. cit.*, p.217; Moxon, S., "Stolypin," *Westminster Review*, February 1912, Vol. 177, pp.143-155.

Family portrait.

(1909)

Monument erected to Stolypin (1912) in Kiev. Demolished by the Kerensky Government.

CHAPTER IV

THE WESTERN ZEMSTVO FIASCO

The law relating to the western zemstvos, Stolypin's last major legislative venture, was fought over closely in both chambers and brought to the surface violent Court intrigues which were then directed against Stolypin's person.[1] The resulting disaster, to which Stolypin reacted intemperately, led to an abrupt decline in his political influence.

The basic idea behind the original measure of 1864 was to devolve power from the central authorities to the local zemstvos, without regard for class privileges. Although confined to the thirty-four provinces of Central Russia, it thus formed a natural complement to the great Emancipation Act of 1861.[2] The zemstvo institutions were given power to levy taxes on land to finance local development and services. The principal activities falling within the scope of zemstvo assemblies were the provision of schools, hospitals, road and water communications; auxiliary interests included organizing fire services, famine and charitable relief. The list of matters of zemstvo concern increased steadily and inevitably each year. Insofar as the work brought tangible benefits and lay within the bounds of local initiative, it encouraged the more positive elements of society--both the progressive members of the nobility and the emerging professional and business classes. It was this concentration of the "third element" which caused the central authorities to be apprehensive.

Members were elected to the provincial and uezd zemstvo assemblies according to three curias governing landowners, townspeople and peasants. The assemblies themselves met annually for a minimum of twenty and ten days respectively.[3] In view of the general indifference of the peasants, coupled with their distrust of any fresh instrument of taxation,[4] the gentry, together with the small numbers of the educated middle class, generally dominated the assemblies. Although legally confined to matters of local interest, the absence of other means of effective opposition to official policy caused the annual meetings of zemstvo assemblies to take on a distinctly political air. They were attended by thousands throughout the country, and anti-government speeches were frequently delivered.[5]

Throughout the existence of the zemstvos, especially during the reigns of Alexander III and Nicholas II, a running struggle continued between the central government and the local zemstvos. In 1890 a new law was enacted,[6] restricting the zemstvos from assuming new powers and giving the gentry an increased majority over the peasantry.[7] By this date, however, the zemstvo organization had taken root, and the restrictions served only to strengthen its feeling of opposition.[8] Any hope that the accession of Nicholas would lead to a relaxation of this legislation was promptly crushed by the new Tsar himself, who informed a zemstvo delegation that further participation in the country's internal government was a matter of more "senseless dreams."[9] Stolypin, dining at the home of Count P. Heyden at the time, stated that the young Monarch had failed to grasp some of the most suitable reins of government.[10]

Despite this setback, by 1904 zemstvo representatives were to be found actively engaged in the majority of political movements.[11] The All-Russian Congress of Zemstvos in November 1904 and a May 1905 zemstvo delegation to the Emperor, under the leadership of Prince Trubetskoi, marked further steps in the growth of the institution.

With Stolypin's accession to the Premiership, official policy became more willing to accede to zemstvo requests. Since Stolypin must be credited with persuading the Tsar of the need to broaden zemstvo activities, it is important to note what his attitude to the institution was. The matter may be summarized in a later comment of one of the zemstvo leaders, that Stolypin's epoch brought the zemstvos into activity as never before and that he, and he alone, placed his trust in the organization.[12] That Stolypin did all he could to vitalize the zemstvos may be evinced from his comments on his 1910 Siberian trip, in which he characterized the lack of zemstvos as an extremely grave shortcoming.[13] The underlying reasons for Stolypin's support are to be found in his fundamental political philosophy. He sought to re-found Russia on the basis of a landowning democracy; an essential part of any attempt to do so must be the growth of a sense of civic responsibility, such as the zemstvo movement could help to promote, at the grass roots of communal life.

Stolypin's first and most important step towards the broadening of zemstvo prerogatives lay in the issue of the law of 5 October 1906,[14] which largely removed the restrictions introduced in 1890. In particular, the restriction prohibiting the zemstvos from raising their annual assessment by more than 3% per annum was annulled, thus encouraging them to increase their efforts. The 1906 legislation undoubtedly served as the major impetus in the growth of zemstvo activity in years to follow.[15] As early as his speech before the Second Duma, outlining his program, Stolypin had stressed the need for expanding zemstvo activity as an essential ingredient of progress.[16]

Stolypin was not seriously disturbed over the zemstvos in Central Russia, however, for they were guaranteed a prosperous future; his main concern was focused on the six western provinces which lacked any regular zemstvo organization and thus tended to fall behind the rest of the country in both social and economic progress.[17] Already as a squire in Kovno he had been convinced of the need to introduce the full zemstvo system into these provinces.[18] By this means a solution might also be found to the struggle between the numerically weak but economically strong Polish population and the numerically strong but economically weak Belorussian peasantry. The root of this problem, however, lay deep in history, in the struggle between Catholicism and Orthodoxy and even, as Vladimir Soloviev, the Russian philosopher noted, in the age-old controversy between East and West.[19]

The proposal to introduce zemstvos into western provinces was not a new one. It had been raised by Goremykin in 1898 and had been rejected by the Emperor in the following year upon the advice of Count Witte that the zemstvo institution was incompatible with autocracy.[20] Pobedonostsov had also played a prominent role in bringing the Tsar to this decision. The latter was undoubtedly motivated by his ultra-reactionary convictions, whereas Witte, as has been noted by several authorities, aimed rather at discrediting Goremykin.[21] Nevertheless, as early as 1892, in a letter to Pobedonostsov, Witte had shown a clear aversion to the principle of local self-government, declaring: "It is one thing to spread this infection, but another to cure it where it became imbued some thirty years ago."[22] Stolypin and Witte thus held opposing views on this point. Despite the apparent attitude of Witte, on 2 April 1903 a law was in fact enacted introducing zemstvos into the western provinces.[23] Considerable Court intrigue surrounds this measure, the credit for which went to Plehve. The law actually introduced zemstvo committees into the six south-western provinces; all members of the provincial committees and chairman of the zemstvo town councils concerned were appointed by the Ministry of the Interior.[24] Although these zemstvos succeeded in performing a measure of material aid, they were a far cry from those operating in the central provinces.

As might be expected, Stolypin was unable to consider this position as satisfactory. His policy of broadening zemstvo rights in the central provinces inevitably prompted the demand to extend the same rights in the western provinces. The problem of introducing the regular zemstvos into these provinces was obviously a delicate one. However, since the Poles as the economically stronger and better educated were likely to get the upper hand if the system were introduced without any refinements, Stolypin decided to solve this problem by splitting the electorate into two electoral groups--thus limiting the Polish representation so that the Russian deputies would always be in a majority. He based this solution on two arguments; firstly, that the Russian population of these regions reached almost 90% of the total; and secondly, that since the regions were historically Russia, it was only natural for the central government to wish to maintain a zemstvo with a Russian character in order to better the lot of the mass of the population. The bill which Stolypin introduced into the Duma in 1910 was designed to give effect to these two objectives.

The Polish opposition in the Duma and the State Council argued that the government was discriminating against the Polish minority. The rightists in the State Council, on the other hand, were against the bill for fear that its liberalizing tendencies would in time be extended to the central provinces.[25] The liberals, insisting on a more radical bill with wider rights for the peasantry, argued against the system of electoral groups, chiefly on the grounds of discrimination against minorities. The extreme left repeated the bulk of the liberal arguments, but in the main used the platform to criticize the government on points which had little concern with the immediate issue.

The western zemstvo question was not raised until 8 May, 1909, when the Chairman of the State Council announced that a proposal had been submitted by thirty-three members of the Council to alter the procedure governing election to the State Council from the nine western provinces.[26] D. Pikhno,[27] elaborating on the proposal, stressed that although all nine of the western provinces' representatives on the State Council were Poles, they formed only 4% of the population. He added, however, that there was no attempt to remove the existing representatives as such; the major objective was to secure better representation for those not now represented, namely the Russian majority.[28] Speaking for the government, Stolypin declared that the existing electoral law for the nine western provinces had always been regarded as imperfect. He agreed to draft an appropriate bill and indicated that the government hoped to try to solve the problem of national representation by introducing zemstvos based on national electoral voting. The system of weighted voting was, he felt, the best way of guaranteeing the interests of the Russian majority.[29] This proposal was accepted by a majority of the State Council.[30]

This question was next raised in the Duma on 30 May 1909, when Stolypin opened the debate with the declaration that, in his view, the existing Polish representation from the western provinces to the State Council was excessive and unfair. In order to help deal with this unhealthy situation the government, he said, intended to submit a bill at the fall session which would introduce zemstvos into the western provinces.[31] This bill would alter the existing electoral system so as to conform to local conditions and peculiarities.[32] Stolypin sought to emphasize that the matter was not being pressed as a sign of hatred towards the Poles, but in order to rectify the lack of balance in the prevailing system. Stolypin's official announcement was followed by only a few speakers; the opposition denounced the intended legislation as directed against minorities and its supporters repeated that it was not designed to eliminate a Polish representation but to give the Russian population a proper voice in the State Council.[33] The sitting closed, both Houses awaiting the government's bill.

Though Stolypin had expected to be able to present the bill on the western zemstvos in the fall of 1909, it was not until 5 May 1910, almost a year after his appearance, that the chairman announced that he had received a suggestion to turn to the bill, a motion which was accepted by a majority of 140 against 90 votes.[34] Consequently, on 7 May, the Duma took up its debates on the western zemstvo bill, which had been in the meantime submitted by the Ministry of the Interior.

The proceedings began with the reading by D. Chikhachev of the report of the special commission on local self-government. Referring to the zemstvo committees established by the Act of 1903, the report stressed those of its inefficiencies and inadequacies which had prompted the present government to introduce an elective zemstvo system into the western region.[35] The major issue, however, confronted the government in its move to do so: should it simply introduce the zemstvo statute of 1890, without any changes, or should it establish national curias for the electors? If complete universal suffrage were introduced, the Poles would be entirely eliminated from zemstvo participation. The government considered this step impractical since it would deny a place to the best educated members of the local community. As a result, the decision had been made to take a middle path, namely to combine two qualifications--that of ethnography and that of taxation. This, Chikhachev proposed, could be done by establishing the average percentage of a given national population in a particular region and the average percentage of immovable property as against the total value of the same possessed by each national group.[36] Two-thirds of the commission had felt that the western region was strictly Russian and that the zemstvo should be a properly Russian one. The only disagreement on the part of the commission, however, was the question of how to protect Russian interests in the face of the united block of Polish landowners. Moreover, most of the industry was in Polish hands, so that the peasants were in complete economic subjugation to the Poles.[37] The commission had eventually decided, therefore, to recommend to the Duma that it should reject the government's bill.[38]

Chikhachev's speech was followed by the report of a special financial commission which had considered the matter. This commission accepted the need to introduce zemstvos in the light of the remarkable results which had been produced by them in Central Russia over the previous four decades.[39] This commission recommended the introduction of the 1890 statute into the western provinces, since this, they felt, would bring much better results than the measure of 1903.[40]

Prior to Stolypin's appearance, two speeches were delivered by members of the opposition, the Social-Democrats and the Polish faction. Though unable to omit the usual revolutionary attacks, Chkheidze, speaking for the Social-Democrats, attempted to summarize some of the major points in dispute. In retracing the zemstvo movement, for example, he dealt with the Goremykin-Witte controversy with due sarcasm; Witte, indeed, received considerable criticism from all sides throughout these debates. Chkheidze's main attack centered on the government's hesitation to introduce any kind of self-government into the western region, for fear the minorities would seize power and direct economic development in their own interests. His contention was that the government was opposed to the zemstvo organization because it had not justified the former's hopes, and therefore perceived in the zemstvos outright sedition and political tendencies. This, in his view, was the reason for the introduction of the 1890 Statute.[41] Chkheidze also criticized the government's attempt to introduce national curias, since it drew a sharp line between national minorities; the true meaning of this was that no matter how good a Pole might be, in the eyes of the government he would always be inferior to any "Russian scoundrel."[42] Chkheidze insisted that local self-government needed to be made fully democratic, for only on that soil could a healthy seed take root. This note elicited the response that this was what the government was attempting to introduce.[43]

E. Montvill, speaking for the Polish group, said that the minority question could not be bypassed. His main query regarding the government's policy towards the Poles was meant to discover whether it was designed to eliminate the local Poles or whether it envisaged the possibility that the Polish population, while preserving its nationality and religion, could become useful and fully fledged citizens of the empire. The bill had been proposed by virtue of a national struggle and involved a political, not an economic problem. Though he did not deny that zemstvos in the western provinces needed revision, he was critical of the government's slogan, "First tranquillity, and then reform," for he felt that this was likely to lead to pacification first, followed by the abolition of all reform.[44]

Stolypin then delivered a long speech dealing with each of the major issues involved in the government's proposals. The State Council, as well as the government, he began, had considered the present elections of the deputies from the western provinces to the Council as unfair and had therefore decided to introduce a new electoral law which would protect the rights of the economically weak Russian majority against the economically and culturally superior Polish minority.[45] As the zemstvo statute had never been introduced into the western provinces, the government had decided to introduce the 1890 zemstvo statute for the Duma's deliberation, with specific alterations befitting local conditions and peculiarities. With an eye to the future, he affirmed that the zemstvos would serve as electoral colleges for the election of deputies to the State Council. Having collected the necessary statistical material from the provinces, the government was now approaching the underlying problem of State Council representation, on which attention had become fixed, with the following question in mind: How could Russian interests be preserved and how far could the government go in creating protective measures that would not affect the independent activity of the zemstvos?[46]

When speaking of restrictions in this way Stolypin was, of course, well aware how likely any such legislation was to rekindle the age-long enmity between the Poles and the Russians, even though the only restriction intended was the establishment of a system of weighted "proportional representation." There was, likewise, no doubt in the government's mind that, in view of the conditions existing in the western provinces, it was imperative that all the local national elements should participate in the work of the zemstvo. Stolypin stressed the need to differentiate the economic from the political aspects, since the former were the major aggravating elements. He also made it clear that the "zemstvo idea" had to conform to overall official policy. Comparing the weakness of the Russian element with the strong citadels of Polish culture, Stolypin asked the Duma whether it would be right for the government to refuse to aid "those weak roots of the Russian state" which were not yet strong enough to safeguard their own interests for themselves. Was it possible under prevailing conditions to permit a free contest of political and economic factors? Stolypin emphasized that the answer to this question could not be found in abstract doctrines but on the basis of past experience and facts. If the Duma agreed that Russian interests had to be upheld in those provinces, then it would obviously be harmful to attempt to introduce a partial measure, basing a judgment on paper facts alone, without taking into consideration the correlation of forces as they actually existed. The government had thus arrived at the following decisions: (1) to delimit Polish and Russian representation for the purpose of zemstvo elections; (2) to establish a percentage relationship of Russian and Polish electors, having regard not only to their property status but also to the historically established dispersal of forces; (3) to take into account the historical role and significance of the Orthodox clergy in the future work of the zemstvo; and (4) to give certain protective rights to Russian representation in the future zemstvos.[47]

Stolypin was emphatic when he stressed the hope that the Duma should not suspect the government of either prejudice or hostility towards the Poles. Such an attitude on the part of the government would have been absurd, and he himself took pride in recalling that he had numerous friends in the western provinces from his own stay there. His only desire was that the Duma should look at the issue with equity, for, in his opinion, the whole region was oriented towards the Polish kingdom.[48]

In tracing the historic strife between Poland and Russia, Stolypin emphasized how the Polish revolts of the nineteenth century had miscarried; he indicated that the Polish population now had an opportunity to go hand-in-hand with the Russians, instead of reacting with antagonism towards anything Russian.[49] The past of the region spoke for itself, indicating the need to protect it against racial struggles during zemstvo elections. It was essential therefore to give zemstvos the full range of independent action, but at the same time to strengthen the Russian viewpoint which, otherwise, would invariably have been pushed aside. According to his view, even national curias, by themselves, would not solve the question of protecting Russian national interests, for that could only be achieved by giving a distinct Russian majority to the zemstvo assemblies.[50] One of the tragedies of the circumstances, in Stolypin's opinion, was that whereas the Poles had remained on the spot for centuries, the Russian nobility had become absentees. Those who did remain were culturally and economically inferior to the Poles and, as a result, had themselves become gradually Polanized.[51] It was the poor peasant class which had, until now, preserved and maintained the national Russian character in the region; however, Stolypin argued, this class of itself was too weak to face the superior Polish influence.

Stolypin had therefore reached the conclusion that, apart from the commission's recommendation just to improve electoral procedure, two major aspects had to be seriously considered: the national and the material, that is, the "property-cultural" aspects. The commission, on the other hand, had insisted upon considering only the aspect of property, which, in Stolypin's opinion, was insufficient by itself to enable satisfactory zemstvo districts to be established, especially where certain uezds were concerned. The property factor might increase the Russian representation in some areas; in others, which were predominantly Russian, it might implant a permanent Polish representation of due proportions. The crux of his argument was that, although the commission's approval might limit the Polish representation to 30%, the remaining 70%--to be made up of Russian peasantry and a mixture of large and small landowners, the poor peasants--would still be under considerable pressure from Polish landlords. Hence, Stolypin reasoned, even though the Polish landlords constituted only 30% of the total in the western provinces, they would undoubtedly retain the dominant role. He therefore insisted on the need to establish a minimum representation of Russians within the zemstvos, such that they would always be in a majority.[52]

Ending his speech, Stolypin again stressed that the aim of the bill was not to subjugate the Polish natives but to defend the rights of Russians living in the same regions. He firmly believed that the bill, as drawn up, would permit all sections of the local population to be fairly represented and to participate in the work of the zemstvos. In this way the bill attempted to put an end to the continuous strife along national lines by instilling the elements of the established Russian state. He thus maintained firmly that the passing of the law might of itself succeed in destroying many illusions and hopes, since it would impress the idea "that the western region is, and always would be, Russian."[53]

As may be seen, Stolypin once again emphasized that the terms of the bill originated from the need to protect "state interests." The situation differed markedly from the Finnish question, for he was here defending the rights of Russians inhabiting a geographic region historically possessed by Russia, with a preponderant Russian population. The ultimate ambition of the Polish faction was to return the region to the Polish domination which it had enjoyed in the 17th and 18th centuries. At the same time, it is likely that Stolypin was sincere in his belief that the government had no intention of seriously infringing the existing rights enjoyed by the Poles. The Poles were still to receive representation out of proportion to their numbers. Stolypin's other apprehension was that the Polish landlords were not interested in bettering the conditions of the Russian peasantry, since this would have defeated their own political and economic aims. However, if the zemstvos were to work to full capacity, they required the genuine participation of all levels of society, and, most important, support of the landlords and the moneyed class. As everyone realized, should the conditions of the masses improve, the political and economic dominance of the Poles would diminish. One factor which was unhesitatingly clear was Stolypin's own unremitting conviction that the whole future of the western provinces, whether they would become or be eventually Polonized, depended on the outcome of this bill.

The heated debates which ensued followed the pattern of previous major bills. After eight sittings, the bill was postponed until the month of June. The Finnish and western zemstvos bills thus overlapped one another and were passed with only a day's interval between them. Although the two issues together caused a rise in the political temperature, they were perceived as separable. The right wing, which chauvinistically defended the Finnish bill, sternly opposed the western zemstvo measure in alliance with the left wing. On this issue therefore, the opposition was seemingly more consistent and organized than over the Finnish question.

The Nationalist Party, the major group supporting the zemstvo bill, reiterated much of what Stolypin had said. Though S. Kryzhanovskii insisted that the western zemstvo bill had been instigated by the Nationalists,[54] the considerable role played by the rightists in the State Council cannot be ignored. The Nationalist S. Bogdanov, who represented one of the western provinces, noted that the roads, schools, and hospitals lacking in his province were being built in significant numbers in adjoining provinces. Attacking the commission's suggested changes, he declared firmly that his party would support only the government bill. He denied that the government was afraid of a handful of Poles, stating that the proposed restrictions were essential if the zemstvo reform was to be a success. He stressed that, since the inception of the Duma, the Poles in the Kievan and other western provinces had organized themselves into separate groups, and not as representatives of their respective provinces; besides issuing constant demands upon St. Petersburg, they took their instructions from Warsaw. The Polish representatives did not consider themselves Russians, but fighters for the "Polish idea."[55] If the Polish influence was to dominate in this way, the zemstvos would be unable to function effectively, for they would be used for Polish political ends and not for local welfare. Speaking from his own experience, Bogdanov declared that the Polish landlords had already shown reluctance to aid the national school program.[56]

Ladomirskii, another member of the same party, although agreeing with the government in the need to protect the interests of the Russian population, insisted that the bill needed many alterations. If the Duma accepted the commission's proposal, then the western zemstvos would definitely fall into Polish hands, and this, in turn, would be a powerful weapon for the Polanization of the area. It was an issue of life and death--"Whether we will remain in this region or not."[57]

The other supporters of the bill were the rightists and the Octobrists. Most of the Octobrists were in favor of the bill, the split occurring because some were for it without any change, whereas others were mainly against the national curias and certain relatively minor points.[58] The rightist argument was based largely around nationalist sentiment, though many of them agreed on the need to introduce the zemstvos into the western provinces. They criticized the Poles for not being able to live side-by-side with the Russians, citing the risings of 1830 and 1863 as examples of their rebellious natures, in spite of the leniency which Russia had shown.[59]

On this occasion, the ultra-reactionaries like Purishkevich could not refrain from attacking the Jews as the second factor for the exploitation of the Russian peasants.[60] Markov, however, managed to present a comparatively constructive speech, albeit with considerable invective. He insisted that he did not hate any nationality, even the Poles, but that he regarded them as the enemies of Russian statehood (russkoi gosudarstvennosti). In his opinion, if any measure were taken to limit Polish participation within the zemstvos it should be not because they were either Poles, or Catholics, but because the persons concerned had fought against the Russian state for centuries.[61]

V. Pakhalchak, a member of the moderate right wing, provided a more lively than average speech by describing various Polish prejudices against the peasants which had been made known to him. He related an incident in which a Polish landlord who had just inherited some land refused to sell it to the peasants because he found out that the majority of them were Orthodox. He had then sold the same land to a German resident for less.[62] Pakhalchak brought to the Duma's attention the actions of Count K. Grokholsky of the Yamnolsk uezd, a Pole who, with influential contacts in St. Petersburg, maintained a police force of

Ingush to watch his property; armed with whips, these police beat peasants almost to death when they crossed into Grokholsky's property. The peasants' complaints to local authorities brought no results, for all trembled before Grokholsky.[63] Turning to another phase of Polish animosity towards the local Russian population, Pakhalchak noted that many Russian small holders who owned 150 to 200 desiatins of land were dependent on more wealthy Poles, since most of the agricultural machinery and services, such as sugar refineries, were in their possession. In order to dispose of his crop the small farmer was forced to comply with every petty demand and whim of the Polish magnates. Such economic exploitation was a well known factor to all who lived in the region. The same situation, he said, also prevailed in the hiring of voluntary employees within the existing zemstvo committees; lawyers, doctors, engineers, and insurance agents were all Poles. The Russians, standing no chance, were being forced out of the region. He concluded that the sentiments which he had just expressed were not his, but the everyday thoughts of those who had elected him to the Duma.[64]

The Octobrists' arguments were closely similar to those presented by the Nationalist deputies; however, a number criticized certain articles in the bill. I. Glebov, while nevertheless supporting the measure,[65] warned that there was an insufficient number of educated Russians to enable the zemstvo to operate. G. Skoropadskii, another member of the Octobrist Party speaking in support of the idea of national curias, insisted that politics was inevitably imposed on the zemstvo, and, as the Russian element was weak, it had to be given a measure of aid. He referred to the zemstvos of the central provinces, within which the gentry and the peasants were working in excellent accord. His main contention, however, lay in the need to increase the Russian element in the sphere of voluntary employment, for the Poles monopolized this aspect of the zemstvo administration.[66]

The major opponents of the bill were, of course, the Poles; their allies on this occasion were the extreme left wing and the Kadets, the latter with a more constructive criticism to offer than the other groups. Polish speakers were, however, by far the most numerous. They naturally stressed the discrimination of the Russian Government against the minority, insisting on the absurdity of the premise that the government had to defend a majority against the minority. How could such a small number of Poles be dangerous to the vast Russian majority? The Pole L. Dymsza pointed out that the only escape from this vicious circle was for the government to call upon both the Poles and the Russians to work for the common cause.[67] W. Jablonowski contended simply that the bill was directed against the Poles as such.[68] J. Swiezynski argued that the Poles who had worked for the government in the past three years had shown undeniable loyalty to Russian statehood, and that the future of Russia greatly depended on the mutual trust and respect of its minority cultures.[69] S. Wankowicz emphasized that the kind of zemstvo envisaged would be unable to fulfill the realistic necessities of the region, for it would only destroy the springs of material cultural well-being.[70] W. Grabski accused the supporters of the bill of using the theme of Polish economic oppression to create artificial tension and to gain political ends.[71] W. Esman argued that, since the government had previously done nothing for the local population of the western provinces, its interests lay in something other than the welfare of the peasantry. He felt that his point was substantiated by the fact that the bill allotted very little place for the local peasantry--a further sign of the government's clandestine motives.[72]

Though some of the Polish speeches underlined certain facts and arguments which had some truth in them--and which would have also applied to earlier governments, such as that of Plehve--on the whole they did not reflect the true attitude of Stolypin's ministry. It cannot be said that

Stolypin discriminated against the Polish element in the western provinces; had that been the case, the Poles would not have received four times the representation to which they were entitled if elected under universal suffrage.

While certain rightists used the rostrum for rousing nationalist feelings, such an accusation could hardly be leveled at Stolypin, or at his aims. To declare, as some speakers did, that Stolypin's government was not interested in zemstvos but in placing restrictions upon them is not supported by fact. Although Esman was right in insisting that the government had not done anything for the peasantry in the past, this, too, did not apply to Stolypin, who used all his efforts to further the economic and political emancipation of the peasants. Although Stolypin considered that the mass of the peasants were not ready to assume the full responsibilities of self-government, since the degree of civic self-awareness required had not yet been attained, there can be no doubt that his main desire was to hasten the evolution of a class of responsible citizens as fast as possible. As he stated on several occasions, the peasants alone could save Russia.

The arguments of the extreme left wing were concentrated on the government's repression of minorities and on the demand for universl suffrage. However, very few of the left wing deputies spoke; the Social-Democrats who did address the assembly reiterated Chkheidze's views. The Social-Democrat I. Pokrovskii accused Stolypin of fomenting a nationalist policy and branded him as an apologist of serfdom.[73] The Trudovik Bulat stated that he was not only certain that the peasantry would be dissatisfied with the proposed zemstvo, for their views were not even being asked, but also that such a zemstvo would fall into the hands of the landlords, resulting in little practical benefit to their tenants. The government's aim, he believed, was to instill hatred of the Poles into the local populace; he nevertheless inferred that the Russian landlords were likely to go hand-in-hand with the Polish landlords against the peasantry.[74] Turning to the deputies of the Duma, Bulat explained that the government had no intention of protecting peasant interests against the Polish economic enslavement, for their concern went deeper, namely, to the preservation of the interest of the Russian landlords.[75]

Among the Kadets, some criticized the bill indiscriminately without any particular arguments, while others presented some sound criticisms. In the main, however, their arguments repeated those already made by the Trudoviks and the Social-Democrats. The Kadet F. Golovin, for instance, reiterated the point which Bulat had made concerning the government's aims, adding that the latter was attempting to gain the support of the local masses in its struggle against the Poles.[76] However, he also stressed the government, and the Polish, contention that the most important factor in the success of the zemstvo work lay in the active participation of all local forces. The main reason his party was against the bill, he declared, was that it would introduce animosity and render amicable work impossible, thus defeating the whole purpose of the reform.[77]

Shingarev was not sure against whom the electoral qualifications were directed and concluded they were therefore directed against the Russian small landowners.[78] The Kadet I. Luchitskii felt that the bill reflected unadulterated nationalism and would produce no good result.[79] The impetuous Rodichev asserted that it was not hard to discern the real significance of the bill--hatred against the Poles--and attacked Stolypin for reverting to the policy of Plehve.[80] Referring to Witte's memorandum on the zemstvos, he agreed that the zemstvo and autocracy were incompatible.[81]

Unexpectedly, the Kadet A. Babianskii adopted the government stand that the Poles occupied the dominant economic and administrative position in the western provinces and pointed to the lack of schools, hospitals, roads, and other public utilities. The western zemstvos were therefore essential for the future of Russia. His consideration of the fact that the western region had to be retained reflected an unusual sense of nationalism for a member of the Kadet Party.[82] As Babianskii was one of the last of the Kadet speakers before the reading of the bill, his speech seemed to indicate that the Kadets might side with the government's point of view.

Chikhachev, the spokesman of the special commission, returned in order to reply to some of the statements which had been made. In answer to Bulat's allegation that peasants in the western zemstvos would not play an active part, he stated that in the near future members of the large landowning class would be the ones to become "decorations" within the zemstvos.[83] This near official comment naturally struck the right wing deeply. Continuing, Chikhachev refuted the Polish and the leftist contention that the bill was directed against either the peasants or the Poles; it could not be directed against the former since the bill extended benefits to the majority of the local population, nor against the latter since it gave them many more electors than they would have under universal suffrage.[84]

By 11 May, even though many of the speakers had grown repetitive in their arguments, a majority declared themselves against a proposal to limit speeches to ten minutes.[85] From then on, however, many speakers declined to speak in the hope of bringing the debates to an end. By the following day, though some deputies expressed themselves against the reading of the bill, a motion to this effect passed by a majority of 196 votes to 140.[86] The Duma, it is interesting to note, exhibited an encouraging reaction when a rightist member proposed a law which would permit Russians alone to buy land being sold by the Poles in the western provinces; this proposition was rejected by an outright majority,[87] demonstrating that the bulk of the assembly, consisting of the Nationalists and the Octobrists, was immune to such crude nationalism. Such a reaction also shows that the Duma was sober in its approach towards the bill and was trying to ascertain the main points of consideration, without discriminating against the Polish economic and political interests in the area. Partiality was much more evident over the Finnish issue. As late as this date, however, the consensus was that the fate of the bill was still dark.[88]

The Duma turned to the reading and debating of the articles of the bill on 15 May, the articles being quickly accepted without much discussion. Article Three, dealing with the national curias and the distribution of electoral candidates on the provincial and uezd levels, caused the longest debate. It was the most important article in the bill, and, in the government's opinion, its rejection would have rendered the whole measure a dead letter. After fifty-eight speakers signed the register, the majority accepted the motion to discontinue the registration of the speakers, but once more rejected the proposal to limit the speakers to ten minutes.[89] During the debate on this article, the opposition's main efforts were directed towards increasing the peasant representation without discriminating against the Poles, while the extreme left stubbornly insisted that the Russian landlords were being favored. All of them, however, agreed on the need for zemstvo institutions in the western provinces. The left wing Octobrist, Prince V. Tenishev, argued against the national curias on the ground that they would lead to Polish separatist sentiment.[90] The Pole Swiezynski insisted simply on the principle of proportionality.[91] The Kadet Shingarev argued that, if the Duma stood for the majority principle, then Article Three reflected a prejudice against the peasantry.[92] The Nationalist M. Andreichuk and the non-party deputy, Count A. Uvarov, submitted two very important amendments. The former suggested the addition of a paragraph to the article which would specifically allot peasant electors; the latter introduced an even more important suggestion, that of lowering the property qualification by half, for he felt that otherwise it would be difficult to recruit a sufficient Russian representation.[93]

Stolypin made a final attempt to evaluate some of the views expressed regarding Article Three. He stressed that the issue was not one concerning the Kingdom of Poland but one concerning a region where the Polish population was estimated at 4.2%. If the government had been guided by national chauvinism, it would have suggested relying on these figures proportionately; however, because it valued the established and educated portion of the population, it had introduced the principle of property into the bill. Calling the Duma's attention to the fact that the western provinces, having developed differently from the other provinces of Russia, had assumed a unique coloring, he said:

> Not by means of natural growth, but by the force of historical squalor which had overtaken this region and toppled in it all that was Russian. . . it is impossible to forget the past, and to give it up as lost. . . If these principles expressed by me are accepted by you as erroneous, as odious, then this odium the government will take upon itself. . . You were told that the government is poisoned with human hatred, that it is attempting to destroy the Polish element and to eradicate it from the western region. . . But, gentlemen, there is no need to elaborate, if the broad framework of the bill within which the government places the Polish populace of the western region is kept in mind.[94]

Throughout his speech, Stolypin stressed that the Poles were being given considerably more places within the electorate than they would have received under universal suffrage; the government was merely attempting to preserve state interests within the historic limits of the empire. Stolypin then expressed the government's agreement with the proposal to lower the electoral qualifications by half,[95] giving further proof that he was not against peasant representation, as the left alleged. In conclusion Stolypin declared that if the bill were not accepted the region would be consigned to economic stagnation.[96]

The debates of Article Three were eventually cut short by acceptance of the chairman's recommendation to limit the speakers' list to twelve. The left wing Octobrists continued their attacks on the bill for its artificial limitations. However, as one of their members noted, the ideal procedure of universal suffrage would be equally artificial, in that it would also limit the Polish electorate. The Octobrists recognized that within the framework of historic circumstances and state interests, the national group which required protection was the Russian.[97] The right wing Octobrists indicated that the only difference of interests which existed between Russian landlords and Russian peasants lay in their relation to property, for in other respects their interests were similar. On the other hand, complete cultural, historical, and religious discord existed between the Polish landlords and the Russian peasants; in the opinion of the Octobrists this created a much greater abyss than did the discord between the Russian landlords and their peasants. National curias which gave the Russian element a majority were justified in their opinion because of Russian predominance; the accusations of discrimination against the Poles were unfounded, for the latter were allotted a reasonable part in the electorate.[98] The Octobrists therefore supported the government's proposal because they felt it guaranteed national interests and was a practical measure. For the purpose of passing the whole bill, certain details, they stressed, had to be sacrificed.[99]

The major opposition, in full force, repeated much of what had already been said. The Poles indicated their willingness to support a zemstvo which would limit Polish influence, but complained that they were being treated as second-class citizens.[100] The Trudoviks repeated that the government's main aim was to limit the influence of the peasantry, since the bill was primarily designed to give preference to the pomeshchiks. Bulat exclaimed: "You know that if the peasants were to be given the major influence, then you will be thrown out of all the zemstvos, and your voice would have no significance."[101] This remark was not addressed only to the right wing and the center, but also to the Kadets, many of whom were landowners. The Social-Democrats repeated the Trudovik allegation that the government's policy was no more than the defense of the "bureaucratic pomeshchiks" in the western provinces. A. Voiloshnikov went so far in his denunciation that the chairman had to ask him to leave the rostrum.[102] Much of the speeches of the extreme left consisted of revolutionary incitements. The Kadets, even at this late stage, made statements which gave reason to suspect that they were veering towards the government's policy. Babianskii, who now spoke in the name of the party, pointed out that even though the bill was directed against the Poles, the representation of the majority of the populace was of prime significance. He agreed that national interests had to be guarded and the peasantry given a chance of educational development. All of these points were, of course, a reiteration of Stolypin's viewpoint. He ended by inviting the Duma to vote for a law which would be fair to the local population, as well as to the Polish minority.[103]

Following these last speakers on Article Three, the chairman announced that the debates were closed and requested the Duma to proceed to the vote.[104] The Duma first voted on the two amendments suggested by Chikhachev and Count Uvarov, namely the stipulation of a peasant electorate and the lowering of the property qualification by half. These were both agreed upon by a majority, after which the whole article was passed.[105] With the passage of Article Three, the press predicted that there was no doubt concerning the passage of the whole bill.[106] The remaining articles were approved quickly so that, by the following day, 18 May, the Duma had completed the second reading.[107] The third reading did not take place until 28 and 29 May, when the bill was presented in full for a final vote and passed by a majority of 168 to 141. Announcement of the balloting results elicited applause from the right and center; the left demanded that the vote should be repeated, that the deputies should actually walk through the left and right doors on either side of the assembly hall for another count. This procedure was accepted, and with eight abstentions, the bill was once again passed by a majority of 165 to 139 votes; the chairman then announced that it would be handed to an editing commission.[108] On 1 June 1910, this commission reported on the changes made and the Duma, having voted on the edited document, finally approved the bill in toto. Following this the Chairman of the Duma announced that it would be forwarded to the State Council.[109] Stolypin was greatly relieved and prepared himself to try to push the bill through the State Council. Having carried the battle through the Duma with comparative ease, he felt that the more conservative body would pass it with even less obstacles. Little did he know what the following months held for him.

On 28 January 1911, almost eight months after it left the Duma, the State Council opened its debates on the western zemstvo bill. This delay on the part of the Council seems to have been considered by Stolypin as in some way deliberate.[110] There was not the air of confidence which prevailed in the State Council during the debates on the Finnish question, but rather one of uncertainty as to what the views of the different groups were and as to what the final outcome would be. The meeting opened with considerable tension, all the ministerial places, the seats of the deputies, and the visitors' galleries being filled to capacity.[111] The debate began with the presentation of the report of the special commission elected on 5 May 1910.[112] Pikhno, the commission's reporter, recalled that the bill had been initiated by thirty-three members of the State Council, who had suggested, on the grounds that not a single Russian deputy had been chosen since the first elections to the State Council, the introduction of a change in the electoral law under which members of the western provinces were elected to the State Council.[113] He then traced the zemstvo history in those provinces, and underscored the main aims pursued by the bill; namely:

(a) To give an appropriate Russian representation from the western provinces in the State Council;
(b) To achieve an efficient zemstvo organization in the western region; and
(c) To assist in uniting and strengthening the Russian population there.[114]

He stressed that there was no disagreement in the Duma or in the Council commissions about the need for zemstvos in the western provinces, for prosperity reigned in all the provinces where these existed. For the first time it was announced that, owing to the lowering of the property qualification, the western provinces contained enough Russians to occupy responsible positions within the zemstvos. Pikhno emphasized that the government was merely proposing the introduction of the zemstvo law which was operating in the central provinces, with minor alterations in the electoral procedure. From the national standpoint it was imperative to imbue the western zemstvos with a Russian character.[115] Turning to the national curias, he considered that they served to protect the interests of a minority and urged the Council to support their institution and not to consider them unjust or harmful as the Polish deputies had done. Pikhno also rebutted the Polish contention that zemstvos should not be concerned with politics, stressing that the political element was inherent in zemstvo activities. The sheer fact, he said, that the zemstvos were given the most important political function--that of electing deputies to the State Council--was proof of that.[116]

A. Stishinskii, the second reporter of the commission, restricted himself largely to the electoral procedure and the system of national curias. The Polish population in the western provinces consisting of 3.7% of the population, was to be allotted 16% of the total number of uezd electoral seats.[117] He maintained, however, that the lowering of the property qualification would remove the better educated, for the small landowners would swamp the large and middle landowners and thus lower the educational level of the zemstvo electorate.[118] In countering the Polish contention that the government was transforming the zemstvo into a political institution, he queried whether the Russian state could in fact be strengthened and developed by non-Russians. Finally, in the hope of convincing his Polish colleagues that it was not important if Russians led such a program, he asserted that bridges, hospitals, roads, and schools were needed by all, irrespective of nationality and political convictions.[119] Stolypin then delivered a short address in which he confirmed his agreement with Pikhno, urged the need to cut the property qualification by half, insisted on allotting electoral seats for the clergy, and stressed that without national curias fruitful results could not be expected of the bill.[120]

The regular debates on the issue then began, the important speakers being the Poles, Stolypin, Witte, and the spokesmen of the commission, Pikhno and Stishinskii. The Polish argument at the State Council was almost a verbatim repetition of that presented in the Duma, with the stress being placed on the allegations that the bill carried the seed of alienation and forced separatism. I. Olizar, speaking for the Polish Kolo, reiterated that it was an illusion to assume that there was a threat of Polanization within the western provinces, where such a vast majority of Russians existed. Challenging Pikhno, he remarked that if the establishment of national curias represented the protection of Polish interests, would it not have been appropriate at least to ask if they desired such a safeguard? He pronounced the bill a blow to those Poles who sincerely wished to be Russian subjects.[121] Another major defender of Polish interests was A. Meysztowicz, who repeated that the Polanization of the western region was a myth. The main problem lay in the fact that the Poles and Russians did not understand each other; he insisted that the Poles had no anti-government feelings towards Russia, even though such an attitude might have existed at one time. Repeating that the Poles were misunderstood in Russia, he called on the State Council to give them a zemstvo with equal rights; until such time, all experimentation should cease.[122]

The views of the left wing of the State Council, little represented by comparison with the position in the Duma, were amply expressed by Professor M. Kovalevskii, who, though agreeing that politics and zemstvos were inextricably interrelated, took a definite stand against the national curias. The main contention of the leftists, however, was that the government distrusted the peasantry, which carried the full burden of resistance to Polanization and Catholization. Kovalevskii also criticized the restriction that only those who had a primary education could be elected. The bill also deviated in his view from the principle of reducing national strife and would force the zemstvos into a position of exacerbating national feelings.[123] In addition, the bill retreated from the principle of the equality of subjects before the law, whereas the zemstvo should be the one hope of bringing the varied nationalities together.[124]

The few extreme right wing speakers who spoke repeated the same epithets and slogans which had been heard in the Duma. Their speeches were overtly nationalistic, with references to the Russian blood spilt for the western provinces, the infidelity of the Poles to the Russian Tsar during the times of political unrest, and the burden on the Russian gentry of carrying out reforms. V. Trepov, the ultra-reactionary, exhibited his outright antipathy to the bill; stressing that he did not belong to any group, he announced that he would vote against the bill for no other reason than that Stolypin's "game was up."[125]

Witte, who had not made a single appearance during the Finnish debates, played the most prominent role in opposing the western zemstvo bill; to a large extent he reflected not so much the views of the rightists as those of the ultra-reactionaries. Not being against the bill because of prejudice towards the Poles, he underlined throughout his speeches his concern for the "poor Orthodox peasantry" and the government's disregard of them. His arguments, unfortunately, were colored with hypocrisy and a certain Machiavellian quality. Because of this his speeches were fiercely attacked, both by his colleagues and by the press. As on previous occasions, and like Trepov in the present instance, Witte emphasized that he was speaking for himself and dissociated himself from any political group. He began by emphasizing that the zemstvo statute of 1864 had recognized the peasantry as citizens sufficiently conscientious to enjoy the same rights within the zemstvo as the gentry. Suddenly, after a quarter of a century, he declared, the government had come to doubt the peasants' capacity.[126] Pointing out that the introduction of the western zemstvos had been proposed as early as the 1860's, he noted that no solution had yet been reached--the reason being that on each occasion the "Polish question" had been encountered. Because of this constant postponement, he concluded that the government had never felt any urgent need to grant zemstvos to the region. Witte declared that he was unable to understand why the Polish influence was feared, for the Russian population was in a great majority. There was, as he said, no need for any "artful designs."[127] If the Polish influence was the main obstacle, the solution was simple; all that was needed was to give "the Russian population more or less equal rights as the Poles; and then the Russians, having the predominant influence and significance, should be able 'to rub it in' to the Poles." He concluded by saying that the Council was being told that this could not be done; this attitude on the part of the government not only indicated distrust towards the Poles, therefore, but also towards the Russians.[128]

The debates of the first sitting ended with Witte's speech. Although passions did not appear to have been aroused, Witte's speech had been well directed to achieving that aim, as was shown at the following sitting. The papers reported that the vote of the State Council would result in the coalition of the most diverse national elements and that the aims of each group were largely personal and not those of principle.[129] *Rech* later commented that the bill would be passed in favor of the government, though by a small majority, predicting that the center, the Poles, and the left wing would vote against the national curias.[130]

The next sitting, on 1 February, was overshadowed by Stishinskii's and Stolypin's speeches. The former was the first to speak and, as during the agrarian debates, he did not hesitate to attack Witte with sarcastic overtones supported by an impressive array of facts. Perhaps knowing that Stolypin and Stishinskii would speak, Witte himself did not appear. Stishinskii's attack on Witte touched off a polemic between the two men which culminated in an exchange of open letters in the press.[131]

Stishinskii's first attack on Witte was directed at the latter's statement that immediately after the emancipation the government had recognized the educational and cultural equality of the peasantry with the private landowners. He expressed bewilderment at such a statement; he could not perceive how, after centuries of serfdom, the peasants would be in a position to make such a big jump in their development that the wise lawmakers could have granted them the same rights as the best educated class. Such a statement, he said, was in any case historically inaccurate; even a quick glance at the zemstvo statute of 1864 showed clearly that the responsibilities of these classes had been carefully differentiated.[132]

The second major attack by Stishinskii was in reference to Witte's comment that the government felt no urgent need to introduce zemstvos into the western provinces. Although the latter had mentioned the government's attempt to do so, he had overlooked Goremykin's efforts in this direction in 1902; Stishinskii then described what had transpired at that date. Goremykin had introduced a bill to the State Council which proposed the introduction of electoral zemstvos in the western provinces; however, it had been withdrawn after a memorandum by the Minister of Finance (i.e., Witte) was distributed to members of the legislative bodies. In this curious memorandum, Stishinskii recapitulated, "though without a sufficient historical foundation," that the idea of local self-government was incompatible with autocracy.[133] Stishinskii ended by insisting that the bill was an essential measure which would put the economy on the right footing and be of the greatest importance to Russia.[134]

Stolypin followed with a long speech in which he analyzed many of the points which had been brought out in the Duma and raised again at the earlier meeting of the State Council. Unlike his speeches on the Finnish question, this address contained that restrained emotion which characterized his views, not only as a defender of local self-government, but as the veritable leader of the movement itself. His attitude and tone of manner declared that his arguments were based on the existing facts and living circumstances of the western provinces, with which he was personally and thoroughly acquainted.[135]

He began by saying that he expected blows from all sides after introducing the bill, touching as it did upon the question of Russo-Polish relations. However, this issue had to be faced if the matter of the western zemstvos was to be dealt with at all.[136] Referring to Witte's comment that the 1903 statute was quite satisfactory,

Stolypin conceded that it marked a step forward, but that he was sceptical whether or not it was sufficient to secure economic prosperity. Anyone who was acquainted with the region, he said, would recognize that conditions in the western provinces were much more suitable for the successful work of the zemstvos than was the case in some of the native provinces of Russia.[137] If the zemstvo statute which operated in the other provinces was introduced into the western region, the area would soon be transformed. While the limitations which he proposed would act as an impediment to some degree, these were necessary for reasons of state. As to the Polish accusation that the government was introducing a zemstvo system which carried with it the seeds of its own destruction, this allegation, said Stolypin, lacked "an essential circumstance known to all living in that region," namely that there was not a single question into which politics did not enter. It was natural enough that the Poles, the former masters of the region, who had lost their rule but kept their wealth, culture, and memories of the past, should seek to retain their present power and domination. Their fewness in numbers was more than balanced by their superior development and economic influence, unless some counterweight existed.[138]

> Take any institution within the region, the credit associations, the agrarian societies, exhibitions and banks; take, for instance, the Vilna Agrarian Bank which was founded in its day for the purpose of upholding Russian agrarian interests, which has turned into a Polish national institution! Everywhere, gentlemen, politics penetrates. And, yet, you wish the government to close its eyes and introduce zemstvos into the region, without taking any measures to counteract this oncoming political avalanche. That which you consider as contaminating the zemstvos with politics is, in fact, a "precautionary innoculation,' an insurance

> against politics and the predominance of any one nationality, or one element, over the other.[139]

Stolypin then declared that, even though it was proposed to lower the property qualification, the qualifications for office would not be greatly affected for, after studying the statistics, the government had found that there would in fact already be sufficient educated Russians to qualify for responsible posts within the zemstvos. The other point of contention was that the government had prepared the bill so as not to be forced to introduce amendments within a few years.[140] Witte had suggested that the statute of 1864 should be introduced instead of the proposed bill, since if it would not give the peasants a predominant position, it would at least give them equal representation. Stolypin reported that this was not the case. The 1864 statute gave the peasants a separate curia by assuring them a third of the vote, whereas the statute of 1890, a facsimile of the bill, allotted 40% to the peasants. The difference between the two statutes really lay in something quite different; whereas the 1864 statute gave the peasants the right to vote for their candidates freely, the 1890 statute gave the governor the power to approve or disapprove the candidates who were to be elected by the peasant assemblies. However, he concluded, the Ukase of 5 October 1906, had placed the peasants on the same footing as other classes.[141] By lowering the property qualification, the existing bill went much further than either of the preceding laws.[142]

Throughout his speech, Stolypin stressed the need to safeguard "state interests." It was necessary to recognize the tendency of the Poles to uphold their culture in the western regions: "Why is it," he exclaimed, "that here in the State Council, or in the State Duma, Polish representatives do not disperse among parties or factions, but organize themselves into a unified national Kolo?" The answer, he suggested, was,

> Because they belong to a nation forged by national sorrow, unified through historic misfortune and bygone ambitious reveries; because they belong to a nation which has only one policy--motherland! And these, I might say 'high incentives,' gave the Polish populace of the western region great political spirit. And yet, against this tempered group, you wish to oppose a mass consisting of peasants, landowners, and small farmers, who only recently populated the region. This unsophisticated, politically uneducated mass, unable to swim, you wish to throw into the sea of political struggle.[143]

The next sitting, on 4 February, again saw Witte as the major speaker, followed by Pikhno. Witte's speech was short and mainly concerned with replying to Stishinskii's attacks. As before, Witte sought to emphasize his concern for the welfare of the "Russian Orthodox peasant." Referring to Stishinskii's remark concerning his memorandum about the incompatibility of zemstvos with autocracy, he observed that he still considered it axiomatic "that the development of local self-government inevitably brought limitations upon an autocracy."[144] He continued,

> If history will say that I played a role in this affair [i.e. the setting of limitations upon absolute rule by the issue of the October Manifesto], then she will not forget that this was not done for the purpose of creating an oligarchy, that is to say, rule by a small group. There is nothing more revolting, nothing more offensive, than limiting autocracy, not for the people but for a small group. I am not guilty of having attempted to create such a state of circumstances. I, gentlemen, have never been, and never will be, for the strong; I always have been and always will be, until my grave, not

> for the strong, but for the weak--the Russian people. The reason I object to the bill under discussion is because, under the banner of patriotism, there is an attempt to create in the western region, instead of the authority of the Tsar, a local oligarchy, with a disgusting disregard for the rights of the Russian Orthodox peasants.[145]

He called upon the State Council to grant the Russian peasants, "at least that measure of influence which the existing bill allots to the Poles," by accepting the same formula for calculating the number of candidates from the Russian Orthodox peasants as was to be applied to the Poles. In conclusion he stressed, "Do not forget that the Russian Orthodox peasants preserved this region."[146]

A careful analysis of this speech is not required in order to perceive instances of hypocrisy in it; indeed, the chance that Witte could have taken his own utterances seriously is slim. Even the most mediocre speaker could refute it upon a basis of known historical facts.

The constant repetition of Witte's concern for the welfare of the "Russian Orthodox peasants" was the most striking instance of a double standard, for he had never previously shown any particular humanitarianism towards them; if anything, indeed, his memorandum of 1902 was directed against the interests of the peasantry. His plea to the State Council to give the peasants at least that measure of influence which had been allotted to the Poles was superfluous, for, with the lowering of the property qualification, the peasants inevitably received a much greater influence than they could have expected. Finally, his remark that he was for the "weak--the Russian people," and not for the "strong," was without doubt directed against Stolypin personally and intended to echo Stolypin's speech on 10 May 1907. However, as Stolypin had shown in that speech, he regarded the majority of the peasantry as the "strong."

Speaking in reply to Witte, Pikhno declared that he felt Witte's argument came close to the basic aims of the bill insuring a firm Russian zemstvo in the western provinces; however, Witte sought to accomplish this aim by other means, relying solely on the peasant force, and ignoring the possibility of a union of Russian forces, landlords and peasants. Witte's desire to give the zemstvo a definite peasant majority had been met by lowering the property qualification by half. The proposal to give the peasants additional votes was unacceptable; not only did the peasant bill guarantee a sufficient Russian majority, but the peasants' lack of competence would make them unsuitable to play an overly dominant role in the zemstvo.[147]

Turning to Witte's remarks on oligarchy, Pikhno commented that while he, too, was no admirer of oligarchy, he could not accept the premise that democratic principles could serve as a complete basis for government where 80% of the population were illiterate.[148] To the argument that the bill was offensive to the Poles, he cited figures which showed that the proportion between population and number of electors allotted could hardly be regarded as unfair to the Poles.[149] The national curias which Witte had attacked so forcefully had been taken from the Law of 6 August 1905, which was solely linked with Witte and had been used for the elections to the First Duma. Aware of the fact that Bulygin and not Witte had drawn up the law, he insisted that the responsibility lay more heavily on the latter than the former, for Witte had employed the law, and yet, after introducing a number of changes, had not deemed it necessary to take any measures to eliminate the national curias which "he [Witte] now considered to be anti-government and so anti-Russian." Pikhno then requested the Council to turn to the reading of the bill.[150]

A month later, on 4 March, the Chairman of the State Council invited the assembly to proceed to the reading of the bill.[151] As in the case of the Duma, the first two articles were immediately accepted by a majority; lengthy debates ensued over Article Three and previous arguments were reiterated. Meysztowicz repeated the Polish contention that the "curial system" was a great blow to them, and that they did not expect either economic prosperity or civil equality, for which reason he would vote against the bill.[152] K. Orlovsky commented that those Poles who had fought and died in Manchuria during the Japanese War had not been discriminated against at that time, yet now they were; he professed to find the microbe of disintegration within Article Three.[153]

The right wing expressed varied views from moderate to extreme. Chauvinists, like N. Balashov, could not understand why there should even be any need for Polish curias in the western provinces which had been Russian from time immemorial. They insisted that all the votes should go to the majority and if necessary the Poles should be left out altogether.[154] The more moderate right wing members, however, such as N. Zinoviev, expressed the view that it was essential to introduce curias in order to protect the interests of this important minority.[155] Prince Trubetskoi, one of the more liberal members of the right wing, disagreed with the article on the grounds that zemstvos with national curias would be concerned with political and not with economic problems.[156] He insisted, nevertheless, on the need for a strong Russian majority, arguing that if one-third of the zemstvos were composed of peasants, half of the remaining two-thirds, plus one, should consist of Russians.[157] As far as the more reactionary members of the State Council were concerned, the truth of the matter was that their opposition to the bill was deep seated, lying in their fear that the lowering of the property qualification would assure a majority influence for the small landowners and the peasants. Pressure for such a change to be introduced into the central provinces would follow inevitably.[158]

The views of the center members who supported the bill were chiefly expressed by Pikhno and Stishinskii. The former replied to the Poles, emphasizing that the bill was an attempt to organize a zemstvo capable of resolving the national-political question.[159] The latter stressed that the Council should not close its eyes to the realities of the situation.[160] Ia. Ofrosimov, an appointed member of the Council from the western region, reiterated the inevitability that the zemstvos would be concerned with political issues, particularly since the Poles had not lost hope of regaining their rule over the region.[161]

At this last opportunity, Witte made a final plea for the interests of the peasants. The bill was harmful to the interests of the empire because of its inherent distrust of "Russian Orthodox peasantry" and because the Poles would follow an anti-government policy. Once again he proposed that the Council should increase the number of peasant electors; for, in his opinion, the places allotted to candidates on the uezd level discriminated against the peasantry.[162]

As the debates on Article Three neared their end, Stolypin returned in the hope of influencing marginal votes. The national curias were the central issue in the bill and of great state significance. The basic ideas behind the government's thinking were that the western provinces were rich but that they were in need of zemstvos; that the region was strictly a Russian one in which the most influential segment of the population were Poles. Their position was such that the Poles would always be able to place the individuals most desirable to them in the zemstvo. The government, on the other hand, wished to equalize the chances of the different national groups in the region.[163]

Shortly after Stolypin's speech, the Chairman of the Council announced that the debates on Article Three were closed and the Council proceeded to the crucial vote. All present, and especially Stolypin, were anxious about the outcome of the ballots on which the passage of the bill depended. The result of the vote was the rejection of Article Three by a vote of 92 to 68.[164] The announcement came as a great shock to Stolypin, who sat "transfixed to his seat" before regaining control of himself and leaving the assembly.[165] The reading of the remainder of the bill continued throughout the next two sittings on 8 and 11 March. For Stolypin, however, the zemstvo issue had ended with the rejection of Article Three. In the meantime, other events were moving rapidly behind the scenes and all sections of society waited anxiously for the final outcome.

The day following the rejection of Article Three in the State Council, Saturday, 5 March, Stolypin set out for Tsarskoe Selo to submit his resignation to the Emperor.[166] His action appears to have been motivated by hearing the full story of Durnovo's and Trepov's intrigue against him, as a result of whose connivance the bill had been rejected. A few weeks prior to the momentous 4 March, Durnovo, the leader of the right wing in the State Council, had written to the Monarch through the Chairman of the Council, giving the reasons why the members of his group were opposed to the bill. A reply to Durnovo's letter was, however, withheld.[167] In the meantime, at Stolypin's request, the Emperor transmitted his wish to the right wing of the State Council through its chairman, M. Akimov, that it should support the government on this issue. Trepov, Durnovo's closest associate, then secured an audience with the Tsar in which he argued that the western zemstvos would fall into the hands of the "petty intelligentsia." At the end of this discussion Trepov asked the Monarch if his wish, passed through Akimov, was to be taken as a direct order. Nicholas retorted it was certainly to be understood that the members of the State Council should vote according to their "consciences."[168] With this tacit imperial approval in hand, Trepov and Durnovo immediately held a meeting of the State Council's right wing on the same evening, 3 March, and Durnovo informed his followers that the Emperor had no objections to their voting as they saw fit. Trepov also had much to say on this occasion, in his endeavor to persuade his colleagues to vote against the bill.[169]

It seems that Stolypin had no knowledge of these happenings, perhaps until his arrival at the State Council on 4 March.[170] The public consensus at the time was that the reactionaries of the State Council had overplayed their hand, that they had sacrificed the interests of the nation in order to gain the removal of Stolypin.[171] The zemstvo issue was close to Stolypin's heart, having been nurtured for many years, and he thought the reactionary clique had used unfair means to influence the Emperor unduly on an issue which he considered of vital significance to the State.

On presenting his resignation to the Monarch, Stolypin declared that he could not "think of sitting in the State Council side-by-side with men who had sponsored such an intrigue against him,"[172] although he was no doubt also perturbed over the Emperor's role in the affair. The outcome was embarrassing to both parties; the Emperor, surprised and disturbed, attempted to conciliate Stolypin by promising to use his influence to have the bill passed through the State Council on its reintroduction. Stolypin, on the other hand, maintained that the Duma would not renounce the idea of a national curia, whereas the Council, reluctant to admit its mistake, would not pass it again. Unwilling to accept Stolypin's resignation, the Tsar asked him to think of another way out of the dilemma. The latter then proposed that the State Council and the Duma should be prorogued for three days so that the bill could be introduced under Article 87 of the Fundamental Laws. He declared that this was the only condition upon which he would withdraw his resignation. Coming from Stolypin, such a demand seemed absurd, and even Nicholas replied with dismay, "Are you not afraid that such a manoeuvre might lead to difficulties with the Duma and the State Council?"[173] Stolypin retorted that such a passage of the bill might cause the Duma to show dissatisfaction, but that it would be reconciled because of the Tsar's personal action; as for the State Council, he felt that it did not matter so much if one considered the amount of good the bill would bring to the region.[174] As Kokovtsov notes, in all probability the argument persuaded the Tsar, whereupon Stolypin presented his third demand, that as a disciplinary measure the Emperor should grant Trepov and Durnovo an unsolicited leave of absence from the State Council until January of the following year. This request surprised the Monarch, who announced that he would require time to determine his reply.

In the course of the following week the press was full of rumors and speculation about the outcome of the government crisis. The first report of Stolypin's resignation appeared on 6 March, and on 9 March Rech confirmed this and published a long article on Kokovtsov as Stolypin's likely successor.[175] Novoe Vremia, the government subsidized organ, speculated on Kokovtsov and Krivoshein as possible candidates for the premiership, and B. Sturmer, Prince A. Shirinskii-Shikhmatov, and A. Makarov as possibilities for Minister of the Interior.[176] Considerable anxiety prevailed in the capital, with political figures and friends attempting to persuade Stolypin to reconsider his stand; the Grand Dukes and the Dowager Empress beseeched Stolypin to remain at this post and attempted to influence the Emperor to comply with Stolypin's requests. On 9 March the Monarch finally acceded to his mother's reasoning and decided to retain Stolypin.[177] Stolypin, on the other hand, remained deaf to the entreaties of his friends and the Imperial Family until his conditions were accepted. Such an uncompromising stand on his part might well have been motivated by the fact that public opinion and sympathy were in his favor at this juncture and that Durnovo and Trepov had received considerable criticism.

On 10 March Nicholas received Stolypin at Tsarskoe Selo and agreed, though reluctantly, to comply with his requests.[178] Despite his verbal consent, Stolypin asked the Tsar to write out the points by hand and to affix his signature to the document. So plain a distrust could not have left a good impression on the Emperor.[179] Following this meeting Stolypin summoned the Council of Ministers and revealed the Emperor's decision.[180] The ministers present, though sympathetic towards Stolypin's cause, attempted to convince him that such actions on his part would be a political error. Kokovtsov went so far as to suggest resubmitting the bill and thus avoiding the unconstitutional approach, even though it might take a year; however, Stolypin, presumably because he felt that much valuable time would be lost, did not agree.[181]

Varied rumors still persisted until 11 March, when the State Council assembled to vote on the whole bill. The ministerial bench was empty and the public gallery was filled to capacity.[182] The announcement that the bill was rejected by the large majority of 134 to 23 came as no great surprise.[183] The Chairman of the Council then set the next meeting for 16 March. As soon as the results were made known in the Duma, the Octobrists and the Nationalists, under the initiative of Guchkov, proceeded to collect signatures to reintroduce the zemstvo bill. Within fifteen minutes over two-hundred signatures had been collected.[184] It was reported that Guchkov announced positively that the motion to reintroduce the bill into the Lower House would come within the prescribed term of thirty days.[185]

On 12 March all further speculation ended with the sudden promulgation of the ukase proroguing the Duma and the State Council for three days, the granting of leaves of absence to Durnovo and Trepov until 1 January 1912, and the announcement that Stolypin would retain his position.[186] Both the State Council and the Duma assembled for their chairmen to read the ukase and to announce that the next sitting would be on 15 March.[187] Neither Trepov nor Durnovo were present.[188] On 14 March the western zemstvo bill was passed under Article 87 of the Fundamental Laws.[189] Although this last act had been rumored in advance (Stolypin had indeed confirmed it to an Octobrist deputation which visited him on 12 March in an attempt to persuade him not to go through with the proposal), the liberal element in the Council and the Duma had not believed that Stolypin would go so far.[190] In their opinion this measure was an insult to the legislative bodies and an abuse of constitutional procedure. Public opinion swung against Stolypin overnight. All the Duma members who had supported him were shocked and all those who had signed the list for the resubmission of the bill on the previous day hurriedly cancelled their signatures.[191] The entire press turned against Stolypin with the exception of Novoe Vremia, which attempted with small success to justify his act.

When the Duma re-convened on 15 March, Guchkov officially presented his resignation,[192] after which followed the reading of the interpellations submitted by the Octobrist, Progressist, Kadet, and Social-Democratic parties.[193] The different groups then attacked Stolypin's action for its disrespect both for the legislative assemblies and for the law. Shulgin and Markov were the only speakers who attempted to justify Stolypin, the former stressing that Stolypin was overburdened and the latter insisting that the action was technically constitutional.[194] The Progressist I. Efremov attacked Stolypin for having gone beyond all bounds in attacking the spirit of national representation. His group would have been glad to support Stolypin's victory over Durnovo if it had represented a victory of liberalism over reaction, but they could not welcome a merely personal victory.[195] Count A. Uvarov, Stolypin's personal friend and long standing supporter, announced that if the Duma supported the Premier on this occasion, it would only destroy itself.[196] Even the ultra-reactionary Purishkevich delivered a long and vehement denunciation of Stolypin's action, accusing him of settling personal accounts with appointed members of the State Council and attempting to turn the Council into part of his administration. He described Stolypin's act as the most unfortunate page in Russian history and praised Durnovo's services to the country during the critical period of 1905.[197] Miliukov then referred to the Duma as having been mortally wounded, and uttered his well known words: "The Third Duma, gentlemen, did not know how to live with dignity. Thus, if need be, let her die with honor."[198] The Social-Democrat Gegechkori predicted the dissolution of the Third Duma and declared that Russia was under Stolypin's dictatorship.[199] Pokrovskii, from the same party, exclaimed that this action threw down a challenge to the whole nation.[200] The Chairman of the Duma then submitted the interpellations to the vote; having been accepted by a large majority, they reflected a nearly unanimous vote of censure against Stolypin's action.[201]

When the State Council met on 24 March, forty-five of its members submitted a similar interpellation, demanding an explanation for the action taken.[202] All speakers emphasized the misuse of Article 87 and the dangers of such a precedent.[203] Even those who were impartial felt that, if the Council let the incident pass unnoticed, this would amount to condonation of a breach of the law.[204]

There were, however, a number who defended Stolypin's stand. Prince P. Golitsyn tried to justify the use of Article 87 and to smooth matters over.[205] N. Shrieber was another, but his point was the more technical one that no interpellation could be submitted to a minister on a matter ordered by the Emperor; provided the bill had been passed by the Duma, the Monarch's prerogative entitled him to take the final decision over the heads of the State Council.[206] Stishinskii asserted that the interpellation did not show that the government's action was illegal, even though it might have been incorrect.[207] Ofrosimov felt that, if the Council had not passed the bill because of national curias, such an action only meant that it had reacted negatively to the Russian national idea.[208] The interpellation was eventually accepted by a majority of 98 to 52.[209]

From then on all waited impatiently for Stolypin's appearance. He appeared before the State Council on 1 April 1911 to announce that, if any violation of the Fundamental Laws had occurred, then the responsibility lay with him and not with the government. The major part of his speech was then devoted to a detailed elaboration on the use of Article 87 in defense of the government's action, stressing that the Monarch had the right, at any time, to interrupt the legislative institutions. The government, he maintained, had felt endangered by the creation of a hopeless situation and had therefore considered it imperative to introduce a law which was vital to the interests of Russia. Such an action was sometimes as indispensable as "tracheotomy to a suffocating man."[210] As might have been expected, the State Council was dissatisfied with Stolypin's reply and those who came to the tribune continued to contend the illegality of the act and its disrespect for the law. Those who voted for the national curias were also critical of Stolypin's explanation, maintaining that the action was a misuse of force on the part of the government.[211]

After seeing the Council's reaction, Stolypin could not have expected any better reception in the Duma. The scene at the Taurida Palace on 27 April, when Stolypin appeared before the Duma, was once again charged with great excitement. The Duma was filled to capacity.

Never before had Stolypin appeared so stolid before the Duma; however, he was much more daring and, to some extent, more aggressive, than he had been before the State Council. He declared that, while both the legislative bodies had the right to submit interpellations, he was sceptical about such a right when applied to legislation already enacted. Legislative institutions could not become arbitrators of the legality of a legislative act of another institution; such a responsibility, under the constitution, lay only with the governing Senate.[212] He was firmly convinced that the millions of Russians inhabiting the western provinces could not be left in despair, simply because of friction within the state machine. Had the law been rejected by both legislative bodies, the government would have been compelled to solve the situation by yet more forceful means.[213] Agreeing that the use of Article 87 was an extreme and exceptional measure, he exclaimed: "But, gentlemen, it gives the Monarch, according to the law, the right to create a way out of a hopeless situation."[214] He then ended his speech by stressing his belief that the action of 14 March did not violate, but "only strengthened the rights of the still young Russian system of representation."[215] This last statement, with its implication that he had fought with the Duma against the reactionary State Council, was the strongest part of his case. Many of the listeners took these words as a meaningless gibe, though Stolypin might have been sincere in pronouncing them, and in conversation with the Duma deputies declared that his action had been a blow aimed at the reactionaries.[216] At the end of his speech he nonetheless managed to receive a healthy applause from the center and the right wing.

Following Stolypin's speech however, opinion continued to condemn his defiance of legality. The Octobrists asserted that, although there might be occasion when the government would have to violate the standard law, there was no foundation for doing so in this case. An Octobrist declaration was read which stated that the passage of the bill under Article 87 did not correspond with the spirit of the laws and was a violation of the Fundamental Laws.[217]

Though much of what was said on this occasion had already been uttered on 15 March, a number of speakers made some original comments. Maklakov, speaking for the Kadets, noted for instance that, when Stolypin presented the Tsar with his demands, he was probably unaware of the insult to the latter's dignity. Criticizing Stolypin's argument concerning the Senate, he said that it had no judicial value and suggested that Stolypin was attempting to hide behind the person of the Monarch, for the will of the latter stood above criticism. He did not wish, he said, to return to discussion of whether or not Article 87 had been violated; this question was irrelevant to the major issue that the ukase was an obvious pressure on the normal operation of the law. It would have been a much more beneficial demonstration on the part of Stolypin if he had humbly bowed his head before the law; Stolypin had not comprehended, Maklakov observed, that the introduction of the western zemstvos was a trivial matter compared to whether, "Russia should be a lawful state or a Stolypin estate."[218]

The Social-Democrat Gegechkori acknowledged Stolypin's act as a "tactical mistake" and declared that even the worst enemy of Russia could not have brought the Russian monarchy such harm as Stolypin had done on this occasion.[219] Chkheidze could not restrain himself from his usual threats and warned the Duma, "you should dread this moment, for it might be that the people will perform a tracheotomy on you, and, perhaps, even a trepanation."[220] This could well have been meant for Stolypin personally.

The ultra-reactionary Purishkevich agreed with the observations of Maklakov, arguing that Stolypin was trying to clear the path so that he would be able to dissolve the representative body whenever he pleased; in the name of the rightists he announced that Stolypin's explanation was unsatisfactory and could not be accepted.[221] The Progressivist Lvov characterized Stolypin's explanation as absurd, emphasizing that the argument was not whether the government had the right to order the Legislative Chambers into recess, but whether it could create a recess artificially in order to use Article 87. As it was, Russia had neither constitutionalism, parliamentarism, nor Fundamental Laws, but only arbitrary rule" and "demagogy."[222]

Baron Meyendorff, speaking for the Octobrists, presented a speech of refreshing originality, not confined to criticism and denunciation. Though opposed to Stolypin's action, his comments were instructive. Although disgusted when he heard of the use of Article 87, upon seeing the response of Russian society and realizing "how deep the roots of legality had penetrated," he had been overtaken with joy, for this reflected the bright symptom that "progress in Russia is feasible without revolution."[223]

The sitting ended with the passing of the Octobrist resolution by a majority of 202 to 82.[224] Stolypin sat motionless, listening to the deputies condemning his action as unconstitutional and probably realizing that they were in the right. He was thus largely isolated, without significant support from any quarter. So the crisis ended. Though Stolypin had triumphed for a day in his blind revenge against his political adversaries, he had begun his political ruination with little chance of regaining his former support in the Chambers. Maklakov rightly notes that, with the Duma's rejection of Stolypin's reply to the interpellation, Stolypin's political career had started to near its end.[225]

Worn out with the strains of the past year,[226] in which he had taken a more than usually active part in pushing through the three major bills--the agrarian, the Finnish, and finally that relating to the western zemstvos--Stolypin was now politically isolated, with only a hollow victory in his hands. His usefulness appeared to be over, for without the confidence of the Chambers he could not continue to hold effective power. After these events, as Kokovtsov notes, "Something inside him seemed to have snapped," and Stolypin appeared to have lost his iron spirit.[227] From then on, the Tsar cooled towards Stolypin and rumors circulated that a new post was being prepared for him; whether this was true or not is unknown, but it is certain that Stolypin's star was on the way down.[228] There are grounds for believing that the Monarch did in fact look for a replacement, but it would have been hard to find anyone who could have filled the place left by Stolypin. The scene was now set for the unexpected final denouement, which took place in Kiev some six months later.

By the beginning of May 1911, the excitement of the western zemstvo fiasco had largely died down and the political life in the capital had begun to return to its usual tempo. On 13 May, both Houses went into recess and Stolypin retired to his estate at Kolnoberge, in the province of Kovno, returning to St. Petersburg only for urgent business.[229]

In the course of the summer, public attention became focused on the festivities to be held in Kiev at the end of August to mark the 50th anniversary of the emancipation of the serfs. Stolypin duly arrived in the city on 27 August, with the Imperial Family following two days later, when the Emperor was to unveil a monument to his grandfather, Alexander II. On 1 September, a gala performance of the opera The Tale of the Tsar Soltan was held. Dmitrii Bogrov,[230] the would-be assassin, succeeded in obtaining a ticket to the performance from Kiev's chief of police, N. Kuliabko, by claiming that he knew two assassins who planned to kill Stolypin and who had tried to persuade him to join in the plot. The police chief accepted the story at its face value since Bogrov had previously proved a reliable police informant.

During the second interval, Bogrov made his way to Stolypin's seat in the front row. Stolypin was standing alone with his back to the stage, scanning the audience. Bogrov passed unnoticed until he was only two or three steps away; as Stolypin glanced at him, Bogrov pulled out a revolver and fired two shots in quick succession. One of the bullets hit Stolypin in the right wrist and ricocheted into the leg of a violinist sitting in the orchestra pit. The second shot, aimed at Stolypin's heart, was deflected by a medallion of St. Vladimir and struck his lower right chest.[231] Amid the consternation which broke out, Stolypin was given first aid and then taken to the Makovsky Clinic, where he died on the evening of 5 September 1911.

Bogrov, who was arrested in the theatre, was tried and sentenced by a military tribunal. At dawn on 11 September he was hanged, in the presence of thirty witnesses, at the Kiev fortress.[232] Stolypin's death has been attributed by some to revolutionaries; others have claimed that it was the work of the police or of the reactionaries. It appears reasonably certain that Bogrov himself was neither a police agent nor a member of the revolutionary party at the time of the assassination, and that his action may be taken as an attempt to expiate himself before the revolutionary party if not before society.[233]

NOTES

1. P.R.O. F.O. 371, Vol. 1214, No. 11048, 23 March 1911.

2. Sliozberg, G., Dorevoliutsionnyi Stroi Rossii (Paris, 1933), p.191.

3. Kliuchevskii, V., Kurs Russkoi Istorii (Moscow, 1956-59), Vol. V, pp.304-305.

4. Veselovskii, B., Istoriia Zemstva za Sorok Let, (SPB, 1909), Vol. 4, p.188.

5. See "O Priemakh Borby Zemstva s Samoderzhaviem," Osvobozhdenie (Stuttgart) No. 22, 8 May 1903, pp.382-385; "Zemtsy-Konstitutsionalisty o Konstitutsionno-Demokraticheskoi Partii, "Osvobozhdenie (Stuttgart), No. 78/79, 5 October 1905, pp.1-14.

6. P.S.Z., Vol. X, No. 6922.

7. Belokonskii, I., Samoupravlenie i Zemstvo (Rostov, 1905), p.25; Pazhitnov, K., Gorodskoe i Zemskoe Samoupravlenie (SPB, 1913), p.91.

8. Belokonskii, I., Zemstvo i Konstitutsiia (Moscow, 1910), pp.32-33.

9. Pushkarev, S., Rossiia v XIX veke (1801-1914) (New York, 1956), pp.383-384; Mirnyi, S., Adresy Zemstv 1894-95, i ikh Politicheskaia Programma (Geneva, 1896).

10. The late Countess Volkov-Muromtsev, the daughter of Count P. Heyden, in an interview with the author.

11. Belokonskii, I., Ot Derevni do Parlamenta (Berlin, n.d.), p.5.

12. Archive of Russian and East European History and Culture, Columbia University, the personal archive of N. Melnikov, Folder 7, Booklet 2, pp.10 and 29; See also Zenkovskii, A., Pravda o Stolypine (New York, 1956), p.204.

13. Stolypin, P., and Krivoshein, A., Poezdka v Sibir i Povolzhe (SPB, 1911), p.121.

14. P.S.Z., Vol. XXVI, No. 28392.

15. Tikhonova, T., Zemstvo v Rossii i na Okrainakh (SPB, 1907), p.12.

16. Gosudarstvennaia Duma, Vtoroi Sozyv, Stenograficheskie Otchety, 6 March 1907, Col. 113.

17. Tverskoi, P., "K Istoricheskim Materialam o Pokoinom P. A. Stolypine," Vestnik Evropy (April 1912), p.192. The six western provinces were: Kiev, Podolia, Minsk, Mogilev, Vitebsk and Volyn.

18. Stolypin, A., P. A. Stolypin 1862-1911 (Paris, 1927), p.68; Oldenburg, S., Tsarstvovanie Imperatora Nikolaia II (Munich, 1939), Vol. II, p.70.

19. Witte, S., Samoderzhavie i Zemstvo (Stuttgart, 1901), see especially pp.9-16, and p.203; for an interesting survey of the Witte-Goremykin controversy see: Shipov, D., Vospominaniia i Dumy o Perezhitom (Moscow, 1918), pp.126-130

and pp.171-177; Shelunin, A., "Graf Witte i Russkoe Samoderzhavie," Krasnaia Letopis, Vol. 7 (1923), p.185; Belokonskii, I., Zemstvo i Konstitutsiia, pp.63-68. Belokonskii points out that this whole affair was conducted in secrecy by Witte and asks why Witte offered to form a commission under the chairmanship of Pobedonostsov; his implication is that Witte was attempting to get this influential figure on his side.

21. It was generally known and assumed within the top hierarchy that Witte's memorandum was directed against Goremykin in order to displace him from the Ministry of the Interior. This Witte achieved. Suvorin, A., Dnevnik (Moscow, 1923), p.330.

22. "Perepiska S. Iu. Witte s K.P. Pobedonostsevym," Krasnyi Arkhiv, Vol. 30 (1928), p.104.

23. P.S.Z., Vol. XXIII, No. 22757.

24. G.S. 28 January 1911, Col. 753; Zenkovskii, A., op. cit., p.369.

25. Kryzhanovskii, S., Vospominaniia. Iz Bumag S.E. Kryzhanovskago. Posledniago Gosudarstvennago Sekretaria Rossiiskoi Imperii (Berlin, 1930), p.138; "P. A. Stolypin i Frantsuzkaia Pressa v 1911 g.," Krasnyi Arkhiv, Vol. 32 (1929), p.209.

26. G.S. 8 May 1909, Col. 1933. The western zemstvo bill which was presented to the Duma was drawn up by the council on local self-government, a body set up by Plehve but which was summoned for the first time by Stolypin in order to do preliminary work on the bill. This council consisted of representatives of both provincial zemstvos and those of the major cities. (Kryzhanovskii, S., op. cit., p.145). As early as 14 October 1907, slightly over two weeks before the opening of the Third Duma, Stolypin sent a circular to all provincial zemstvo

assemblies, requesting them to nominate representatives to the Council when the question of the western zemstvos would be discussed. (Veselovskii, B., op. cit., Vol. 4, p.169). It may be noted that the idea of national curias for the western provinces was supported by a majority of zemstvo members, especially the Russian deputies of the western provinces.

27. Professor D. Pikhno, an appointed member of the State Council from Kiev, was the editor of the newspaper Kievlianin and evidently with a group of Kievan nationalists played a prominent role in instigating the drafting of the bill. See Oldenburg, S., op. cit., Vol. II, p.68; Izgoev, A., P. A. Stolypin - Ocherk Zhizni i Deiatelnosti (Moscow, 1912), p.90.

28. G.S. 8 May 1909, Cols. 1935, 1941. Of course, "Russian majority" really meant a small number of Russian landowners and peasants, and great masses of Ukranians and Belorussians.

29. Ibid., Cols. 1941-42.

30. Ibid., Col. 1949.

31. G.D. 30 May 1909, Col. 2751.

32. Ibid., Col. 2756.

33. Ibid., Col. 2825.

34. G.D. 5 May 1910, Col. 671. Throughout the months of March and April, while the Special Commission was discussing the proposed bill, Novoe Vremia incited national sentiment against the Poles. It noted on 3 April, for instance, that the commission had rejected all of the articles which guaranteed a Russian majority, stressing that this was what the Poles wished. It also asked: "What is left of the principle of a Russian zemstvo?" Novoe Vremia, 3 April 1910 (No. 12234), p.4.

35. G.D. 7 May 1910, Cols. 731-33; 737. Owing to the property qualificaton which was set, the arrangements made in 1903 for the western provinces provided almost exclusively for Polish representation. The problem was intensified by the fact that most of the Russian landlords who did own land within the franchise were absentees.

36. Ibid., Col. 738.

37. Ibid., Cols. 740-742.

38. Ibid., Cols. 746-747.

39. For a thorough account of zemstvo work for the first forty years of its existence see Veselovskii, B., op. cit. His numerous statistics in four volumes afford a good insight into the colossal accomplishment of the zemstvos. See also Makeev, N., and O'Hara, V., Russia (New York, 1925), pp. 111-116.

40. G.D. 7 May 1910, Cols. 748-751.

41. Ibid., Cols. 752-754.

42. Ibid., Col. 755.

43. Ibid., Cols. 760-761.

44. Ibid., Cols. 763-774.

45. Ibid.

46. Ibid., Col. 775.

47. Ibid., Cols. 775-778.

48. Ibid., Col. 779.

49. Ibid., Col. 784.

50. Ibid., Col. 787.

51. _Ibid._, Col. 788.

52. _Ibid._, Cols. 788-790.

53. _Ibid._, Col. 791.

54. Kryzhanovskii, S., _op. cit._, p.218.

55. _G.D._ 7 May 1910, Cols. 792-794.

56. _Ibid._, Cols. 794-795.

57. _G.D._ 8 May 1910, Cols. 869-871.

58. Of the whole Octobrist Party only sixteen members were against the bill for one reason or the other; among these N. Khomiakov, Baron Meyendorff, and Bennigsen voted against the passing to the reading of the bill, declaring that the bill was directly opposed to the program of the Octobrist Party. Kizevetter, A., _op. cit._, p.510.

59. _G.D._ 10 May 1910, Col. 1052; 11 May 1910, Cols. 1146-1152.

60. _G.D._ 15 May 1910, Col. 1400; 10 May 1910, Col. 949.

61. _G.D._ 8 May 1910, Cols. 912-914.

62. _G.D._ 12 May 1910, Col. 1201; Zavarzin, P., _Rabota Tainoi Politsii_ (Paris, 1924), p.140-143. The attempt to Polanize the western provinces was a distinct possibility and gave the Ministry of the Interior real concern. This author (Zavarzin), noting that the Poles held the Russian peasants in dire poverty, cites an incident in 1908 when the government decided to collect the vote of certain uezds in the western provinces. During the voting procedure the Polish landlords applied considerable pressure to the peasants. In one case they threatened to throw the poor peasants off their estates if they did not accept Catholicism

within two weeks. As a result, tens of thousands became Catholics. This movement, according to the author, was directed by the Polish Kolo in the Duma and headed by R. Dmowski. For verification, he cites a secret meeting of this organization in Warsaw; when the police broke in they found many incriminating papers and Dmowski.

63. G.D. 12 May 1910, Cols. 1202-1203.

64. Ibid., Cols. 1203-1206.

65. G.D. 8 May 1910, Cols. 858-868.

66. G.D. 10 May 1910, Cols. 1022-1027.

67. G.D. 8 May 1910, Cols. 930, 932-933.

68. G.D. 10 May 1910, Col. 967.

69. G.D. 7 May 1910, Cols. 821, 824.

70. G.D. 11 May 1910, Col. 1119.

71. G.D. 12 May 1910, Cols. 1214, 1216, 1218.

72. Ibid., Col. 1221.

73. G.D. 11 May 1910, Cols. 1094-1099.

74. G.D. 8 May 1910, Cols. 849-851.

75. Ibid., Cols. 853-855.

76. G.D. 7 May 1910, Col. 806.

77. Ibid., Col. 809.

78. G.D. 10 May 1910, Col. 984.

79. Ibid., Col. 1038.

80. G.D. 8 May 1910, Cols. 873-874.

81. *Ibid*., Cols. 880-881.

82. *G.D.* 12 May 1910, Cols. 1188, 1194, 1197.

83. *G.D.* 10 May 1910, Col. 1006.

84. *Ibid*., Cols. 1007-1009.

85. *G.D.* 11 May 1910, Col. 1117. The press rightly observed that little new was said during the debates of 11 May 1910, *Novoe Vremia*, 12 May 1910 (No. 12271), p.2.

86. *G.D.* 12 May 1910, Cols. 1227-1233.

87. *Ibid*.

88. As late as this date, however, the general consensus was that the fate of the bill was still undecided. *Rech*, 12 May 1910 (No. 128), p.2.

89. *G.D.* 15 May 1910, Cols. 1361-1363.

90. *Ibid*., Cols. 1363-1364.

91. *Ibid*., Cols. 1369-1377.

92. *Ibid*., Cols. 1376-1387.

93. *Ibid*., Cols. 1368, 1389-1390.

94. *Ibid*., Cols. 1391-1392.

95. *Ibid*., Col. 1392.

96. *Ibid*., Col. 1393.

97. *Ibid*., Cols. 1394-1395.

98. *G.D.* 17 May 1910, Cols. 1452-1454.

99. *Ibid*., Cols. 1456, 1459-1460.

100. *G.D.* 15 May 1910, Col. 1410.

101. Ibid., Cols. 1402, 1406.

102. G.D. 17 May 1910, Cols. 1470-1473.

103. G.D. 15 May 1910, Cols. 1396-1398.

104. G.D. 17 May 1910, Col. 1477.

105. Ibid., Cols. 1499-1500.

106. Novoe Vremia, 18 May 1910 (No. 12277), p.2.

107. G.D. (Evening Session), 18 May 1910, Col. 1752.

108. G.D. 29 May 1910, Cols. 2829-2839.

109. G.D. 1 June 1910, Cols. 2979-2981. For the complete text of the bill see Cols. 3061-3072. P.S.Z., Vol. XXXI, No. 34903.

110. This point was brought out by Stolypin in his letter to the Tsar and Izwolsky. To the latter Stolypin wrote that under the wings of the State Council reactionaries, legislation was being purposefully delayed or simply rejected after it had been successfully passed in the Duma. Both letters were written after the fiasco. See "Iz Perepiski P. A. Stolypina s Nikolaem Romanovym," Krasnyi Arkhiv, Vol. 30 (1928), pp.85-86; "P. A. Stolypin i Frantsuzkaia Pressa," Krasnyi Arkhiv, Vol. 32 (1929), pp.210-211.

111. Rech, 29 January 1911 (No. 28), pp.5-6.

112. G.S. 5 May 1910, Col. 2607.

113. G.S. 28 January 1911, Col. 752.

114. Ibid., Col. 756.

115. Ibid., Cols. 757-758.

116. Ibid., Cols. 760-762.

117. *Ibid*., Col. 771. Professor Kovalevskii gives the following population figures for the six western provinces: out of a total population of 17 million, 14 million were Russians, and the Poles numbered 644,500, or 3.7%. Kovalevskii, M., "Zemstvo v Shesti Guberniiakh Zapadnago Kraia," *Vestnik Evropy* (March 1911), p.255.

118. *G.S.* 28 January 1911, Col. 777.

119. *Ibid*., Cols. 782, 784.

120. *Ibid*., Cols. 790-791.

121. *Ibid*., Cols. 794-808.

122. *G.S.* 1 February 1911, Cols. 902-903, 904, 912.

123. *Ibid*., Cols. 854-856. In one of his articles, Professor Kovalevskii clarifies the reasons why he was opposed to the national curias while noting that he supported the introduction of zemstvos similar to those operating in the Russian central provinces. He felt that the bill introduced a militant zemstvo which would produce a political struggle and national strife. He was also against any limitations being placed upon the electorate. Vestnik Evropy, *op*. *cit*., p.258.

124. *G.S.* 1 February 1911, Cols. 860-865.

125. *G.S.* 4 February 1911, Col. 927. Trepov was one of the thirty-three members of the State Council who signed the motion to alter the electoral law which precipitated the western zemstvo bill. E.V., *op*. *cit*., Vol. II, p.75.

126. *G.S.* 28 January 1911, Cols. 808-809. This last statement by Witte is ironic in that it was he who initiated any government doubts of the peasantry through his memorandum on the zemstvo.

127. It is of interest to note that, in Witte's memorandum, he was quite aware of the Polish influence, insisting that Goremykin's project did not restrict the Poles sufficiently and pointing out that there were considerable grounds for fearing that these zemstvo councils would become nothing less than Polish Seim. Witte, S., _op_. _cit_., p.181.

128. _G.S._ 28 January 1911, Cols. 815-816.

129. _Rech_, 30 January 1911 (No. 29), p.2.

130. _Rech_, 3 February 1911 (No. 33), p.4.

131. _Rech_, 12 February 1911 (No. 42), p.6.

132. _G.S._ 1 February 1911, Cols. 824-826.

133. _Ibid_., Col. 830.

134. _Ibid_., Col. 835.

135. Baron Meyendorff.

136. _G.S._ 1 February 1911, Col. 866.

137. _Ibid_., Cols. 868-869.

138. _Ibid_., Cols. 870-871.

139. _Ibid_., Col. 871.

140. _Ibid_., Cols. 872-873.

141. _Ibid_., Col. 875.

142. The basic difference between the different legislative Zemstvo Acts above should be clarified. The Statute of 1864 was a liberal one extending a wide franchise to all estates. The Ukase of 1890, which introduced significant restrictions on the 1864 Act, considerably hampered the freedom of expansion of zemstvo activity. With Stolypin's Ukase of

5 October 1906, the restrictions of 1890 were eliminated and the zemstvo statute reverted to read like that of 1864, with a few additional but minor, privileges. These zemstvo statutes operated only within the central provinces of Russia. The first ukase to introduce zemstvos into the six western provinces, that of 1903, was limited to these provinces only. The bill which Stolypin introduced largely reproduced the arrangements operating in the central provinces, national curias dividing the Polish and the Russian electorate comprising the major change. However, when the law was passed in the Duma in June 1910, property qualifications used in the central provinces was cut by half. This western zemstvo statute now differed from that operating in the central provinces in that the latter had no national curias and retained the franchise of 1864.

143. G.S. 1 February 1911, Col. 878-879.

144. G.S. 4 February 1911, Col. 933.

145. Ibid., Col. 934.

146. Ibid., Col. 955.

147. Ibid., Cols. 939-940.

148. Ibid., Col. 941.

149. In the Kiev province, with a 2% Polish population, the bill suggested the Poles receive 16% of uezd electors. The relationship of Polish population to Polish representation in the other western provinces was to be as follows: Volyn 6% vs. 24%, Podolsk 2.3% vs. 20%, Vitebsk 3.4% vs. 24%, Minsk 3% vs. 25%, Mogilev 1% vs. 12%.

150. G.S. 4 February 1911, Col. 944. After this proposal had been accepted, Stishinskii informed the State Council that changes introduced into the bill by the Duma had not yet been discussed by the special commission.

He proposed that the commission should make an oral report on these amendments. This motion was accepted, however, the intended report by the commission was defeated; namely, that the Council should proceed with the reading of the bill and avoid returning to the general debates of the bill. (See also Cols. 978-984).

151. G.S. 4 March 1911, Col. 1197.

152. *Ibid*., Col. 1217.

153. *Ibid*., Col. 1207.

154. *Ibid*., Col. 1212.

155. *Ibid*., Col. 1218.

156. *Ibid*., Col. 1201.

157. *Ibid*., Col. 1203.

158. "P. A. Stolypin i Frantsuzkaia Pressa," *Krasnyi Archiv*, Vol. 32 (1929), p.209.

159. G.S. 4 March 1911, Col. 1226.

160. *Ibid*., Col. 1232.

161. *Ibid*., Col. 1236.

162. *Ibid*., Cols. 1257-1260.

163. *Ibid*., Cols. 1240-1241.

164. *Ibid*., Col. 1256.

165. Dillon, E., "Foreign Affairs," *Contemporary Review*, Vol. 99 (May 1911), p.632.

166. *Rech*, 7 March 1911 (No. 64), p.2; Kokovtsov, V., *op*. *cit*., Vol. I, p.451.

167. *Contemporary Review*, *loc*. *cit*.

168. Oldenburg, S., *op. cit.*, p.72.

169. *Novoe Vremia*, 6 March 1911 (No. 125650), p.2.

170. Rein, G., *Iz Perezhitago: 1907-1918* (Berlin, 1935), p.127.

171. Tikhomirov, L., *K Reforme Obnovlennoi Rossii* (Moscow, 1912), p.206.

172. Kokovtsov, V., *op. cit.*, p.453. In a letter to the Emperor of 1 May 1911, Stolypin recollected that when the Monarch had asked him to remain at his post, he was confronted with the question of the unsurmountable obstruction of the State Council, as well as Durnovo's unceasing efforts to increase that obstruction. "Iz Perepiski P. A. Stolypina s Nikolaem Romanovym," *Krasnyi Archiv*, Vol. 30 (1928), p.86.

173. Kokovtsov, V., *op. cit.*, p.454.

174. *Ibid.*

175. *Rech*, 6 March 1911 (No. 63), p.3; *Rech*, 9 March 1911, (No. 66), p.304; *Novoe Vremia*, 7 March 1911, (No. 12566), p.1; *P.R.O.* F.O. 371, Vol. 1214, No. 10270, 20 March 1911.

176. *Novoe Vremia*, 9 March 1911 (No. 12568), p.2.

177. Bok, M., *Vospominaniia o Moem Otse P. A. Stolypine* (New York, 1953), pp.325-326; *The Times*, 24 March 1911, p.5.

178. E. V., *op. cit.*, Vol. II, p.72.

179. "Iz Perepiski P. A. Stolypine s Nikolaem Romanovym," *Krasnyi Arkhiv*, Vol. 30 (1928), p.80; Strakhovsky, L., "The Statesmanship of Peter Stolypin: A Reappraisal," *Slavonic & East European Review*, Vol. 37 (June 1959), p.367. It illustrates, however, that in all probability the Tsar must have forced Stolypin

into similar predicaments in the past, Stolypin bearing full responsibility before the public on each occasion. Baron Meyendorff felt strongly that this was the case.

180. _Rech_, 11 March 1911 (No. 68), p.3.

181. Kokovstsov, V., _op_. _cit_., pp.457-458.

182. _Rech_, 12 March 1911 (No. 69), p.5.

183. _G.S._ 11 March 1911, Cols. 1361-1362.

184. _Novoe Vremia_, 12 March 1911 (No. 12571), p.2.

185. _The Times_, March 1911, p.5.

186. _P.S.Z._, Vol. XXXI, Nos. 34898 and 34899; _Rech_, 12 March 1911 (No. 69), pp.2-3.

187. _G.S._ 12 March 1911, Cols. 1365-1366.

188. _Rech_, 13 March 1911 (No. 70), p.5.

189. _Novoe Vremia_, 14 March 1911 (No. 12573), p.1; _Rech_, 14 March 1911 (No. 71), p.1; _P.S.Z._, Vol. XXXI, No. 34903.

190. _Novoe Vremia_, 13 March 1911 (No. 12572), p.2; _Rech_, 15 March 1911 (No. 72), p.4.

191. _The Times_, 28 March 1911, p.5.

192. _G.D._ 15 March 1911, Col. 670.

193. _Ibid_., Cols. 719-722.

194. _Ibid_., Cols. 763, 800.

195. _Ibid_., Cols. 740, 742.

196. _Ibid_., Col. 770.

197. _Ibid_., Cols. 785-792.

198. Ibid., Col. 751.

199. Ibid., Cols., 752, 756, 758.

200. Ibid., Col. 785.

201. Ibid., Col. 812.

202. G.S. 24 March 1911, Col. 1403.

203. Ibid., Col. 1410.

204. Ibid., Col. 1411.

205. Ibid., Col. 1419.

206. Ibid., Cols. 1424-1428.

207. Ibid., Cols. 1447-1448.

208. Ibid., Col. 1445.

209. Ibid., Col. 1456.

210. G.S. 1 April 1911, Cols. 1781-1795.

211. Ibid., Cols. 1847-1851.

212. G.D. 27 April 1911, Col. 2851.

213. Ibid., Col. 2860.

214. Ibid., Col. 2861.

215. Ibid., Col. 2863.

216. Rech, 15 March 1911 (No. 72), p.4; Izgoev, A., op. cit., p.94.

217. G.D. 27 April 1911, Cols. 2864-2868.

218. Ibid., Cols. 2869-2878.

219. Ibid., Cols. 2917, 2930.

220. Ibid., Col. 2986.

221. Ibid., Col. 2891.

222. Ibid., Cols. 2946, 2951.

223. Ibid., Col. 3015.

224. Ibid., Cols. 3024-3025.

225. Maklakov, V., Rechi Sudebnyia, Dumskiia i Publichnyia Lektsii: 1904-1926 (Paris, 1949), p.115.

226. P.R.O. F.O. 371, Vol. 1214, No. 10572, 22 March 1911.

227. Kokovtsov, V., op. cit., p.463: The Times, 28 March 1911, p.5.

228. Izgoev, A., op. cit., p.103.

229. Padenie Tsarskogo Rezhima. Stenograficheskie Otchety (Leningrad, 1924), Vol. VII, p.91.

230. Dmitrii Bogrov, a Christianized Jew, was born on 29 January 1887, of a respectable and a well known family in Kiev. His father was a wealthy lawyer with an estate amounting to some half a million rubles; in 1910 alone he had donated 85,000 rubles for a hospital. Though anti-semitism was strong in Kiev, the father had long been a member of the Kievan Gentry Club, and was well liked and respected by members of the city elite. As might be expected, the children of the family received the best education. As early as 1901-1902, however, while still a youth in the gymnasium, Dmitrii had paid visits to revolutionary circles, showed sympathy for the revolutionary cause, and even done small favors for the Socialist-Revolutionaries. These activities presumably stemmed from his oldest brother, who was already a member of the Social-Democratic Party. See: Novoe Vremia,

3 September 1911 (No. 12743), p.4; Bogrov, A., *Dmitrii Bogrov i Ubiistvo Stolypina* (Berlin, 1931), pp.28-29, 35; Knizhnik, I., "Vospominaniia o Bogrove, Ubiitsa Stolypina," *Krasnaia Letopis*, Vol. V (1922), p.288; Mushin, A., *Dmitrii Bogrov i Ubiistvo Stolypina* (Paris, 1914), p.104.

231. Gan, L., "Ubiistvo P. A. Stolypina," *Istoricheskii Vestnik*, Vol. 135 (1914), p.983; Mushin, A., *op. cit.*, p.162; *Rech*, 3 September 1911 (No. 231), p.3.

232. *Novoe Vremia*, 11 September 1911 (No. 251), p.2; *Istoricheskii Vestnik*, *op. cit.*, pp.996-997.

233. For a more detailed account of the assassination and Bogrov's motives, see my article: "Stolypin's Assassin," *Slavic Review*, Vol. XXIV, No. 2, June 1965.

CHAPTER V

EPILOGUE

During the years he held power, Stolypin embodied the most hopeful aspects of the age as well as the divisions within it. Before his political downfall, brought about by the reactionaries who schemed against him, he symbolized the alternative courses that stood before the country: part of him looked to the nineteenth century and venerated the institution of the monarchy, the other looked forward to the growth of a modern state, ruled by party government and an elected assembly. Perhaps because of this very mixture, he held firmly to the belief that the imperial system could be rehabilitated and brought into harmony with the needs of an emerging modern Russia without destroying entirely the fabric of the old order.

The obstacles to the gradualist reforms he favored included, as ever, the vastness of the country, which made communications and the implementation of the new measures extremely difficult, and the weakness and unresponsiveness of the existing executive machinery. It represented the only power he had, but it was incapable by itself of acting as the lever by which Russia could be brought into the modern world.

Throughout this period, the opposition clung to its convictions that no progress could be achieved until the existing order had been eradicated, and that the new one could be built only on the ruins of the old. Stolypin himself was treated as the representative of an absolute monarchy rather than as a would-be liberal politician. In consequence he never received the support of the parties to the left of the Octobrists, those whose backing he needed if he were to make a peaceful transition to the new order. The right meanwhile believed that he was betraying their interests. During the whole of his ministerial career Stolypin had to fight two foes: on the one hand, an entrenched reactionary opinion, active in the administration and at Court, and on the other hand, a revolutionary opposition, determined to work only partly within the established constitutional framework--and in any case unwilling to cooperate with him. He thus had to work with no sure base of support, with little room to maneuver, and with criticism at every step he tried to take.

The Tsar, a complex and weak individual, stood at the center of the political vortex. He warily regarded the issues confronting him, suspicious that they contained threats to him or to his prerogatives. Overcome by sudden moods and easily influenced by those around him, he would declare himself on one day in favor of liberties, and on the next abruptly retreat from his promises. These swings in his opinions caused some of the ablest men in the country to retire from politics, disheartened and convinced that progress was impossible under Nicholas II. Even Stolypin, monarchist though he was, came finally to lose trust in the Tsar. Dealing with him was a task in itself, and Stolypin's description of Nicholas as "romantic" and "byzantine" (vizanteits) reflected his own experiences.[1]

Much of the commentary upon Stolypin is distorted by authors who want to prove a predetermined case; those who label him a reactionary, without making any effort to analyze him within the framework of the Russian reality of the time, ignore the difficulties he faced. The Soviet Government has published numerous documents and a number of works about Stolypin in an effort to establish him as a reactionary, although the arguments and data do not stand up to examination. Those who refer to Stolypin's epoch as one of "brutal reaction"[2] betray political or ideological considerations which produce a distortion of history that goes beyond the bounds of mere scholarly disagreement. Stolypin wished, no doubt, to build a stronger base for a future monarchy, but he was firmly opposed to the idea of the monarchy as it had existed in the past.[3] How can he be classified as a reactionary in this context? There is ample evidence to show that he was transforming tsarism, a goal quite incompatible with "reaction."

Whatever differing views may be held on the merits of Stolypin's policies, there is little disagreement among most scholars and observers in the West regarding his impressive characteristics as a man. He was determined, self-confident, capable, and possessed of a fair share of courage--he was well aware of the difficulty of the task he was undertaking and prepared to summon up all the support his personal eloquence could evoke--a man, in short, who gained power by his individual qualities and would succeed, if succeed he could, by force of personal example, in a setting where established institutions could turn against him and where independent public opinion was far from a major force. Tributes were paid to his qualities by a wide spectrum of his contemporaries, including his opponents and his admirers. He did not compromise at the first sign of opposition or hesitate to assume responsibility. As Sir Donald Mackenzie Wallace observed at the time, Stolypin had a large "reserve of quiet determination, energy, and perseverance--qualities in which the Russians are too often very deficient."[4] He was given power at an extremely difficult time and it was his abilities and his belief in a viable future for Russia which made him, as Sir Arthur Nicholson noted, "the most notable figure in Europe."

The center of Stolypin's political philosophy was the belief that Russia could evolve into a constitutional monarchy. As a constitutionalist he attempted, as he himself said, to strengthen the new order as it was defined in the October Manifesto, and in the new Fundamental Laws. While he was more moderate in his aims than the majority of his Western contemporaries, Russia's constitution was embryonic, threatened both from the left and the right.[5] Stolypin was acutely aware that a constitutional form of government could not be secured until the appropriate institutions had been firmly established. He thus stands as an institutionalist who wanted to create the machinery for constitutional government, and was engaged in conducting a transitional phase from "autocratic" to constitutional rule.

Russian parliamentarism in history was far from being an indigenous, slowly-evolved phenomenon, and it suffered many setbacks; too many political pressures with varying motives were at work. The reactionaries were opposed to any representative body; in their view the tranquillity of the country could be maintained only by subjecting the masses to autocratic rule. The extreme left, and the splinter groups which advocated the same aims, wanted nothing less than the destruction of the existing order and the institution of a socialist utopia. The Kadet Party, regarded by Stolypin as containing the "best minds of the country," was as impetuous as the others and demanded the immediate transformation of the country to a parliamentary system on the British pattern.

Stolypin, while soberly aware that changes were imperative, emphasized "moderation" and "gradualness." The liberals refused nevertheless to cooperate with him, reluctant to compromise or to gain experience in dealing with immediate problems. Despite this he sought the support of men such as Miliukov and others who had ties with the emergent public opinion. He made it a point also to keep in touch with the leaders of the various political factions in the Kadet Party and those to their right,[6] even though they continued to scorn him, blinded as they were by an ideology more revolutionary than evolutionary,[7] dreaming of a democracy and of an open society which would be achieved in a single dialectic leap. Their own way of defining problems kept them from seeing that Stolypin, too, was sincere in wishing to better the lot of the masses. In terms of political action Stolypin was thus thrown back on his original aim, to bring the promises of the October Manifesto--the basic liberal freedoms--into life and to create as rapidly as possible a peasant majority that possessed economic sufficiency and political education, even if it could not be done in a year or even a decade.[8]

Although the Emperor had control of foreign policy, there is some evidence that even here Stolypin left his mark, although his first concern was with internal restoration rather than foreign policy. During his Ministry he sought to keep Russia out of hostilities and acted as a pacifying influence on the militaristic elements. About a month before his death, Stolypin expressed his sentiments in a letter to Izwolsky, then Russian Ambassador to France:

> You know my point of view. We need peace: a war during the approaching year, and especially in the name of a cause which the people would not understand, would be fatal for Russia and for the dynasty. Conversely, every year of peace fortifies Russia not only from the military and naval point of view, but also from the economic and financial one. Besides, and that is more important, Russia is growing from year to year; self-knowledge and public opinion are developing in our land. One must not scoff at our parliamentary institutions. However imperfect, their influence has brought about a radical change in Russia, and when this country's time will come, it will meet its enemy consciously. Russia will hold out, and be victorious, only in a popular war.[9]

Stolypin, unlike the monarch and the right wing reactionaries, was a firm supporter of the Duma. There is enough documentation to show that he was a moderator of reaction--which was anxious to see the abolition of the Duma--and that he preferred a weak Duma to no Duma. During the days of revolutionary upheaval the right wing looked to Stolypin as its salvation, but when the emergency was over it showed increasing concern about his democratic leanings. In the face of pressure from the reactionaries and the Court, Stolypin nevertheless strove to raise the authority of the representative body. Despite high-handedness in the use of Article 87, his principal long-range objective was to secure the place of a truly representative regime. By May 1908 Stolypin was able to say that "blind reaction is becoming far less possible" and that the "representative regime was already taking root."[10]

The failure of the First Duma was not solely due to the stand of the opposition. It is true that Goremykin, the spokesman for the administration, was inept and failed to establish contact with the assembly, and that the government as a whole lacked enthusiasm for the newly launched experiment. But the Kadets, who had the majority of seats, were responsible for much of the tone, attitude, and general behavior of the assembly. Nevertheless, despite evident flaws, the Duma still offered national representatives the opportunity to speak freely in a public forum so as to make the assembly a focus of attention in the empire, and acted as a bond for various political and national groups.

Stolypin's program, submitted to the Second Duma in March 1907, was certainly an ambitious endeavor to bring about wide reforms in almost every aspect of national life.[11] Stolypin was the driving force behind this undertaking, having initiated major reforms during the short interval between the first two Dumas--perhaps the busiest and the most crucial period of his career. In the Second Duma he showed himself at his best. Through his speeches and his skill in dealing with the Duma he was able to dispel much of the distrust of the Kadets. At first he was hopeful that the Duma would accept his program, since it was largely what the opposition had itself demanded earlier. The adamant rejection of his program made him aware that the Duma had no intention of collaborating; the radical deputies wished to overthrow the existing order no matter what was offered. His last hope lay with the Kadets; with their support he felt that not only the Second Duma but the very concept of constitutionalism itself could yet be saved. However, the Kadets wanted too much and Stolypin could not meet their price.

The first two Dumas were dissolved, but in different circumstances and for different reasons. In the case of the First, Stolypin, as Minister of the Interior, did not have to urge dissolution, for from the first week of its existence the Emperor and Goremykin saw no other alternative. As regards the Second Duma, Stolypin did not disguise the fact that he would seek a dissolution if the assembly proved unworkable. However, the manner in which the dissolution came about was perhaps a surprise even to him, for he had hoped for a reconciliation based on the decision of the Kadets to cooperate with the government. Despite these setbacks, even Stolypin's critics have admitted as a "point d'honneur" that he guided the country to the Third Duma when all possible pressure from the reactionary circles was applied on the monarch to resist such a move. Stolypin's action at this time provides the best evidence of his commitment to representative government and his determination to guide the Duma towards constitutionalism, if it proved itself a practical instrument. Despite mistakes on both sides during the first two Dumas, Stolypin saved the country from a critical political impasse by the adoption of the Act of 3 June 1907, and guided the Third Duma towards productive ends.[12] From that point on, Russia began to recover from the preceding chaos; the Third Duma produced results and gained increasing recognition both inside the country and without.[13]

Together with his efforts to establish a viable representative body, Stolypin's main achievement was the adoption of the agrarian laws. His insight into the problem was illustrated by his shrewd remark, "Razreshit etogo voprosa nelzia, ego nado razreshat!" (To solve this problem is an impossibility, we must begin to solve it!). By the time the Third Duma convened, Stolypin was more strongly convinced than ever that the salvation of Russia depended upon the well-being of the peasant. His agrarian program was designed to help reduce the poverty and misery under which the majority of the peasants suffered and to enable them to improve their conditions by their own efforts. His aim was to establish a free and prosperous peasantry, occupying individual farms and supporting on its shoulders the rich industrial potential of the country. He proposed to modernize agriculture by fostering the small independent proprietors, who, through initiative and drive, could lift the economic level of the countryside to that of the European countries, thus giving the towns and industry the impetus for expansion and development they needed in order to absorb the growing urban population. Such a policy snatched the initiative from the hands of the revolutionary parties, who claimed to defend the interests of the peasants.

Though some, like Gurko, have sought to devalue the originality of Stolypin's ideas on the agrarian question, originality is not the important point. For that matter, one could argue convincingly that the idea of breaking down the communal structure was not even Witte's, but Bunge's, who pushed the idea a couple of decades earlier and who was then sharply attacked by Witte. Long before Stolypin became a public figure, and under the influence of his uncle's agrarian ideas, he began to form the intellectual development of his approach to the agrarian question. It was Stolypin who was prepared to take action and to shape general notions into a specific policy which the government could implement. The most notable feature of Stolypin's administration was his endeavor to raise the standard of living of the peasants, so that they could be brought into the mainstream of national life, exercising the same rights and opportunities as others. His program was on a scale which had never previously been witnessed elsewhere, and after only a few years' trial foreign observers considered that the effect might well be such as to transform Russia within a few decades.

Tranquility and normalcy did not return, as his opponents contended, by police action and suppression alone, but by his meeting the wishes of the mass of the peasantry with action instead of words.[14] Stolypin did not in any case have an army large enough to suppress over a hundred million peasants. It was not through coercion that peasant disturbances largely died down by the end of 1907. It seems reasonable to suggest that the peasantry--never a radical body--turned their attention away from revolutionary slogans and agitation until they could see whether or not Stolypin would be able to implement his promise of economic emancipation.

The Finnish and the western zemstvo issues, relics of the pre-1905 period, were still awaiting solution. Both were pushed to the fore by the rightists at a moment most unfavorable for Stolypin--apparently as part of a series of attempts by the reactionaries to impede his program, to embarrass him politically, or better still, to drive him from office. Once the Finnish question was brought into the open, however, the passing of the law of 14 June 1910 became a necessity. Although this issue, like that relating to the western zemstvo, concerned the government's policy towards minorities and therefore provoked nationalist feelings in the Duma and the State Council, Stolypin managed to pursue a solution without jeopardizing his political position, an outcome which served only to increase further the antagonism of the right wing.

The most significant element revealed in Stolypin's speeches at the time was his avoidance of crude nationalism--his language in the Council and Duma remained moderate in tone. He was earnest in his desire to protect imperial interests without further restricting those rights enjoyed by Finland, but he was by no means immune to nationalist feelings. At the same time he was too clear-sighted to use the law for curtailing Finnish autonomy or for purposes of Russification; such a policy would have created more antagonism. He felt nationalism was a less important issue than agriculture; the one was a slogan to rouse popular emotions, the other held the key to the whole of Russia's political future.

The nineteen points contained in Article Two of the Finnish law no doubt constitute an encroachment, or, more correctly, a limitation on Finnish legislative prerogatives. In terms of imperial interests, however, there could be little choice between allowing Finland almost as much freedom as before in fields where a fair degree of autonomy had been exercised, and preserving Russian discretionary rights, above all in defense and external relations. Stolypin felt, moreover, that the system of enumeration could not be objected to, for this had been recommended after the 1899 manifesto by the Finnish Senate itself. The law might have been a practical solution if the Finns had been willing to accept on its face value Article One, which stated that only legislation of a general nature would fall under the imperial jurisdiction and that local legislation would remain unaffected. The Finns, for their part, had certainly infringed on imperial prerogatives in the past, no doubt often rashly, in a number of matters of considerable importance. These instances included the adoption of the 1879 military statutes, the establishment of an independent Finnish army, the Criminal Code of 1899, the military laws passed by the Finnish Senate in 1896 without consulting the Ministry of War, a 1906 law concerning the use of Russian in government offices, the attempt by the Finnish Senate to introduce a law in 1907 establishing a new form of administration, the importation of arms into Finland, and, finally, the partiality shown to the Russian revolutionaries on Finnish soil. The accumulated burden of these events could not be ignored by the imperial government and finally brought the Finnish question to its climax.

Thus, in dealing with Finland Stolypin's action was governed by a host of important factors, including Russia's comparative weakness and the paramount importance of "state necessity and interest." Perhaps in a different day and age he might have opted for the complete independence of Finland. In 1908 such a policy would have been a disaster--a sudden loosening of a hitherto frozen sea--which would have swept Russia from her precarious position as a world power, with minorities and revolutionaries, soon aided from the outside, joining to destroy the empire. How much of this was seen by Stolypin himself cannot now be clearly proved. As for his Russian contemporaries, they seem to have both under- and over-estimated the speed at which the empire could proceed. On looking back, although modern sympathies may favor greater liberty for the Finns, it is hard to ignore the difficulties of his actual position and the danger inherent in whatever move he made.

The western zemstvo issue, though tied to the whole question of zemstvos in Russia, was of concern principally to the Polish landed interests in the western provinces and was bound up with the government's policy towards the Polish minority. The Poles had less substance for their arguments than the Finns, for Stolypin's legislation on the western zemstvos did not discriminate against the Poles as a nationality; if anything, it favored them. The bill discriminated against the economic interests of the Polish landlords and benefited the vast majority of the peasantry in the provinces. The introduction of the zemstvos there, and the broadening of zemstvo rights by the halving of property qualifications, increased indeed the apprehensions of the Russian landowners, who feared that similar action would follow in the central provinces of the empire.[15]

Stolypin's bill would have been passed easily by the Duma had it been reintroduced following the State Council's rejection; the decision in the State Council depended on the Emperor's will, and he would have supported the measure if the alternative had been Stolypin's resignation. Stolypin would then have triumphed, not only over his adversaries in Court circles, but also in the eyes of liberal opinion. As it was, neither the Duma nor public opinion reacted as strongly to the proroguing of the Duma and the dismissal of the members of the Council as they did to the passing of the bill under Article 87 during the artificially created interim period. Stolypin pinned his hopes on the degree of support for the measure in the Duma, which he expected would note approvingly that the law was adopted in the form that the Duma itself had approved the previous June.[16] He ignored the fact that his action would be interpreted as a bypassing of the constitution, which could be used against the Duma at a later date.[17] The explanation for his action is perhaps to be found in his reaction to the Monarch's behavior, for he believed that the Tsar had entered into a compromise with right wing elements. It was this fear which no doubt prompted the written promise, Stolypin's only way of limiting double-dealing on the part of the Emperor.[18] Such a request, however, must have been resented by the Tsar.[19]

In considering Stolypin's actions at this time it is necessary to recall the burden of government, the overwhelming amount of work he undertook in person, and the long hours which had begun to affect his health.[20] Even among social peers, he was increasingly conscious of isolation. He had created numerous enemies while attempting to clear the administration of corruption by means of senatorial investigating committees. Such investigations involving men in high places strengthened the resolve of ultra-reactionaries to intrigue against him. The Durnovo-Trepov plot was an open one and everyone knew that it was directed against Stolypin personally. This plot, however, was hatched by individuals, and Stolypin should have seen things in the right perspective--yet by now he was physically exhausted.[21] The episode revealed that, although Stolypin might fall, constitutionalism and parliamentary procedure were taking root.

After this last political crisis Stolypin's career declined, although the assassination which followed lifted him momentarily to an even higher pedestal than that on which he had stood before the tragedy--for he died an apparent political martyr. Although it would seem to fit the political scene of the time better to attribute the assassination to the revolutionary parties or the ultra-reactionaries, Stolypin was assassinated by a man who performed the deed out of a desire for self-expiation rather than from a sense of political necessity.[22]

In the final analysis Stolypin was, despite his inadequacies, a man of courage and scruple who understood the needs of his country and its people. The situation he inherited in 1906 was disastrous, but he rose to meet the challenge. He was the only member of the government during the reign of Nicholas who attempted to check the Tsar's absolutist tendencies, even though his efforts were not always successful. Under his leadership the Cabinet held the political initiative and carried through major social, economic, and political reforms--virtually the only Russian constitutional government of which this can be said. In the light of the power still held by the Monarch, the reluctance of the inexperienced members of the Duma to compromise the purity of their ideas, and the relative novelty of the constitutional system for most of the people, Stolypin's efforts and achievements are truly deserving of credit.

In addition, he was moved more by devotion to his country than by self-seeking, workaday political ambition. The program of reform upon which he embarked was a phenomenon which had not been seen in Russia since the days of Alexander II. It is also apparent that he acted in the interests neither of the landowners nor of the bureaucracy; if he had, the reactionaries would not have been so eager for a confrontation with him from 1907 on, an effort which succeeded in isolating him and making his political end inevitable.[23]

Such behavior on the part of the reactionaries was caused by his cooperation with the Duma in efforts to strengthen constitutional government, and by the creation of the commission of inquiry to eliminate corruption. This body exposed and at least in part reduced the peculation prevailing in the upper civil and military echelons, and it led to the arrest and prosecution of a number of civil and military officials. This is a tale that will be fully told only if and when the Soviet Union opens its archives without impediment to foreign scholars. Even without access to the documents, we can see clearly that this effort on Stolypin's part was a principal contributing factor to the vindictive reactionary enmity towards him.

His labors set in motion an epoch of worthy reforms. The results, while they lasted, were in themselves impressive. Yet, to attempt an evaluation of his epoch by tallying the laws passed by the Duma during his years in power would be simplistic. Future archival work will probably show to what extent his efforts affected almost every aspect of Russian life. Besides the adopted bills, others were shelved because of the strength of forces beyond his control. He must have known that many of these bills could not be enacted, but he pushed them nonetheless in order to show concern for the vital areas of national life. It was largely due to him that the Duma had by 1911 earned for itself a measure of respect and had passed an undeniably impressive list of legislation. Stolypin's powers of organization, his commitment to political integrity, his tenacity of purpose, and his industry made themselves felt throughout his administration. He saw clearly enough the extent of the changes that would be required, and he sought strenuously to provide the required bases for a transformed society--he acted, in his words, with the aim to build "a great Russia."

NOTES

1. Baron Meyendorff. That is what Stolypin told Baron Meyendorff, implying that the Emperor

could not be depended on.

2. Davidovich, A., Samoderzhavie v Epokhu Imperializma (Moscow, 1975), p.302.

3. Testifying after the fall of the monarchy, Guchkov observed that the liberals considered Stolypin a reactionary, whereas in the ultra-reactionary circles of the day he was regarded as the most dangerous revolutionary. That was why, as he notes, the reactionaries spent much of their energies, not in fighting the radical movements, but in seeking to overthrow Stolypin. Padenie, Vol. V, p.253.

4. P.R.O., F.O. 371, Vol. 127, No. 27,544, 13 August 1906.

5. Stolypin told Sir Arthur Nicolson that his "own ideal was the British Constitution," but that it was impossible to cast Russia at once into that mould. In some years she might possibly reach that goal, but sudden and impetuous changes would work ruin. P.R.O., F.O. 371, Vol. 126, No. 23,110, 2 July 1906.

6. Bestuzhev, I., Borba v Rossii po Voprosam Vneshnei Politiki 1906-1910 (Moscow, 1961), pp.78 and 119.

7. In a letter written on 12 September 1906, Sir Donald MacKenzie Wallace referred to the Kadets as a group of "learned professors and unpractical doctrinaries" who were naive enough to think that as soon as they would come to power, revolutionary activity would cease. The revolutionaries, for their part, were determined to seize control and were totally irreconciled to the "aims of Parliamentarians in general and the Kadets in particular." Wallace Correspondence.

8. Kryzhanovskii testified years after the events that the basis of Stolypin's policy was to raise both the intellectual and economic level of the masses. See Padenie, Vol. V, p.391; and P.R.O.,

F.O. 371, Vol. 126, No. 23,110, 2 July 1906.

9. Izwolsky, A., *Au Service de la Russia* (Paris, 1937), Vol. II, p.304. The letter is dated 28 July 1911.

10. *P.R.O.*, F.O. 371, Vol. 1219, No. 46,360, 17 November 1911.

11. Leontovitsch describes Stolypin's program speech as one of the most decisive liberal advances in Russian history. Leontovitsch, V., *Geschichte des Liberalismus in Russland* (Frankfurt, 1959), p.400.

12. The Electoral Law of 3 June 1907 was of course not democratic in the Western sense of the word, but it at least ensured that the liberal aspects of the government's program would be carried out. Nevertheless, the Third Duma was far from having been in "Stolypin's pocket." Nor is there convincing evidence to substantiate the charge that it was the new electoral law that brought the conservative landlords into the Third Duma. The peasants still remained the majority of the electorate, and there is reason to suspect that the peasants veered towards the center when they voted for the Third Duma.

13. By 1909 the Duma began to assert its importance and was gaining recognition as an essential part of the machinery of government. *P.R.O.*, F.O. 371, Vol. 727, No. 6047, 15 February 1909.

14. After the western zemstvo affair Sir Bernard Pares wrote a brief report entitled "Politics and Parties in Russia" in which he noted that the agrarian reform was proceeding very rapidly with "the healthy cooperation of the best of the peasantry;" it was "killing theoretic revolution and establishing a new race of sturdy and independent farmers." School of Slavonic and East European Studies Library, University of London. *Papers of Sir Bernard Pares*, pp.1 and 7.

15. For a more detailed account of the gentry's concern over the introduction of western zemstvos, see Korros, A., "The Landed Nobility, the State Council, and P.A. Stolypin," in Haimson, L., ed., The Politics of Rural Russia, 1905-1914 (Indiana University Press, 1979). See also Chmielewski, E., The Polish Question in the Russian State Duma (University of Tennessee Press, 1970), p.99.

16. So certain was Stolypin of the Duma's support that he did not even find it necessary to tell the leaders of his supporting parties of his final decision, which might have been the culminating reason for Guchkov's resignation. Kliachko, L., Povesti Proshlogo (Leningrad, 1920), p.36.

17. Maklakov, V., op. cit., p.114. As regards this issue Pares felt at the time that this artificial prorogation was worse than a coup d'etat because it set a precedent which could be dangerous to the new constitutional order. Such action might "mean in the end no Houses at all." Pares, B., op. cit., p.4.

18. The misunderstanding between Stolypin and the Tsar may have been further complicated in that the former was under the impression that the Tsar had not even considered his request to exert his influence in the first place. When, in addition, he heard that the Emperor had had talks with Trepov, of which Stolypin was not informed, Stolypin, in all probability assumed that the Tsar was scheming against him and compromising his position with the reactionaries. It may well be that the Emperor had placed Stolypin in a compromising position on previous occasions as well.

19. Kryzhanovskii, S., op. cit., p.213.

20. Dr. Zeitler, who performed Stolypin's autopsy, told Baron Meyendorff "on byl ne zhilets" (he

was not long for this world) and that Stolypin could not have lived much longer owing to the state of his liver and heart. See also the Tsar's letter to his mother on 4 March 1909, in which he comments on Stolypin's ill health due to trouble with his heart. "Iz Perepiski Nikolaia i Marii Romanovykh v 1907-1910 g.," *Krasnyi Arkhiv*, Vol. 50-51 (1932), p.187; Skripitsyn, V., *Bogatyr Mysli, Slova i Dela* (SPB, 1911), p.65; Kryzhanovskii, S., *op. cit.*, p.232; *Rech*, 8 September 1911 (No. 246), p.3.

21. Shidlovsky, S., *Vospominaniia* (Berlin, 1923), Vol. I, p.191.

22. For more detail see my article "Stolypin's Assassin," *Slavic Review*, Vol. XXIV, No. 2.

23. See Pronin, D., "Soprotivlenie Stolypinskoi Reforme Sprava (Zapisano so Slov Pokoinogo Ottsa)," *Russkaia Zhizn* (San Francisco), 10 March 1973, No. 7691. The author notes that his father boarded a train in Moscow on 4 February 1908 and found himself in a compartment with several members of the reactionary Union of the Russian People who were openly discussing the need of Stolypin's removal. Sir Donald MacKenzie Wallace noted in a letter to Knollys on 25 October 1906 that the "ultra-monarchical and violently reactionary parties likewise give him a good deal of trouble." He continued by saying that they would like to see the return of "pure autocracy" and insisted that Stolypin was "betraying the Emperor." *Wallace Correspondence*.

SELECTED BIBLIOGRAPHY

Documents

Columbia University. Archive of Russian and East European History and Culture. The following collections were consulted: Bok, B., Bok, M., Bark, P., Girs, A., Globachev, K., Prince Golitsyn, A., Gurliand, I., Liubimov, D., Melnikov, N., Mendeleev, P., Meyendorff, A., Shlippe, F., Zenkovskii, A.

Chernovskii, A., ed. Soiuz Russkogo Naroda. Po Meterialam Chrezvychainoi Sledstvennoi Komissii Vremennogo Pravitelstva 1917 g. Moscow, 1929.

Derenkovskii, G., ed. Vtoroi Period Revoliutsii: 1906-1907 gody. Chast Pervaia. Ianvar-Aprel 1906 goda. Kniga Pervaia. Moscow, 1957.

______. Vtoroi Period Revoliutsii: 1906-1907 gody. Chast Pervaia. Ianvar-Aprel 1906 goda. Kniga Vtoraia, Moscow, 1959.

______. Vtoroi Period Revoliutsii: 1906-1907 gody. Chast Vtoraia. Mai-Sentiabr 1906 goda. Kniga Pervaia. Moscow, 1961.

Dobrovolskii, A., ed. Svod Zakonov Rossiiskoi Imperii. 2nd Edit. SPB, 1913.

Finland. National Archive. The following collections were consulted: KKK (1908-1912), VSV (1909-1912), A. Guchkov, Baron A.F. Meyendorff, and Trudovik (S.R.).

Great Britain. Public Record Office. Foreign Office General Correspondence with the British Embassy in St. Petersburg, Russia. Series No. 65 and No. 371, 1905-1912.

Ioffe, M., ed. Vazhneishie Zakonodatelnye Akty: 1908-1912. SPB, 1913.

Izwolsky, A. Au Service de la Russie: Correspondence Diplomatique 1906-1911. Vol. II. Paris, 1937.

Kalinychev, P. Gosudarstvennaia Duma v Rossii v Dokumentakh i Materialakh. Moscow, 1957.

Krasnyi Arkhiv, 106 vols. Moscow, 1922-1941.

Lazarevskii, B. Zakonodatelnye Akty: 1904-1908 g. SPB, 1909.

Obninskii, V. Polgoda Russkoi Revoliutsii. Sbornik Materialov k Istorii Russkoi Revoliutsii (Oktiabr 1905-Aprel 1906 g.g.). Moscow, 1906.

Piatkovskii, A., ed. Vtoroi Period Revoliutsii: 1906-1907 gody. Chast II. Mai-Sentiabr 1906 goda. Kniga Tretia. Moscow, 1963.

Russia. Gosudarstvennaia Duma: Stenograficheskie Otchety. Sozyvy I, II, III. SPB, 1906-1912.

_____. Izdanie Tzentralnago Statisticheskago Komiteta M.V.D., Statisticheskii Ezhegodnik Rossii: 1911g. SPB, 1912.

_____. Izdanie Ministerstva Vnutrennikh Del, Vysochaishche Utverzhdennoe 3 Iunia 1907 g. Polozhenie o Vyborakh v Gosudarstvennuiu Dumu. SPB, 1907.

_____. Krestianskii Pozemelnyi Bank, Svedeniia o Deiatelnosti: Vypusk 13-20, 28. SPB, 1912-1915.

_____. Ministerstvo Zemledeliia, Denezhnyi Otchet po Prodazhe Kazennykh Zemel v Poriadke Vysochaishago Ukaza 27 Avgusta 1906 g. za 1915 god. Petrograd, 1916.

_____. Obzor Deiatelnosti Gosudarstvennoi Dumy Tretiago Sozyva. SPB, 1912.

______. Osobennaia Kantseliariia po Kreditnoi Chasti Ministerstva Finansov, Russkii Denezhnyi Rynok 1908-1912. SPB, 1913.

______. Osobye Zhurnaly Soveta Ministrov. SPB, 1907-1912.

______. Otdel Selskoi Ekonomii i Selskokhoziiaistvennoi Statistiki, Sbornik Statistiko-Ekonomicheskikh Svedenii po Selskomu Khoziaistvu Rossii i Inostrannykh Gosudarstv. Petrograd, 1915.

______. Padenie Tsarskogo Rezhima: Stenograficheskie Otchety. ed. P. Shchegolev. 7 vols. Leningrad, 1924.

______. Polnoe Sobranie Zakonov Rossiiskoi Imperii. Sobranie Tretie. 34 vols. SPB, 1885-1916.

______. Prilozheniia k Stenograficheskim Otchetam Gosudarstvennoi Dumy. SPB, 1907-1912.

______. Rossiiskaia Eksportnaia Palata: Otchet za 1912 god. SPB, 1913.

______. Sbornik Deistvuiushchikh Postanovlenii Izdannykh v Poriadke Stati 87-oi Osnovnykh Gosudarstvennykh Zakonov 1906-1911 g.g. SPB, 1913.

______. Stenograficheskii Otchet: Gosudarstvennyi Sovet. SPB, 1907-1912.

Simonov, M., ed. Vtoroi Period Revoliutsii 1906-1907 gody. Chast II. Mai-Sentiabr 1906 goda. Kniga Vtoraia. Moscow, 1962.

______. Vtoroi Period Revoliutsii 1906-1907 gody. Chast III. Oktiabr-Dekabr 1906 goda. Moscow, 1963.

The Bodeleian. V. Maklakov-B. Elkin Correspondence.

The Times, London. Printing House Square. *Correspondence between the Secretary of King Edward VII, Francis Knollys, and Sir Donald MacKenzie Wallace, the Times correspondent in Russia (1903-1909)*.

Tiatkovskii, A., ed. *Vtoroi Period Revoliutsii, 1906-1907 gody. Chast II. Mai-Sentiabr 1906 goda. Kniga Tretia*. Moscow, 1963.

Trusov, N., ed. *Revoliutsionnoe Dvizhenie v Rossii Vesnoi i Letom 1905 goda (Aprel-Sentiabr). Chast Pervaia*. Moscow, 1957.

_____. *Nachalo Pervoi Russkoi Revoliutsii: Janvar-Mart 1905 goda*. Moscow, 1955.

University of London. School of Slavonic and East European Studies Library. *Private notes and letters of Sir Bernard Pares*.

Viktorov, V., ed. *Soiuz Russkogo Naroda. Po Materialam Sledstvennoi Komissii Vremennogo Pravitelstva 1917 g*. Moscow, 1929.

Newspapers

Moskovskie Vedomosti, Moscow.
Novoe Vremia, St. Petersburg.
Oko, St. Petersburg.
Proletarii, Moscow.
Rech, St. Petersburg.
Russkoe Slovo, Moscow.
Svoboda, Warsaw.
The Times, London.
Za Narod, Paris.

Periodicals

Space limitations prohibit specific citation of articles on the Stolypin epoch used for this study. Most helpful have been the following serial publications:

Atlantic Monthly
Byloe (Leningrad)
Byloe (Paris)
Byloe (Petrograd)
California Slavic Studies
Istoricheskii Vestnik
Istoricheskie Zapiski
Krasnaia Letopis
Oxford Slavic Papers
Political Science Quarterly
Russkaia Mysl
Russkoe Bogatstvo
Slavic Review
The American Economic Review
The American Slavic and East European Review
The Journal of Modern History
The Russian Review
The Slavonic and East European Review
Vestnik Evropy
Volia Rossii
Voprosy Istorii
Vozrozhdenie (Paris)

Books

A.B. Za Kulisami Okhrannago Otdeleniia. Berlin, 1911.

Adamovich, G. V.A. Maklakov - Politik, Iurist, Chelovek. Paris, 1959.

Akselrod, P. and Martov, Iu. Pisma P.B. Akselroda i Iu.O. Martova - 1901-1916. vol. I. Berlin, 1924.

Aleksandrov, N. Sotsialdemokraticheskaia Fraktsiia v Tretei Gosudarstvennoi Dume. Paris, 1910.

Alexinsky, G. Modern Russia. London, 1913.

Alektorov, A. Inorodtsy v Rossii. SPB, 1906.

Antsiferov, A. A. Bilimovich, M. Batshev, and D. Ivantsov. Russian Agriculture During the War. New Haven, 1930.

Arkhangelskii, P. Ocherki Po Istorii Zemelnogo Stroia Rossii. Kazan, 1920.

Atsarkin, A. Stolypinskaia Reaktsiia. Borba V.I. Lenina za Teoreticheskie Osnovy Marksistskoi Partii. Moscow, 1956.

Avrekh, A. Tsarizm i Treteiunskaia Sistema. Moscow, 1966.

_____. Stolypin i Tretiia Duma. Moscow, 1968.

Babov, A. Vozroditsiia Rossiia. Constantinople, 1924.

Balakshin, A. Otchet Ministerstva Zemledeliia i Gosudarstvennykh Imushchestv, SPB, 1908.

Barandov, G. Stolypinskaia Reaktsiia, Moscow, 1938.

Baturinskii, D. Agrarnaia Politika Tsarskogo Pravitelstva i Krestianskii Pozemelnyi Bank, Moscow, 1925.

Bazylow, L. Ostatnie Lata Rosji Carskiej: Rzady Stolypina. Warsaw, 1972.

_____. Polityka Wewnetrzna Caratu i Ruchy Spoleczne v Rosji na Poczatku XX Wieku. Warsaw, 1966.

Bebutov, Prince. Poslednii Samoderzhets. Berlin, 1912.

Beletskii, S. Grigorii Rasputin. Petrograd, 1923.

Belokonskii, I. Samoupravlenie i Zemstvo. Rostov, 1905.

_____. Ot Derevni Do Parlamenta. Berlin, n.d.

_____. Zemskoe Dvizhenie. 2nd Edit. Moscow, 1914.

_____. Zemstvo i Konstitutsiia. Moscow, 1910.

Berendts, R. The Rights of Finland. SPB, 1910.

Bestuzhev, I. Borba v Rossii po Voprosam Vneshnei Politiki 1906-1910. Moscow, 1961.

Betskii, K. and Pavlov, P. Russkii Rokambol. Leningrad, 1925.

Bilimovich, A. Zemleustroitelnaia Zadacha i Zemleustroitelnoe Zakonodatelstvo Rossii. Kiev, 1907.

Bing, E., ed. The Letters of Tsar Nicholas and Empress Marie. London, 1937.

Bobrov, V. 62 Rechi Ministrov vo Vtoroi Gosudarstvennoi Dume. Moskva, 1908.

Bogdanovich, A. Tri Poslednikh Samoderzhtsa, Moscow, 1924.

Bogrov, A. Dmitrii Bogrov i Ubiistvo Stolypina. Berlin, 1931.

Bok, M. Vospominaniia o Moem Otse P.A. Stolypine, New York, 1953.

Bolshakov, A. and Rozhkov, N. Istoriia Khoziaistva Rossii v Materialakh i Dokumentakh. 3rd Edit. Moscow, 1926.

Borodin, N. _Gosudarstvennaia Duma v Tsifrakh._ SPB, 1906.

Borodkin, M. _Iz Noveishei Istorii Finliandii._ SPB, 1905.

_____. _Finland--Its Place in the Russian State._ SPB, 1911.

Broidko, E. _Memoirs of a Revolutionary._ London, 1967.

Brutskus, B. _Agrarnye Voprosy v Rossii._ Petrograd, 1917.

_____. _Obobshchestvlenie Zemli i Agrarnaia Reforma._ Moscow, 1917.

_____. _Agrarnyi Vopros i Agrarnaia Politika._ SPB, 1922.

Brianchaninov, A. _Mezhdodume._ SPB, 1907.

_____. _Pochemu Narod ne Verit Kadetam._ Moscow, 1917.

_____. _Rospusk Gosudarstvennoi Dumy._ Pskov, 1906.

Buchanan, Sir George. _My Mission to Russia and other Diplomatic Memories._ 2 vols. London, 1923.

Burtsev, V. _Kalendar Russkoi Revoliutsii._ Petrograd, n.d.

_____. _Borba Za Svobodnuiu Rossiiu._ Berlin, 1923.

Butmi, G. _Konstitutsiia i Politicheskaia Svoboda._ SPB, 1906.

Chebyshev, N. _Blizkaia Dal. Vospominaniia._ Paris, 1933.

Chelintsev, A. _Sbornik Statisticheskikh Materialov._ Odessa, 1922.

_____. Selsko-Khoziaistvennaia Geografiia Rossii. Berlin, 1923.

Chermenskii, E. Burzhuaziia i Tsarizm v Pervoi Russkoi Revoliutsii. 2nd Edit. Moscow, 1970.

Chernov, V. K Voprosu o Vykupe Zemli. SPB, 1906.

_____. The Great Russian Revolution. New Haven, 1936.

_____. Pered Burei. New York, 1953.

Chernyshev, I. Lesitskii, A. and Maslov, P. Krestianskoe Pravo i Obshchina. SPB, 1907.

_____. Obshchina Posle 9 Noiabria 1906 g. Petrograd, 1917.

_____. Agrarno-Krestianskaia Politika Rossii za 150 Let. Petrograd, 1918.

Chertov, V. Finliandskii Razgrom. Essex England, 1900.

Chuprov, A. Po Povodu Ukaza 9 Noiabria 1906 g. Moscow, 1908.

_____. Krestianskii Vopros. Moscow, 1909.

_____. Melkoe Zemledelie i Ego Osnovnyia Nuzhdy. Berlin, 1921.

Churberg, W. The Situation of Finland. SPB, 1911.

Chmielewski, E. The Polish Question in the Russian State Duma. University of Tennessee Press, 1970.

Conroy, M. Peter Arkad'evich Stolypin: Practical Politics in Late Tsarist Russia. Colorado, 1976.

Curtiss, J. ed. Essays in Russian and Soviet History in Honor of Geroid T. Robinson.

New York, 1963.

Dan, F. Proiskhozhdenie Belshevizma. New York, 1946.

Davidovich, A. Samoderzhavie v Epokhu Imperializma. Klassovaia Sushchnost i Evoliutsiia Absoliutizma v Rossii, Moscow, 1975.

Denikin, A. Ocherki Russkoi Smuty. Paris, 1921.

Deutscher, I. The Prophet Armed. Oxford, 1954.

Diakin, V. Samoderzhavie, Burzhuaziia, i Dvorianstvo v 1907-1911 g.g. Leningrad, 1978.

Dietze, C. Stolypinsche Agrarreform und Feldgemeinschaft, Leipzig, 1920.

Dillon, E. The Eclipse of Russia. London, 1918.

Dobrodomova, L. Borba Bolshevikov v Gody Stolypinskoi Reaktsii Za Sokhranenie i Ukreplenie Nelegalnoi Revolutsionnoi Partii. Moscow, 1955.

Dolgorukov, P. and Shakhovskoi, D. Melkaia Zemskaia Edinitsa. SPB, 1902.

Dolgorukov, P. and Petrukevich, I. Agrarnyi Vopros. Moscow, 1905.

Dubrovskii, A. Stolypinskaia Reforma. Leningrad, 1925.

Dubrovskii, A. and Gravl, B. Agrarnoe Dvizhenie v 1905-1907 g.g. Moscow, 1925.

Duff, J. ed. Russian Realities and Problems. Cambridge, 1917.

Durante, K. Sergei Yulevich Witte, Kak Glavnyi Vinovnik Narusheniia Vysochaishago Poveleniia ot 4-go Marta 1891 g., Sovmestnago Uchastiia v Dele Ogrableniia Krymskago Pomeshchika K.A. Durante i Khishcheniia Kazennoi Zemli. Odessa, 1908.

E.V. (E. Verpakhovskaia), Gosudarstvennaia Deiatelnost Predsedatelia Soveta Ministrov Stats-Sekretaria Petra Arkadievicha Stolypina, 3 vols. SPB, 1909-1911.

Edelman, R. Gentry Politics on the Eve of the Russian Revolution. The Nationalist Party, 1907-1919. Rutgers University Press, 1980.

Efremov, P. Stolypinskaia Agrarnaia Politika. Moscow, 1941.

Efremov, R. Vneshniaia Politika Rossii: 1907-14 g.g. Moscow, 1961.

Egiezarova, N. Agrarnyi Krizis Kontsa XIX veka v Rossii. Moscow, 1959.

Elpatevskii, S. Pravitelstvo i Duma. SPB, 1906.

Ermolov, A. Nash Zemelnyi Vopros. SPB, 1906.

_____. Slovo o Zemle. SPB, n.d.

Evreinov, G. Natsionalnye Voprosy Na Inorodcheskikh Okrainakh Rossii. SPB, 1908.

Ezerskii, N. Gosudarstvennaia Duma Pervago Sozyva. Penza, 1907.

Feodoroff, E. The Finnish Revolution in Preparation 1889-1905. SPB, 1911.

Ferguson, A. and Levin, A., eds. Essays in Russian History. A Collection Dedicated to George Vernadsky. Connecticut, 1964.

Finland. The Finnish Question in 1911. London, 1911.

_____. Finland and Russia. London, 1911.

_____. Finliandskaia Okraina v Sostave Russkago Gosudarstva. SPB, 1906.

Finn-Enotaevskii, A. Sovremennoe Khoziaistvo Rossii: 1890-1910. SPB, 1911.

Firsov, D. and Yakobei, M. K Peresmotru Agrarnoi Programmy i Eia Obosnovaniia. Moscow, 1908.

Fischer, G. Russian Liberalism. Harvard University Press, 1958.

Footman, D. The Russian Revolutions. London, 1962.

Futrell, M. Northern Underground, Episodes of Russian Revolutionary Transport and Communications through Scandinavia and Finland 1863-1917. London, 1963.

Gerassimov, A. Tsarisme et Terrorisme. Paris, 1934.

Gernet, M. Istoriia Tsarskoi Tiurmy. 5 vols. Moscow, 1960-1963.

Gertsenshtein, M. Natsionalizatsiia Zemli, Krestianskii Bank i Vykupnaia Operatsiia. SPB, 1906.

Gessen, S., ed. Arkhiv Russkoi Revolutsii. 22 vols. Berlin, 1922-1939.

_____. Okrainnye Gosudarstva. Berlin, 1926.

Glavnoe Upravlenie Zemleustroistva i Zemledeliia, Obsledovanie Zemleustroennykh Khoziastv, Proizvedennoe v 1913 godu v 12 Uezdakh Evropeiskoi Rossii. Petrograd, 1915.

Glavnyi Zemelnyi Komitet, Trudy Komissii Po Podgotovke Zemelnoi Reformy. Petrograd, 1917.

Goldstein, J. Russia: Her Economic Past and Future. New York, 1919.

Golovanov, V. Zemelnyi Vopros vo Vtoroi Gosudarstvennoi Dume. SPB, 1907.

Golubev, V. Po Zemskim Voprosam 1901-1911. SPB, 1913.

Goodhart, A. Poland and the Minority Races. London, 1920.

Goremykin, M. Agrarnyi Vopros. SPB, 1907.

Gorky, M., Andreyev, L., and Sologub, F. The Shield. New York, 1917.

Grand Duke Alexander. Once a Grand Duke. London, 1932.

Greenberg, L. The Jews in Russia. New Haven, 1945.

Grii, S. Kadety Vo Vtoroi Dume. SPB, 1907.

Guerrier, V. Vtoroe Raskreposhchenie. Moscow, 1911.

_____. Pervaia Russkaia Gosudarstvennaia Duma. Moscow, 1906.

_____. Vtoraia Gosudarstvennaia Duma. Moscow, 1907.

Guerrier, V. Pervye Shagi Byvshei Gosudarstvennoi Dumy. Moscow, 1907.

Gurko, V. Features and Figures of the Past: Government and Opinion in the Reign of Nicholas II. Stanford University Press, 1939.

Gwynn, S., ed. The Letters and Friendships of Sir Cecil Spring Rice. A Record. 2 vols. New York, 1929.

Haimson, L., ed. The Politics of Rural Russia, 1905-1914. Indiana University Press, 1979.

Hare, R. _Portraits of Russian Personalities Between Reform and Revolution_. Oxford, 1959.

Harper, S. _The Russia I Believe In_. Chicago, 1945.

Harrison & Sons. _The Russo-Finnish Conflict_. London, 1910.

Hoetzsch, O. _Russland_. Berlin, 1913.

Hortz, F. _Die Agrarischen Fragen im Verhaltnis zum Sozialismus_. Wien, 1899.

Hosking, G. _The Russian Constitutional Experiment. Government and Duma 1907-1914_. Cambridge, 1973.

Iakushin, V. _Gosudarstvennaia Vlast i Proekty Gosudarstvennoi Reformy v Rossii_. SPB, 1906.

Iurskii, G. _Pravye v Tretei Gosudarstvennoi Dume_. Kharkov, 1912.

Iuzhanin, V. _Za Chto Razognali Gosudarstvennuiu Dumu_. SPB, 1906.

Ivanova, L. _Vserossiiskaia Politicheskaia Stachka v Oktiabre 1905 goda. Pervaia Chast._ Moscow, 1955.

Izdanie Amurskago Pereselencheskago Raiona, _Obzor Zemledelcheskoi Kolonizatsii Amurskoi Oblasti_. Blagoveshchensk, 1913.

Izdanie Pereselencheskago Upravleniia, _Aziatskaia Rossiia_. 3 vols. SPB, 1914.

Izdanie Golosa Sotsialdemokrata, _Ternii Bez Roz_. Geneva, 1908.

Izgoev, A. _Russkoe Obshchestvo i Revolutsiia_. Moscow, 1910.

_____. P.A. Stolypin: Ocherk Zhizni i Deiatelnosti. Moscow, 1912.

Jackson, J. Finland. New York, 1940.

Jussila, O. Suomen Perustuslait Venalaisten ja Suomalaisten Tulkintojen Mukaan 1800-1863. Helsinki, 1969.

Kablukov, N. Ob Usloviiakh Razvitiia Krestianskago Khoziaistva v Rossii. Moscow, 1908.

Kaledin, V. High Treason. Four Major Cases of the St. Petersburg Personal Court Branch. London, 1936.

Kaminka, A. and Nabokov, V. Vtoraia Gosudarstvennaia Duma. SPB, 1907.

Karpov, N. Agrarnaia Politika Stolypina. Leningrad, 1925.

_____. Krestianskoe Dvizhenie v Revolutsii 1905 goda v Dokumentakh. Leningrad, 1926.

Karpovich, M. Imperial Russia, 1801-1917. New York, 1932.

Kaufman, A. Agrarnyi Vopros v Rossii. Moscow, 1908.

_____. Pereselenie i Kolonizatsiia. SPB, 1905.

_____. Russkaia Obshchina v Protsesse Eia Zarozhdeniia i Rosta. Moscow, 1908.

_____. Agrarnyi Vopros v Rossii. 2 vols. Moscow, 1909.

_____. Sbornik Statei. Moscow, 1915.

Kennard, H. The Russian Year Book for 1911. London, 1911.

Kerensky, A. The Crucifixion of Liberty. London, 1934.

Khlebnikov, N. Gosudarstvennaia Duma. SPB, 1906.

Khromov, P. Ekonomicheskoe Razvitie Rossii v XIX - XX vekakh. Moscow, 1950.

Khrushchev, A. Andrei Ivanovich Shingarev. Moscow, 1918.

Kirby, D., trans. and ed. Finland and Russia 1808-1920. From Autonomy to Independence. A Selection of Documents. New York, 1976.

Kirilov, V. Bolsheviki vo Glave Massovykh Politicheskikh Stachek v Period Podema Revoliutsii 1905-7 g.g. Moscow, 1961.

Kizevetter, A. Na Rubezhe Dvukh Stoletii. Prague, 1929.

Kliucharev, S. Krestianskaia Nishcheta i Finansovo-Ekonomicheskaia Sistema S. Iu. Witte. Kiev, 1906

Klopov, A. V Chem Spasenie Derevenskoi Trudiashchesia Rossii. SPB, 1908.

Kliachko, L. Povesti Proshlogo. Leningrad, 1929.

Kofod, A. Borba s Chrespolositseiu v Rossii i Za Granitseiu. SPB, 1906

_____. Khutorskoe Razselenie. SPB, 1907.

_____. Russkoe Zemleustroistvo. 2nd Edit., SPB, 1914.

Kokovtsov, V. Iz Moego Proshlago. 2 vols. Paris, 1933.

Koni, A. Na Zhiznennom Puti. SPB, 1914.

Korewo, N. The Finnish Question. SPB, 1911.

Kovalevskii, P. Natsionalizm i Natsionalnoe Vospitanie v Rossii. SPB, 1912.

Kossovskii, V. Voprosy Natsionalnosti. Vilna, 1907.

Kostomarov, G. Moskovskii Sovet v 1905 godu. Moscow, 1955.

Kozyrev, I. Borba Bolshevikov za Armiiu i Flot v Period Revoliutsii 1905-1907 g.g. Moscow, 1955.

Kramarzh K. Russkii Krizis. Prague, 1925.

Krechetov, P. Petr Arkadievich Stolypin: Ego Zhizn i Deiatelnost. Riga, 1910.

Kretov, F., ed. Bolsheviki vo Glave Pervoi Russkoi Revoliutsii, 1905-7 g. Moscow, 1956.

Kriukov, N., ed. 1907 - Ezhegodnik Glavnago Upravleniya Zemleustroistva i Zemliadeliia. SPB, 1908.

Krivoshein, K. A. V. Krivoshein. Ego Znachenie v Istorii Rossii Nachala XX Veka. Paris, 1973.

Kryzhanovskii, S. Vospominaniia. Iz Bumag S.E. Kryzhanovskago, Posledniago Gosudarstvennago Sekretaria Rossiiskoi Imperii. Berlin, 1930.

Krzywicki, L. Agrarnyi Vopros. SPB, 1906.

Kulakovskii, P. Politika i Vopros Ob Avtonomii Polshi. SPB, 1906.

Kuplevaskii, N. Spravka o Mneniiakh 25-ti Russkikh Uchenykh, Spetsialistov Prava, Po Voprosu o Iuridicheskom Polozhenii Finliandii v Sostave Russkoi Imperii. SPB, 1910.

Kurlov, P. Gibel Imperatorskoi Rossii. Berlin, 1923.

_____. Konets Russkogo Tsarizma. Petrograd, 1923.

Kuzmin, S. Vtoraia Duma. SPB, 1907.

Lavrinovich, Yu. Itogi Rossiiskoi Konstitutsii. SPB, 1907.

Lazarevskii, N. Russkoe Gosudarstvennoe Pravo. Petrograd, 1917.

Levin, A. The Second Duma. Yale University Press, 1940.

_____. The Third Duma, Election and Profile. Archon Books, 1973.

Leontovitsch, V. Geschichte des Liberalismus in Russland. Frankfurt, 1959.

Liashchenko, P. Ocherki Agrarnoi Evoliutsii Rossii. SPB, 1908.

Lipskii, A. O Poriadke Izdaniia Kasaiushchikhsia Finliandii Zakonov Obshchegosudarstvennago Znacheniia. SPB, 1910.

Litvinov, I. Ekonomicheskie Posledstviia Stolypinskogo Agrarnogo Zakonodatelstva. Moscow, 1929.

Logachev, V. Sbornik Rechei Petra Arkadevicha Stolypina - Proiznesennykh v Zasedaniiakh Gosudarstvennago Soveta i Gosudarstvennoi Dumy, (1906-1911). SPB, 1911.

Lokot, T. Pervaia Duma. Moscow, 1906.

_____. Politicheskiia Partii i Gruppy v Gosudarstvennoi Dume. Moscow, 1907.

_____. Opravdanie Natsionalizma. Kiev, 1910.

Lopukhin, A. Otryvki Iz Vospominanii. Po Povodu Vospominanii Gr. S. Iu. Witte. Moscow, 1923.

Lositskii, A. Vykupnaia Operatsiia. SPB, 1906.

Lvovich, A. Partii i Krestianstvo v Gosudarstvennoi Dume. 1907.

Makeev, N. and O'Hara, V. Russia. New York, 1925.

Maklakov, V. and Pergament, O. Nakaz Gosudarstvennoi Dumy. SPB, 1907.

Maklakov, V. Pervaia Gosudarstvennaia Duma. Paris, 1939.

_____. Vtoraia Gosudarstvennaia Duma. Paris, 1944.

_____. Vlast i Obshchestvennost Na Zakate Staroi Rossii. 3 vols. Paris, 1936.

_____. Rechi Sudebnyia, Dumskiia i Publichnyia Lektsii 1904-1926. Paris, 1949.

_____. Iz Vospominanii. New York, 1954.

Martov, L., Maslov, P. and Petrosova, A. Obshchestvennoe Dvizhenie v Rossii v Nachale XX-go Veka. 4 vols. SPB, 1909-1914.

Maslov, P. Agrarnyi Vopros v Rossii. Vol. II. SPB, 1908.

_____. Teoriia Razvitiia Narodnago Khoziaistva. SPB, 1910.

_____. Krestianskie Dvizheniia v Rossii v Epokhu Pervoi Revoliutsii. Moscow, 1924.

Maslov, P., et. al. Vopros Momenta. Sbornik Statei. Moscow, 1906.

Mazour, A. Finland Between East and West. New York, 1956.

Mekhelin, L. K Voprosu o Blizhaishem Opredelenii Pravovykh Otnoshenii Mezhdu Rossieiu i

Finliandieiu. Helsingfors, 1909.

_____. Raznoglasiia Po Russko-Finliandskim Voprosam. SPB, 1908.

_____. K Voprosu o Blizhaishem Opredelenii Pravovykh Otnoshenii Mezhdu Rossieiu i Finliandieiu. Helsinki, 1909.

Melnik, I. Sibir. SPB, 1908.

Menshchikov, L. Otkrytoe Pismo P.A. Stolypinu Russkomu Premier-Ministru. Paris, 1911.

Migulin, P. Vozrozhdenie Rossii. Kharkov, 1910.

_____. Ekonomicheskii Rost Russkago Gosudarstva Za 300 Let (1613-1912). Moscow, 1913.

Miliukov, P., et. al. M. M. Vinaver i Russkaia Obshchestvennost Nachala XX Veka. Paris, 1937.

Miliukov, P. God Borby. SPB, 1907.

_____. Kak Proshli Vybora vo 2-iu Gosudarstvennuiu Dumu. SPB, 1907.

_____. Vtoraia Duma. SPB, 1908.

_____. Tri Popytki. Paris, 1921.

_____. Natsionalnyi Vopros. Prague, 1925.

_____. Rossiia Na Perelome. Paris, 1927.

_____. Vospominaniia. 2 vols. New York, 1955.

Miliutin, V. Sotsialism i Selskoe Khoziaistvo. Moscow, 1919.

Miller, M. The Economic Development of Russia 1905-1914. London, 1926.

Milonov, Iu. Moskovskoe Professionalnoe

Dvizhenie v Gody Pervoi Revoliutsii. Moscow, 1926.

Mintslov, S. *Peterburg v 1903-1910 Godakh*. Riga, 1931.

Mirnyi, S. *Adresy Zemstv 1894-1895 i Ikh Politicheskaia Programma*. Geneva, 1896.

Mogilianskii, M. *Pervaia Gosudarstvennaia Duma*. SPB, 1907.

Mosolov, A. *At the Court of the Last Tsar*. London, 1935.

Muromtsev, S. *Delo o Vyborskom Vozzvanii. Stenograficheskii Otchet*. SPB, 1908.

Mushin, A. *Dmitrii Bogrov i Ubiistvo Stolypina*. Paris, 1914.

Myhrman, A. *The Swedish Nationality Movement in Finland*. Chicago, 1939.

Mysli o Sovremennom Polozhenii Finliandii. London, 1900.

Naumov, A. *Iz Utselevshikh Vospominanii 1868-1917*, 2 vols. New York, 1954.

Nazanskii, V. *Krushenie Velikoi Rossii i Doma Romanovykh*. Paris, 1930.

Nicholas II. *Dnevnik Imperatora Nicholaia II*. Berlin, 1923.

Nicolson, H. *Lord Carnock*. London, 1930.

Nikitin, K. and Smirnov, L. *Deiatelnost Vtoroi Gosudarstvennoi Dumy*. Moscow, 1907.

Nisselovich, L. *K. Voprosu o Taktike Kadetskoi Fraktsii v Gosudarstvennoi Dume*. SPB, 1906.

Nolde, B. Dalekoe i Blizkoe. Istoricheskie Ocherki. Paris, 1930.

Nosov, N., ed. Problemy Krestianskogo Zemlevladeniia i Vnutrennei Politiki Rossii. Dooktiabrskii Period. Leningrad, 1972.

Obninskii, V. Novyi Stroi. Moscow, 1909.

Obolenskii, S. One Man in His Time. New York, 1958.

Obshchii Gerbovnik Dvorianskikh Rodov Vserossiiskoi Imperii. SPB, 1836.

Obzor Deiatelnosti Ministerstva Zemledeliia i Gosudarstvennykh Imushchestv Za Sedmoi God Ego Suschestvovaniia. SPB, 1901.

Oganovskii, N. Zemelnyi Perevarot v Rossii. Ego Prichiny i Sledstviia. SPB, 1907.

_____. Zakonomernost Agrarnoi Evolutsii. Saratov, 1911.

_____. Individualizatsiia Zemlevladeniia v Rossii i Eia Posledstviia. Moscow, 1917.

_____. Revolutsiia Naoborot. Petrograd, 1917.

_____. Zemelnyi Vopros i Zemelnaia Politika. Odessa, 1917.

_____. Otkuda Poshla Krestianskaia Zemelnaia Nuzhda, 2nd Edit. Moscow, 1917.

_____. Agrarnaia Evolutsiia v Rossii Posle 1905 g. Moscow, 1918.

Oldenburg, S. Tsarstvovanie Imperatora Nikolaia II. 2 vols. Belgrade/Munich, 1939.

Owen, L. The Russian Peasant Movement 1906-1917, London, 1937.

Oznobishin, A. Vospominaniia Chlena IV-i Gosudarstvennoi Dumy. Paris, 1927.

Pakharnaev, A. Mezhdudumskiia Rasporiazheniia Pravitelstva v 1906 godu. SPB, 1907

Pares, B. Russia and Reform. London, 1907.

_____. My Russian Memoirs. London, 1931.

_____. The Fall of the Russian Monarchy. London, 1939.

_____. A Wondering Student. Syracuse University Press, 1948.

Paskhalov, K. O Merakh k Prekrashcheniiu Bezporiadkov i Uluchsheniiu Gosudarstvennago Stroia. Moscow, 1905.

Pavlov, M. Dumskaia Taktika Bolshevikov v Revolutsiiu 1905-1907 g.g. Leningrad, 1947.

Pavlov, N. Ego Velichestvo Gosudar Nikolai II. Paris, 1927.

Pavlovsky, G. Agricultural Russia on the Eve of the Revolution. London, 1930.

Pazhitnov, K. Gorodskoe i Zemskoe Samoupravlenie. SPB, 1913.

Pershin, P. Uchastkovoe Zemlepolzovanie v Rossii. Moscow, 1922.

_____. Zemelnoe Ustroistvo Dorevoliutsionnoi Derevni. Moscow, 1928.

Peshekhonov, A. Agrarnaia Problema. SPB, 1906.

_____. Sushchnost Agrarnoi Problemy. SPB, 1906

Petergofskoe Soveshchanie o Proekte Gosudarstvennoi Dumy. Berlin, n.d.

Pinchuk, B. The Octobrists in the Third Duma, 1907-1912. Seattle, 1974.

Podolinsky, S. Russland vor der Revolution. Die Agrarsoziale Lage und Reformen. Berlin, 1971.

Pogromy v Rossii. Berlin, 1908.

Pokhlebnik, V. SSSR-Finliandiia. 260 Let Otnoshenii 1713-1973. Moscow, 1975.

Polezhaev, P. Za Shest Let 1906-1912. SPB, 1912.

Polivanov, A. Iz Dnevnikov i Vospominanii Po Dolzhnosti Voennogo Ministra i Ego Pomoshchnika 1907-1916. Moscow, 1924.

Polner, T., Obolensky, V., and Turin, S. Russian Local Government During the War and the Union of Zemstvos. Yale University Press, 1930.

Polnyi Sbornik Vsekh Russkikh Politicheskikh Partii. SPB, 1906.

Popov, I. Duma Narodnykh Nadezhd. Moscow, 1907.

Preobrazhenskii, E., ed. Russkie Finansy i Evropeiskaia Birzha v 1904-1906 g.g. Moscow, 1926.

Preyer, W. Die Russische Agrarreform. Jena, 1914.

Prokopovich, S. Agrarnyi Vopros i Agrarnoe Dvizhenie. Rostov, 1905.

_____. Kooperativnoe Dvizhenie v Rossii Ego Teoriia i Praktika. Moscow, 1913.

_____. Krestianskoe Khoziaistvo. Berlin, 1924.

Protopopov, D. Chto Sdelala Pervaia Gosudarstvennaia Duma. Moscow, 1906.

Puntila, L. The Political History of Finland 1809-1966. Helsinki, 1975.

Purishkevich, V. Dnevnik. Riga. 1924.

Pushkarev, S. Rossiia v XIX veke, (1801-1914). New York, 1956.

Radkey, O. The Agrarian Foes of Bolshevism. New York, 1958.

Raeff, M. Michael Speransky. Statesman of Imperial Russia 1772-1839. Hague, 1957.

Rashin, A. Naselenie Rossii za 100 let (1811-1913 g.g.). Moscow, 1956.

Reade, A. Finland and the Finns. New York, 1917.

Rein, G. Iz Perezhitago 1907-1918. 2 vols. Berlin, 1935.

_____. Ubiistvo Stolypina. Nice, 1933.

Renwick, G. Finland To-Day. London, 1911.

Rittich, A. Zavisimost Krestian Ot Obshchiny i Mira. SPB, 1903.

_____. Krestianskii Pravoporiadok. SPB, 1904.

Robinson, G. Rural Russia Under the Old Regime. New York, 1949.

Rodzianko, M. The Reign of Rasputin. London, 1927.

Rozanov, V. Pisma A.S. Suvorina k V.V. Rozanovu. SPB, 1913.

Rozental, E. Diplomaticheskaia Istoriia Russko-Frantsuzkogo Soiuza v Nachale XX veka. Moscow, 1960.

Russkii Russkim: Chto Znachit Polskaia Avtonomiia. SPB, 1907.

Rutenberg, P. Ubiitsvo Gapona. Leningrad, 1925.

Sack, A. The Birth of the Russian Democracy. New York, 1918.

Savinkov, B. Memoirs of a Terrorist. New York, 1931.

Savinkov, B., Ulianitskii, V. and Filosofov, G. Stati Po Natsionalnomu Voprosu. Warsaw, 1921.

Savich, G. Novyi Gosudarstvennyi Stroi Rossii. SPB, 1907.

Sazonov, G. Obzor Deiatelnosti Zemstv Po Narodnomu Prodovolstviiu 1865-1892. SPB, 1893.

Sazonov, S. Vospominaniia. Paris, 1927.

Sbornik Statei: Intelligentsiia v Rossii. SPB, 1910.

Schelking, E. Recollections of a Russian Diplomat. The Suicide of Monarchies (William II and Nicholas II). New York, 1918.

Schybergson, M. Politische Geschichte Finnlands 1809-1919. Gotha, 1925.

Seeger, C., trans. The Memoirs of Alexander Iswolsky, by A. Iswolsky. London, 1920.

Semennikov, V., ed. Revoliutsiia 1905 g.i Samoderzhavie. Moscow, 1928.

Sementkovskii, R. Sovremennaia Rossiia: Nash Parlament. SPB, 1912.

Sergeenko, P. Pisma L.N. Tolstogo 1848-1910. Moscow, 1910.

Sergeevskii, N. K Voprosu o Finliandskoi Avtonomii i Osnovnykh Zakonakh. SPB, 1902.

_____. Zaprosy Po Finliandskomu Upravleniiu v Gosudarstvennoi Dume 1908 goda. SPB, 1908.

Shakhovskoi, D. S.A. Muromtsev. Moscow, 1911.

Shakhovskoi, L. Partiia Bolshevikov v Pervoi Russkoi Revoliutsii: 1905-1907 g.g. Moscow, 1959.

Shanin, T. The Awkward Class. Political Sociology of Peasantry in a Developing Society: Russia 1910-1925. Oxford University Press, 1972.

Shearman, H. Finland: The Adventures of a Small Power. London, 1950.

Shcheglo, V. O Podderzhke Levykh. SPB, 1906.

Shchegolev, S. Ukrainskoe Dvizhenie Kak Sovremennyi Etap Iuzhnorusskago Separatizma. Kiev, 1912.

Shelukhin, S. Ukraine, Poland and Russia and the Right of the Free Disposition of the Peoples. Washington, 1919.

Shestakov, A. Krestianskaia Revoliutsiia 1905-1907 g.g. v Rossii. Moscow, 1926.

Shidlovsky, S. Vospominaniia. 2 vols. Berlin, 1923.

Shingarev, A. Vymiraiushchaia Derevnia. SPB, 1907.

Shipov, D. Vospominaniia i Dumy o Perezhitom. Moscow, 1918.

Shotwell, J. and Deak, F. Turkey at the Straits. New York, 1940.

Shtein, V., ed. Mestnyi Agronomicheskii Personal Sostoiavshii Na Pravitelstvennoi i Obshchestvennoi Sluzhbe 1 Ianvaria 1915 g. Petrograd, 1915.

Shulgin, V. Dni. Belgrade, 1925.

Sidelnikov, S. Obrazovanie i Deiatelnost Pervoi Gosudarstvennoi Dumy. Moscow, 1962.

Sidorov, A. Polskaia Avtonomiia i Slavianskaia Ideia. Kiev, 1908.

Simanovich, A. Rasputin i Evrei. Riga, 1928.

Simmons, E. Continuity and Change in Russian and Soviet Thought. Massachusetts, 1955.

Skripitsyn, V. Bogatyr Mysli, Slova i Dela. SPB, 1911.

Skvortsov, I. K Zemelnoi Reforme Novoi Rossii. 2 vols. 1955-1956.

Sliozberg, G. Dorevoliutsionnyi Stroi Rossii. Paris, 1933.

Smirnov, A. Kak Proshli Vybory vo 2-iu Gosudarstvennuiu Dumu. SPB, 1907.

_____. Pobeda Kadetov i Levyia Partii. Moscow, 1907.

Smirnov, A., ed. P.N. Miliukov: Sbornik Materialov po Chestvovaniiu ego Semedesiatiletiia 1859-1929. Paris, 1929.

Smith, J. Finland and the Russian Revolution 1917-1922, University of Georgia Press, 1958.

Snodgrass, J. Russia. A Handbook on Commercial and Industrial Conditions. Washington, D.C., 1913.

Soiuz Russkikh Evreev. Kniga o Ruskom Evreistve ot 1860-kh godov do Revolutsii 1917 g. Sbornik Statei. New York, 1960.

Sokovnin, P. Kulturnyi Uroven Krestianskago Polevodstva Na Nadelnoi Zemle i Ego Znanie v Agrarnom Voprose. SPB, 1906.

Soloviev, V. Natsionalnyi Vopros v Rossii. SPB, 1891.

Soloviev, Iu. Dvadtsat Piat Let Moei Diplomaticheskoi Sluzhby 1893-1918. Moscow, 1928.

_____. Vospominaniia Diplomata 1893-1922. Moscow, 1959.

Souvoroff, P. The Finnish Question. SPB, 1910.

Spiridovich, A. Istoriia Bolshevizma v Rossii. Paris, 1922.

_____. Zapiski Zhandarma. 1928.

_____. Les Dernieres Annees de la Cour de Tsarskoie-Selo. Paris, 1929.

Stenback, M. Finland: The Country, Its People and Institutions. Helsinki, 1926.

Stolypin, A. P.A. Stolypin 1862-1911. Paris, 1927.

Stolypin, D. Ocherki Filosofii i Nauki, Nash Zemledelcheskii Krizis. Moscow, 1891.

_____. Ob Organizatsii Nashego Selskago Byta. Moscow, 1892.

_____. Essais de Philosophie des Sciences. Geneva, 1888.

Stolypin, P. and Krivoshein, A. Poezdka v Sibir i Povolzhe. SPB, 1911.

Struve, P. Patriotica. SPB, n.d.

Sturzo, L. Nationalism and Internationalism. New York, 1946.

Sukhomlinov, V. Vospominaniia. Berlin, 1924.

Suvorin, A. Dnevnik, Moscow, 1923.

Sviatlovskii, V. Mobilizatsiia Zemelnoi Sobstvennosti v Rossii. SPB, 1911.

_____. K Voprosu o Sudbakh Zemlevladeniia v Rossii. SPB, 1907.

Sytin, I. Pervye Shagi Gosudarstvennoi Dumy. Moscow, 1907.

Szeftel, M. The Russian Constitution of April 23, 1906. Political Institutions of the Duma Monarchy. Brussels, 1976.

Taube, M. La Politique D'Avant Guerre et la Fin de l'Empire des Tsars. Paris, 1928.

Teitel, Ia. Iz Moei Zhizni za Sorok Let. Paris, 1925.

Thadden, R., ed. Das Verangene und die Geschichte. Festschrift fur Reinhard Wittram. Goettingen, 1973.

Tikhomirov, L. K Reforme Obnovlennoi Rossii. Moscow, 1912.

Tikhonova, T. Zemstvo v Rossii i Na Okrainnakh. SPB, 1907.

Timberlake, C., ed. Essays on Russian Liberalism. University of Missouri Press, 1972.

Tiumenev, A. Ot Revoliutsii k Revolutsii. Leningrad, 1925.

Tolstaia, A. Otets: Zhizn Lva Tolstogo. 2 vols. New York, 1953.

Tolstoi, L. Edinstvennoe Vozmozhnoe Reshenie Zemelnago Voprosa. Moscow, 1907.

_____. Ne Mogu Molchat. Berlin, 1908.

Trotsky, L. 1905. 4th Edit. Moscow, n.d.

Tsetkov, A. Mezhdu Dvumia Revoliutsiiami. Moscow, 1957.

Tsitron, A. 72 dnia Pervago Russkago Parlamenta. SPB, 1906.

_____. 103 Dnia Vtoroi Dumy. SPB, 1907.

Tsvetkov-Prosveshchenskii, A. Na Putiakh Bolshevizma. Moscow, 1930.

Tsyavlovskii, M. Bolsheviki. Moscow, 1918.

Tsytovich, N. Selskoe Obshchestvo kak Organ Mestnago Upravleniia. Kiev, 1911.

Tyrkova-Williams, A. Na Putiakh k Svabode. New York, 1952.

Valiszevsky, K. Finnish Question: The Ostrich and the Sparrow. SPB, 1910.

Varshavskii, S. Zhizn i Trudy Pervoi Gosudarstvennoi Dumy. Moscow, 1907.

Vasilev-Iuzhin, M. V Ogne Pervoi Revoliutsii. Moscow, 1955.

Vasilevskii, E. Ideinaia Borba Vokrug Stolypinskoi Agrarnoi Reformy. Moscow, 1960.

Vasilevskii, I. Graf Witte i Ego Memuary. Berlin, 1922.

Vasiliev, N. Vtoraia Duma. SPB, 1907.

_____. Pravda o Kadetakh. SPB, 1907.

Veniaminov, P. Krestianskaia Obshchina. 1908.

Veselovskii, B., ed. Iubileinyi Zemskii Sbornik: 1864-1914. SPB, 1914.

_____. Istoriia Zemstv Za Sorok Let. 4 vols. SPB, 1909.

_____. Krestianskii Vopros i Krestianskoe Dvizhenie v Rossii. SPB, 1907.

Vikhliaev, P. Kak Uravniat Polzovanie Zemlei. Petrograd, 1917.

Vinaver, M. Konflikty v Pervoi Dume. SPB, 1907.

_____. Nedavnee. Paris, 1926.

Vishniak, M. Dan Proshlomu. New York, 1954.

Vitenberg, K., ed. Chego Khotel Narod. Paris, 1914.

Vladislavlev, I. Mozhet li Gosudarstvennaia Duma Pomoch Krestianam. SPB, 1906.

Vodovozov, V. Kak Proizvodiatsia Vybory v Gosudarstvennuiu Dumu Po Zakonu 3 Iiunia 1907 goda. SPB, 1907.

Vodovozov, V. Graf S.Iu. Witte i Imperator Nikolai II. Petersburg, 1922.

Voeikov, V. S Tsarem i Bez Tsaria. Helsinki, 1936.

Voitinskii, V. Gody Pobed i Porazhenii. 2 vols. Berlin, 1923-24.

Volkov, A. Okolo Tsarskoi Semi. Paris, 1928.

Voshchinin, V. Ocherki Novago Turkestana. SPB, 1914.

Walkin, J. The Rise of Democracy in Pre-Revolutionary Russia. Political and Social Institutions Under the Last Three Czars. London, 1963.

Wioth-Knudsen, K. Bauernfrage und Agrarreform in Russland. Munich, 1913.

Williams, H. Russia of the Russians. London, 1917.

Winter, N. The Russian Empire of To-Day and Yesterday. London, 1914.

Witte, S. Samoderzhavie i Zemstvo. Stuttgart, 1901.

_____. Zapiska Po Krestianskomu Delu. SPB, 1905.

_____. Vospominaniia Tsarstvovanie Nikolaia II. Berlin, 1922.

Wolfe, B. Three Who Made a Revolution. Boston, 1955.

Wrangel, N. From Serfdom to Bolshevism. The Memoirs of Baron N. Wrangel 1847-1920. Philadelphia, 1927.

Wrede, R. Prava Russkikh v Finliandii. Helsingfors, 1910.

Wuorinin, J. Nationalism in Modern Finland. New York, 1931.

Yaney, G. The Systematization of the Russian Government. Social Evolution in the Domestic Administration of Imperial Russia 1711-1905. University of Illinois Press, 1973.

Zaichikov, G. Borba Bolshevikov Protiv Militarizma i Imperialisticheskoi Voiny v 1907-14 g.g. Moscow, 1964.

Zaionchkovskii, P. Krizis Samoderzhaviia na Rubezhe 1870-80-kh godov. Moscow, 1964.

Zavarzin, P. Rabota Tainoi Politsii. Paris, 1924.

Zenkovskii, A. Pravda o Stolypine. New York, 1956.

Zenskovsky, S. Pan-Turkism and Islam in Russia. Massachusetts, 1960.

Zenzinov, V. _Perezhitoe_. New York, 1953.

Zurabov, A. _Vtoraia Gosudarstvennaia Duma_. SPB, 1908.

INDEX